The Eye of the Poet
Six Views of the Art and Craft of Poetry

David Baker

David Citino

Billy Collins

Yusef Komunyakaa

Maxine Kumin

Carol Muske

Ann Townsend

edited by
David Citino

New York   Oxford
OXFORD UNIVERSITY PRESS
2002

Oxford University Press

Oxford   New York
Athens   Auckland   Bangkok   Bogotá   Buenos Aires   Calcutta
Cape Town   Chennai   Dar es Salaam   Delhi   Florence   Hong Kong   Istanbul
Karachi   Kuala Lumpur   Madrid   Melbourne   Mexico City   Mumbai
Nairobi   Paris   São Paulo   Shanghai   Singapore   Taipei   Tokyo   Toronto   Warsaw

and associated companies in
Berlin   Ibadan

Published by Oxford University Press, Inc.
198 Madison Avenue, New York, New York 10016
http://www.oup-usa.org

Oxford is a registered trademark of Oxford University Press

Library of Congress Cataloging-in-Publication Data

The eye of the poet : six views of the art and craft of poetry / Billy Collins . . . [et al.];
edited by David Citino.
    p. cm.
  ISBN 0-19-513255-6 (pbk. : acid-free paper)
    1. Poetry—Authorship.   I. Collins, Billy.   II. Citino, David, 1947–

PN1059.A9 E93 2001
808.1—dc21   00-062387

9   8   7   6   5   4   3   2   1

Printed in the United States of America
on acid-free paper

The Eye of the Poet

Contents

Preface

This is a book of advice about the writing and reading of poetry, written by practicing poets and teachers of poetry.

I've been teaching poetry writing and literature classes on the university level for nearly thirty years. It occurred to me that a collection of relatively informal discussions of some of the principles of poetry writing by experienced poets from around the country could be of value to creative writing students who want to bring their own writing closer to the light, or to those "general readers" we're always hearing about who feel the urge to know more about this thing called poetry. Every day I meet readers who can't get enough fiction or biography, say, but read little poetry. Why is this? I wondered. Why has poetry disappeared from the lists of many of the major publishing houses, even though poetry seems to be undergoing something of a renaissance these days? Certainly more and more people are writing it. PBS is regularly putting poetry on the small screen. Former Poet Laureate Robert Pinsky has been leading a crusade of sorts to bring poetry back into the national consciousness. Still, relatively few readers seem to be reading poetry, and fewer still are buying it. A book about the workings of the poem, I reasoned, directed at the woman or man new to poetry or strayed from it, might help to enhance the experience of readers, teachers—and poets themselves.

It has been suggested that poets are rare birds with strange markings and plumage; that they see the world in particularly insightful, acute, or just strange ways. Poets, this argument suggests, are "seers" with arcane reports to file for the benefit of the rest of humankind.

Another view of poetical vision is more democratic. Poets see what every woman and man is capable of seeing—in fact, actually do *see*, each and every day—but poets are more adept than others at describing what they see. In this view, the news of the poem is a depiction of this world, and not some other.

This book examines both views of poetical viewing, and others besides. You have before you a book of advice on writing and reading poetry, and at the same time a celebration of what the poet sees, before, during, and after the poem. It is not a "cookbook," a paint-by-numbers how-to that leads the reader through the process of poetry writing. Such textbooks seek to reduce poetry to a formula as straightforward as mixing the perfect Manhattan or dropping a four-speed transmission into a '57 Chevy. Rather, this book is a lively colloquy in which practitioners of the poem share with the reader their enthusiasm, knowledge, and their vision, as well as their estimation of the near-limitless possibilities of the poem. Working, teaching poets speak their minds about their life-long relationship with their art and craft.

The reader will find six sections written by seven widely published American poets who are at the same time experienced teachers and presenters of poetry and literature. The poets, who speak for the most part in prose, are Billy Collins, Carol Muske, David Baker and Ann Townsend (who collaborate on their section, as they do on their life together), Yusef Komunyakaa, Maxine Kumin, and myself. Most days, in addition to paying passionate attention to their own poems, these poets speak to others in workshops and classrooms about the possibilities, probabilities, and certainties (though there are precious few of this last one) of a poem.

This book is a course in poetry writing and reading. The authors have things to say to readers of various levels of experience, from beginners to veteran writers. The authors of these essays are poet-teachers and teacher-poets. They travel the country giving poetry readings, lectures, and talks to various audiences, college students, library patrons, residents of assisted-living houses, community centers, prisons, the man and woman in the street.

I've long thought that the roles of poet and teacher are similar in important ways. The poet explores some territory, inner or outer, and composes a travelogue of her or his insights for the reader. The student seeks understanding from the teacher, one who is more experienced or experienced in different ways. The reader of a poem is, for as long as it takes to enter the country of a poem, a student of the poet.

Each expansive section in this collection is intended for that reader who is interested in, or fascinated by, or obsessed with, poetry, as writer, reader, or one who wants to know more about both roles. These seven poets offer students of poetry a sense of the wide variety of options available to them when they sit down to work. The poets include in their essays examples of poems—written by themselves and others—to illustrate the points they are making. The poets range over many topics, including personal ones—how they do what they do is something readers will find interesting—but the emphasis on the pages that follow is always on the almost endless potentialities, and also the exigencies, of the poem.

In the first section, "Poetry, Pleasure, and the Hedonist Reader," Billy Collins explores a quality of poetry often overlooked but obvious to the ardent practitioner. Poetry, the reading of it, the writing of it, gives pleasure. We know that poetry differs from prose in significant ways. How do we read a poem? Collins asks. His answer is "Very carefully," but the care we take ensures that we experience the satisfaction of poetry. Collins elucidates the primary ways that moving around inside the borders of a poem provide the mind and soul, and even the body of the reader, with rewards. Collins helps us understand what it means to read like poets.

Well, what is a poem, as opposed to an essay or story? A poem begins, and ends, in silence, the whiteness of the page, though today the emphasis seems to be on what the reader brings to the poem—his or her own stillness. Between the two silences (or personal, reader-response interference), what happens? Carol Muske provides a wise and engaging exploration of the question in "What Is a Poem?" She explains to us her complex yet accessible vision of the poem, using, as examples, the words of several poets, including Rainer Maria Rilke, John Keats, W. B. Yeats, Gertrude Stein, and Enheduanna, daughter of a king of Sumer, who, though she wrote her poetry in 2300 B.C.E., still sings to us today.

David Baker and Ann Townsend, in "The Line/The Form/The Music," take as their concerns the shapes and the sounds of poetry. Because their realm is the most technical of the six essays, Baker and Townsend include suggested exercises and directions to further reading on the topic of the formal and musical aspects of making and reading poems. In their section, Baker and Townsend, who in "real life" are husband and wife (and the parents of Kate), comment on aspects of their topic and on the work of one another, thereby helping the reader to understand better the way a poet composes his or her music and how the reader listens to it. What are the implications of the fact that poets break their lines?

In "Kit & Caboodle," Yusef Komunyakaa enrolls readers in a virtual poetry workshop, inaugurates them into the promises and demands of the course, and then pays particular attention to the way words can work, in the air, in the room, on the page. Like David Baker and Ann Townsend, he suggests specific assignments for the poet serving an apprenticeship. The reader takes the course and is afforded the opportunity to take his or her own art farther. This section is another example of the closeness of the roles of poet and teacher, student and reader.

Maxine Kumin, calling on years of experience as a major contemporary American poet who has performed for countless audiences in her distinguished career, considers the necessities and demands of "Audience." Who is listening to the poet? How does the poet connect with the hearer? What is the connection between the writer and performer, the reader and auditor? Kumin enlists the help of John Crowe Ransom, Donald Hall, Maggie Dietz, Lawrence Raab, and her own poetry to delight and instruct the reader. Full of fascinating anecdotes drawn from her career as itinerant performance artist, illustrating the way poetry can fill the air between poet and audience, Maxine Kumin performs as only she can.

In my section, I consider the role poets play as they conceive and execute their poems. Who in the world does Shakespeare think he is when he writes, in a sonnet, "Let me not to the marriage of true minds admit impediments," or "My Mistress' eyes are nothing like the sun?" He can be said to see himself as lover, sonneteer, wit, traditionalist, revolutionary, remaker of the past. The poet is sometimes historian and at other times an advocate for the fall of history. Considering the poet as intellectual and anti-intellectual, singer and squawker, truth-teller and liar, I look at both classical and modern conceptions of the poet. "Who am I?" the poet would like to know. I suggest several answers.

Each of these six essays is meant to be a self-contained exploration, yet at the same time each is part of the larger whole. Maxine Kumin talks back to Billy Collins and Yusef Komunyakaa who are picking up on something Carol Muske, David Baker and Ann Townsend are mulling over. Poets take care of their own business but feel the compulsion to follow where their musings lead. They invite you, the reader, to go with them across the border of the here and now into the vast country of poetry.

David Citino
The Ohio State University

The Eye of the Poet

Poetry, Pleasure, and the Hedonist Reader

Billy Collins

If it is true, as Frost once said, that a poem begins with a lump in the throat, perhaps a study of poetry begins with a bubble in the head. In this case, what inflated my interest was the question, not of how to read a poem, but rather what exactly—or even vaguely—happens to us when we *do* read a poem. How can one describe the psychological, even physiological effects a poem is having on a reader? How does poetry alter consciousness? Emily Dickinson said when she read a good poem she could feel the top of her skull coming off—and, I would like to think, a soft breeze wafting over her exposed brain. And Whitman claimed a strong poem could send a charge of static electricity into his beard. But apart from such chills and thrills, what is the effect of poetry on the reader's state of mind? Can the deeply subjective experience of reading poetry be described in a way  that touches a common ground shared by many readers? Much has been written about the more widely experienced effects of fiction on its readers, particularly about the power of fiction to lure the reader out of his present surroundings and into an alternate reality. The reader with a novel open on his lap is seen as having one foot in his living room and the other in a Parisian bedroom or on the English moors. But comparatively little has been written on the mental changes that take place in the consciousness of the reader of poetry, the psychic sensations that poetry is best at delivering. Does a poem displace our ordinary sense of reality the way fiction does? To what degree do we leave our own world to enter the world of a poem? How does a poem lure us away from our daily rhythms into the cadence of its own metrical dance? How does it affect our patterns of thinking?

I sense that the answers to some of these questions lie within the broader question: What are the pleasures of poetry? What special kinds of pleasures does poetry inject into the consciousness of its reader? How does poetry stimulate the reader's attention? It is no accident that the word "pleasure" occurs nearly fifty times in Wordsworth's *Preface to Lyrical Ballads,* in which he is busy assembling a new audience for a new kind of poetry that wants to deliver a new kind of pleasure. And Borges, for all the labyrinthine complexity of his writings, has described himself as a "hedonist reader," one who is driven to the page simply by the need for pleasure.

Pleasure, of course, is a slippery word, and literary pleasures are very bound up with that faculty about which there can be no dispute—taste. Our pleasures ultimately belong to us, not to the pleasure's source. It's not about the pill—it's about how the pill makes you feel. Also, as poetry has changed in style and methodology, each "age" or "school" has held a very different notion of the pleasures that poetry offers. A random flip through an anthology of well-known poems will confirm this. If the book falls open to John Donne, we are prepared to experience a very circumscribed set of pleasures, largely dependent on our fondness for wit and convolution of image. If we find Whitman on the next page we flip to, our expectations shift drastically. We prepare ourselves to hear that capacious voice rolling over the American landscape while singing the song of itself. We trade in our appreciation of the perfectly deployed conceits of a persona for a need to hear the intonations of that distinctive, open-throated Whitmanesque voice, so public and intimate at the same time. Every poet with a distinctive voice offers a pleasure discreetly different from that of any other poet. But surely there are pleasures that almost all poetry offers, root-pleasures that finally provide a way of distinguishing poetry from prose, other than noticing that poetry does not go out to the end of the page while prose, as you see here, invariably does.

To list some of the pleasures of poetry in a series is surely to give the false impression that they occur separately or sequentially. In the act of reading, these pleasures, and perhaps others I am not even aware of, overlap, intermingle, and form the gestalt of poetic gladness. The sensations that a poem produces in us do not occur in isolated compartments of the brain, and, like the dancer and the dance, they can be cleaved only by a willful act of analysis such as that which follows. Here then is an attempt to clarify a few of the more prominent aspects of poetry that convey the kind of pleasures that call the reader to the page.

THE PLEASURE OF THE DANCE

Perhaps the most immediate sensation that lets us know we are "someplace else" when we read a poem is based on our feel for the music of the poem. The poet is, above all, a song and dance man, and he invites his readers into a kind of ballroom whose dance floor is the site of the poem's rhythm and sound. William Matthews remarked that one of the most basic appeals of poetry is to our desire to slow down, and surely we can feel the pace of our thoughts begin to decelerate when we say the first few lines of a poem. The rhythm that the lines of the poem insist upon replaces the more hectic, jumpier rhythms of our thinking and our behavior, or it supplies a cadence where there was none.

It was many and many a year ago,
   In a kingdom by the sea,
That a maiden there lived whom you may know
   By the name of Annabel Lee;—

Reading such jaunty, sure-footed metrical lines, we submit to the poet's orchestration; we get in step and willingly slip into the light harness of the poem's cadence. But even in less insistently metrical poems, there is a speech-rhythm that we hearken to:

Deep in the grounds of a burnt-out hotel,
Among the bathtubs and the washbasins
A thousand mushrooms crowd to a keyhole.
This is the one star in their firmament
Or frame a star within a star.

What should they do there but desire?
So many days beyond the rhododendrons
With the world waltzing in its bowl of cloud.
They have learnt patience and silence
Listening to the rooks querulous in the high wood.

[Derek Mahon, "A Disused Shed in Co. Wexford," from *Poems 1962–1978*
(Oxford University Press, 1978)]

The pacing of the voice, the careful phrasing, the affinity of sounds, and the lineation of the words control the speed of our reading and cast a modest spell over us. These two excerpts, plucked from the nineteenth and the twentieth centuries, also illustrate the most noticeable change that has occurred in poetry over the past century, that is, the decreased reliance on metronomic meter and end rhyme.

After a poetry reading I gave in a rural community in the English Midlands a few years ago, an elderly man rose from the audience during the question and answer session that followed and asked "Mr. Collins, are *all* your poems written in prose?" If this had taken place at a convention of so-called New Formalists, everyone would have been rolling on the floor. But his question was ingenuous, and it seemed he spoke for many people in the audience who simply were not hearing in my poems the kind of tune they had been raised on.

That man's question was a way of asking what happened to rhyme and regular meter. Noticing their absence, some readers may think that these elements, so basic to poetry, were simply dispensed with, that the music simply fled. But in fact, rhyme and meter were stirred more thoroughly into the concoction of poetry so as to occupy a still important but less conspicuous place. Regulated rhythms such as the iambic tetrameter that we respond to immediately ("Whose woods these are I think I know") gave way to less metronomic cadences that were closer to the rhythm of speech. Pound's injunction was that the iambic must be broken so that poetry could move to more natural rhythms. Williams declared his independence from strict meter when he introduced the "variable foot." And when rhymes deserted their traditional posts at the ends of lines, they did not desert poetry; rather they took up residence inside the poem's body. Here is the first stanza of a short, well-known poem by Robert Hayden:

THOSE WINTER SUNDAYS

Sundays too my father got up early
and put his clothes on in the blueblack cold,
then with cracked hands that ached
from labor in the weekday weather made
banked fires blaze. No one ever thanked him.

[*The Collected Poems of Robert Hayden,* Frederick Glaysher, editor (Liveright, 1966)]

Despite the lack of end rhymes, the lines are rich in sound, thick with assonance (blueblack, cracked/ached, labor, weekday, made, blaze/ banked, thanked). By moving from the ends of lines to the interior of the poem, the rhymes have become a more integral part of the poem's texture. The ear that misses the more predictable sequence of terminal rhyme must adjust to the less patterned occurrences of interior rhymes.

A regular meter and the use of end rhymes give to a poem two predictable elements that are then set against the surprises of the poem's utterance. This interplay between the familiar and the unfamiliar creates a tension or a balance that is basic to the experience of poetry. Readers are treated to a happy mixture of novelty and repetition. Such patterns also give us the feeling of being somewhat at home in a poem. We might not know where the poem is going or what effect it will finally have on us. We don't even know what the next line or word will be, but we do know after the first few lines that the poem is running to a certain meter and that rhymes will occur at known intervals. This is why with formal poetry the reader never feels like a complete stranger. Besides the harmonious tune that rises from such poems, the comfortable feeling of being in a known or knowable place is what many readers really miss when they lament the decline of formal verse.

I said that end rhyme and metrical regularity create a reassuring predictability in poetry, but I need to add a qualifier. This predictability is not absolute, only partial. In the case of meter, the reader never knows when the poet may choose to toss in a variation. A poem might be breathing steadily to an iambic beat, when suddenly two trochees or a spondee might appear. Variation is actually not possible unless a pattern of regularity has been established. Take the dramatic change of pace that occurs in the opening lines of this Shakespeare sonnet:

> That time of year thou mayst in me behold
> When yellow leaves, or none, or few do hang
> Upon those boughs which shake against the cold,
> Bare ruined choirs where late the sweet birds sang.

Three lines of perfectly accented iambic pentameter establish the beat of the poem, but they also set up the reader for the modulation in the fourth line, which begins with three heavy accents ("Bare ruined choirs"), creating a drag on the progress of the iambic beat until it is allowed to continue bouncing along with "where late the sweet birds sang." Two adjectives of desolation, then the brilliant metaphor of a branch as a choir loft. A regular cadence creates a pattern against which variation can stand out. A "perfect" sonnet would be composed of exactly 70 iambs (5 feet times 14 lines), and it would produce a monotony no more desirable than the work of a jazz drummer who never varies the beat, never lays down an extra riff, never knows when a little syncopation might help things along.

The predictability of rhyme must also be qualified. The reader might know what sound is coming up, but not what word. Frost could have written

> Whose woods these are I think I know.
> His name is Henry Bigelow.

Or,

> My little horse must think it queer.
> He acts as skittish as a deer.

And when you allow for inexact rhymes such as off rhymes or slant rhymes, the degree of predictability is lowered further:

> My little horse must think it queer
> That I am here without a car.

If we notice how the pleasure of reassurance guaranteed by predictable patterns of rhyme and meter works with the pleasure of the uncertainty about what is actually coming next, we get a more kinetic picture of the ways that poetry offers its metrical and aural delights.

THE PLEASURE OF THE PAGE

Much has been said about the importance of the oral roots of poetry. The precedence of song over writing is often used as a reason to applaud the popularity of the spectacle known as the poetry reading. But for the past few hundred years, readers have encountered poetry primarily in print, and even today with the ubiquity of public readings, poetry is most commonly received by means of the medium on which it was set down—the page. True enough, speech came before print, but putting aside the figure of the Orphic singer, poems come into being first on a page; thus, to read a poem is to be brought into contact with its paper-and-ink origins. Typing out a poem that interests you is not only about the best way to know a poem more intimately; it is a physical re-enactment of the poem's composition. The poet typed or hand-wrote every letter just as you can do any time you wish.

On the page, the physical shape of the poem is visible. It presents itself as the container for the poem's language and a spatial guide for the reader's passage through the poem. This aspect of the poem is lost if the poem is only listened to. Philip Larkin said that one reason he did not enjoy attending poetry readings is that he could never tell when the poem was going to end. The reader can see the ending up ahead and prepare for it. The printed poem retains its bodily shape, which is formed as the poet writes. The shape is specifically the result of 1) the poem's length, 2) the poet's use of stanzas to subdivide the poem and, most essentially, 3) his reflexive habit of turning the line back before it reaches the right side of the page. And that shape, as Larkin knew, tells the reader where he is in the poem: beginning, middle, end, middle of the middle, beginning of the end, etc. Many commentators have offered explanations of how poetry is different from prose (I like prose as rain and poetry as snow), but perhaps Christopher Ricks put it most baldly when he put forth as the most reliable measure the fact that prose continues out to the end of the page and poetry does not. It is true that a page of poetry, held ten feet away from a viewer, will be recognized as poetry by its shape whether that viewer is the Poet Laureate or a schoolchild. Poetry does not simply fill the space of a page; it exploits it by creating a physical shape. Prose, it has been said, is like water; it will take the shape of any vessel into which it is poured. The author of a short story will care little about how many pages his work may occupy in a magazine. But poetry, like sculpture, will always retain its own shape. The poet, not the typographer, makes the call. Insofar as the poem's shape influences our reading of it, all poetry is concrete poetry.

For the poet, the poem's contours are the result of the way he composed it, but for the reader, the shape of the poem is a space to be inhabited. To read a poem is to enter a protective enclosure, a shape of words surrounded by blankness, an echo chamber surrounded by silence. The poem's room-like aspect appeals to what Bachelard called "topophilia," our desire to dwell in a felicitous space. Notice the sensation that you are about to experience when you are released from the ongoing, page-filling rattle of my prose and allowed to enter a piece of poetic space, in this case, one occupied by a short lyric of Louise Bogan's:

THE DREAM

O God, in the dream the terrible horse began
To paw at the air, and make for me with his blows.
Fear kept for thirty-five years poured through his mane,
And retribution equally old, or nearly, breathed through his
    nose.

Coward complete, I lay and wept on the ground
When some strong creature appeared and leapt for the rein.
Another woman, as I lay half in a swound,
Leapt in the air, and clutched at the leather and chain.

Give him, she said, something of yours as a charm.
Throw him, she said, some poor thing you alone claim.
No, no, I cried, he hates me; he's out for harm,
And whether I yield or not, it is all the same.

But, like a lion in a legend, when I flung the glove
Pulled from my sweating, my cold right hand,
The terrible beast, that no one may understand,
Came to my side, and put down his head in love.

[Louise Bogan, "The Dream," from *The Blue Estuaries*, Farrar, Strauss & Giroux, Inc., 1968.]

Notice the familiar feeling we get as poetry readers of being turned back regularly before the end of the page. What ultimately tells the poet she must turn back is Poetry with a capital P. If she continues recklessly to the edge of the page, she will be writing—God forbid—Prose. The poet, in that sense, is a kind of Prose Avoidance System. The poet keeps turning back and beginning new lines (thus maintaining her status as a Poet), but from the reader's point of view each return points him back into the poem, returning him to its interior so as to make him stay within the territory it insists on inhabiting. Of course, the original motive for turning back was metrical. A pentameter line must end with the fifth foot. But without the guidelines of meter, each line ending must be decided by the poet. Any line can end anywhere before the far end of the page. Actually, it can even go past the end of the page as long as the rest of the line is tucked into the next line, with its own indentation to indicate that the poet intends this to be one line. Bogan's poem might be considered a semiformal poem; it favors a five-foot line, but many of the lines spill over the lip of the pentameter. It should be added that some poems are shaped better than others. A carefully contoured poem will help to guide our reading, but a careless, haphazard shape will only add to the potential confusion. Pointlessly disruptive line breaks ("the/ cat") make it feel as though the poem has the hiccups and distract from a clear reading. Auden said writing "free verse" was more difficult than formal poetry because, like Robinson Crusoe, the free-verse poet must do everything for himself. If he has a taste for rabbit stew, he must first catch a rabbit. Lacking the prefabricated box of the sonnet to inhabit, he must build a shelter on his own.

Notice, also, that before you began to read the Bogan poem, it had already made a physical impression on you. You saw in a flash, as if glancing down to see what someone you are being introduced to is wearing, that the poem falls neatly into four stanzas of equal length. We expect from such an orderly looking poem a certain amount of organizational and material tidiness. We are prepared, perhaps at a level less than conscious, to tour the four rooms of the poem, and we may anticipate—correctly here—that each room will be different from the others. In "The Dream," the first stanza presents the nightmarish situation, the second introduces the intercessor, the third contains her command to the dreamer, the fourth shows the redemptive action and resolution. And each stanza ends with a period.

The shape of the poem guides our reading of it. To the extent that the shape holds us, we experience the pleasure of being embraced. In Bogan's poem, the frightening and mysterious content is brought under the control of the poet as she recounts this fearsome experience in a finely delineated space. The poem wants us to be alarmed at the chaos of the terrifying horse and the strange apparitional Other who clutches helplessly at the "leather and chain." But the poem, unlike a short story containing such a scene, also wants to reassure us by the way it holds us in, clasps us to its form. It is not until the last line that we realize how appropriate the orderly quatrains are to the frightening poem when the beast, tamed by the act of faith, and the poem itself find a peaceful place to settle.

Poems, it must be said, come in all shapes and sizes from a twelve-book epic to a haiku to Aram Saroyan's notorious one-word poem "lighght"—from the long, relaxed lines of Whitman and C. K. Williams to the sawed-off lines of William Carlos Williams and Robert Creeley. But in every case, if we receive the poem in print, its shape will not only influence our reading of it, but it will hold us in its embrace as we read, guiding our passage over its special terrain. Unlike the arbitrary sprawl of prose, poetry presents itself as a vessel, a defined space, a house we will gladly inhabit in the course of our reading. One of the underestimated pleasures of poetry is the pleasure of being held in the grip of the poem's distinctive form.

THE PLEASURE OF THE MIRROR

We may read poems because we are interested in the poet as a biographical creature who existed in a historical and cultural context, but we mostly read poems because we are curious about ourselves. In the short span of time it takes to read a typical lyric (under a minute in many cases), some aspect of ourselves is stimulated and brought to the fore. Poems that fail to have that effect may be justifiably considered by a reader to be worthless, though perhaps that particular reader is not quite ready for that particular poem. Maybe he will be ready in a few years. Maybe he will never be ready. Maybe by the time he is ready, the poem will have tumbled out of the circle of his experience. But worthwhile poems—the ones we *are* ready for—arouse our sympathies the way an appealing song might make us want to sing along. Such poems can have an almost epiphanic effect on us by showing us, say, a whole new way of understanding grief. Don't all the great elegies teach us, for one thing, that grief is a form of self-reflection that has less to do with the deceased than the survivor?

Usually, the effect is more subtle. Talking about a poem, for me, is always preferable to talking about poetry, so let us take a look at this short lyric by the Song dynasty poet Mei Yao-chen:

> The hard rain rang as it dashed on the window,
> I was just going to sleep by the dying lamp.
>
> Insects voices kept up terribly long,
> the echoes were carried to my lonely pillow.
>
> The rest were all drunk, seemed not to hear,
> I was forced to listen, and it was awful.
>
> The night was short, I never slept—
> my eye was irritated by a dust speck.
>
> [Mei Yao-Chen: "In the Rain, Spending the Night at the Library of Messrs. Xie, Xu, and Pei," from *An Anthology of Chinese Literature* edited and translated by Stephen Owen, (W. W. Norton, 1996) p. 650.]

The poet is spending the night in the library of three friends, the title informs us, and the presence of the sleeping others—"The rest"— works to intensify the speaker's isolation. They have all gotten drunk together, but now everyone except the speaker has found sleep. The initial pang I felt when I first read this poem has to do with the limits of friendship. The poem draws forth from me nights of sleeplessness away from home in the company of other sleepers, an especially poignant form of insomnia. An objective vocabulary of insects, rain, window, lamp, and pillow mixes with an emotional vocabulary— dying, terribly, lonely, awful—creating a balance of exterior and interior worlds. But the finer pleasures of the poem lie in its two surprises: the fact that the "night was short," when it would have been so easy to lie for effect and say that the night was unendurably long. And then there is the surprise of the last line, which perfectly undercuts the whole poem and leaves me smiling. All the terrible loneliness is nothing compared to the irritation of a speck in his eye. When the philosopher has a toothache, the poem wants to remind us, he puts his philosophy aside. The lamp may have *seemed* to be "dying," the insect noises *seemed* to be terribly long, the pillow *seemed* to be lonely; but there is no doubt about the truth that the night was short and the sleepless man had something in his eye. The poem rests on the tension between the vast intangibility of his loneliness and the ordinary but real speck in his eye.

Insofar as the poem has produced these reactions in me, the poem has read me as I was reading it. Each reader will accommodate a poem in a somewhat different way, which is to say that a poem can have many different interpretations of *us*. The conscious intelligence of a poem meets that of the reader at a half-way point creating a kind of field where the exchanges between reader and poem—their readings of each other—take place. The recognition that a poem is able to shuffle itself into our consciousness produces a feeling of kinship with the page, an intimacy that pulls us pleasurably out of our isolation and places us in the company, not only of the poet and his poem, but of all other readers of the poem, past and future. The poem is a mirror in which we see an aspect of ourselves; it is also a hall of mirrors in which we see images of our fellow readers regressing into time.

THE PLEASURE OF TRAVEL

Like the reader of fiction, the reader of poetry comes to the event ready to be enthralled, but the way a poem possesses us is very different from the pull exerted on us by fiction. What draws us into a short story or a novel is first the tug of the plot, that is, the possibilities offered by an ongoing narrative. As we enter a story, we begin to follow a timeline of events that replaces the timeline of our surrounding reality. Driven by curiosity, we turn the pages seeking the outcome, but perfectly willing to be teased. "Make them laugh, make them cry, but most of all, make them wait," advised Nelson Algren. Further, the story seems to know where it is headed, which is more than many of us can say of ourselves. Here's the way a Raymond Carver story opens:

> Vera's car was there, no others, and Burt gave thanks for that. He pulled into the drive and stopped beside the pie he'd dropped the night before.

Raymond Carver, "A Serious Talk" from *Where I'm Calling From: New and Selected Stories* (Atlantic Monthly Press, 1986) p. 122.

A simple enough beginning, but still, we are hooked. Who is Vera? What is her relationship to Burt? Why is he thankful? What happened the night before? What pie? We read on with the anticipation that all these questions will be answered and most of our initial curiosities sated. The earliest poetry, we might suppose, had the same enthralling effect on its listeners. Such poems would tell stories about the history of the people listening, the exploits of their heroes, or the fantastic behavior of their gods. But that was before narrative adventure was replaced by the lyric, the short song of a single voice lifted by an intensity of language and usually transmitted, again, in print.

The literary term for the mesmerizing charm that absorbs us so completely as we read fiction is realism. The introduction of social realism into literature by way of the novel was equivalent, Tom Wolfe thinks, to the introduction of electricity into the Industrial Revolution. Most poetry since the Renaissance has had to get along without that power. We are not drawn into a poem in the same way that we are drawn into a novel. The "state we achieve when immersed in a novel," writes Sven Birkerts, "is powerful, pleasure-inducing and very nearly hypnotic." Reading fiction, according to Birkerts, produces in the reader "a change of state and inner orientation. . . . . To read . . . is to make a volitional statement, to cast a vote; it is to posit an elsewhere and to set off toward it." [Sven Birkerts, *The Gutenberg Elegies* (New York, 1994) p. 80] Story has the power to take us rather immediately to "the other place." In realistic fiction, that is a place that greatly resembles ours, a place where human characters are behaving in typical human ways, engaging in dialogue, eating sandwiches, riding elevators, taking off their clothes—a place that for the duration of our reading becomes a substitute reality. By silencing, even erasing the self, Birkerts asserts, "we suspend our sense of the world at large, bracket it off, in order that the author's implicit world may declare itself." [Birkerts, p. 93]

Poetry, like fiction, is also a means of transportation—and a cheap one at that—but the question is where does it take us? Unlike a novel or a short story, a poem does not usually convey us to an alternative place, a geographical elsewhere—say, a butcher shop in nineteenth-century London or a motel room in Phoenix, made vivid and convincing by the use of realistic detail. But when we read a poem, some alteration does take place in us; some adjustment occurs in our state of mind. The "elsewhere" that a poem leads us to is not a physical place; rather it is the very consciousness of the speaker/poet. We gain access to that other consciousness by submitting to the speech-world of the poem, which is composed of a certain vocabulary, diction, syntax, and tone. Listen to the first stanza of Hart Crane's "The Broken Tower:"

> The bell-rope that gathers God at dawn
> Dispatches me as though I dropped down the knell
> Of a spent day—to wander the cathedral lawn
> From pit to crucifix, feet chill on steps from hell.

To read these lines is to be caught in a web of language spun from the diction of religion and trembling with the sound of bells and a feeling of religious despair. The lines employ many of the devices associated with poetic expression: rhyme, meter, assonance, alliteration, and metaphor, to name a few. Whatever small pleasure each one of these devices provides, they work together as a group to maintain our concentration on the poem itself. Our normally wandering attention is focused and held fast by the body and diction of the poem. Our sense of the world as chaotic is replaced by a unit of language that is deliberate and intelligible. The employment of such poetic devices imparts to the poem a kind of self-consciousness, and this poetic self-consciousness replaces our own self-consciousness as we read. We slip from the sensory world around us into a purely verbal dimension in which words are pointing at themselves as much or more than they are referring to their actual equivalents outside the poem. Thus, to read a poem is to indulge in self-forgetting. In accepting the poem's language, we move from the realm of our own daily speech sounds and allow ourselves to be lifted into a higher, more self-contained, deliberate version of the language we are used to speaking and hearing every day. Finally, we immerse ourselves in the mind that has so deliberately fashioned the language. If a poem succeeds for us, we reach a point at which our consciousness sinks into the speaker's. We might even feel that we have replaced the poet and that we, not he, are uttering the words. This is close to what we tend to do when we sing along with a popular song. Instead of just accompanying the singer, we replace the singer, karaoke-style. For as long as the song lasts, I am Mick Jagger—I am Martha and, on a good day, I am even her Vandellas. So too, I am Wallace Stevens. I am John

Clare. What's more, in reading a poem we may fantasize that we have written it. We get what Edward Hirsch calls "the eerie feeling that we are composing what we are responding to." [Edward Hirsch, *How to Read a Poem* (Harcourt, Brace, 1999) p. 29] Or as Gaston Bachelard put it: ". . . in reading we are re-living our temptations to be a poet. All readers who have a certain passion for reading, nurture and repress, through reading, the desire to become a writer." [Gaston Bachelard, *The Poetics of Space* (Orion Press, 1964) p. xxii]

Rather than engrossing us through the deployment of a realistic fictional world, a poem pulls us in through the power of the speaker's consciousness, which temporarily replaces our own reader-consciousness. Another way that poetry can transport us out of our selves is to spirit us off to imaginary places or hypothetical zones— what Keats might have meant by "realms of gold." In epics such as *The Divine Comedy, The Faerie Queene,* and *Paradise Lost,* much of the poet's energy is expended in conjuring up and maintaining the fantastical world which is the grand theater of the poem's action—some poetic Erewhon. "Kubla Khan" offers a good example of a shorter poem that is largely devoted to placing in our minds a dimensional landscape of the imagination. A more discrete kind of travel is to be found in poems that begin in one place and slide into another more remote, sometimes impossible place. A *locus classicus* for this kind of maneuver can be found in the fourth stanza of Keats' "Ode on a Grecian Urn."

Who are these coming to the sacrifice?
    To what green altar, O mysterious priest,
Leads't thou that heifer lowing at the skies,
    And all her silken flanks with garlands drest?
What little town by river or sea shore,
    Or mountain built with peaceful citadel,
Is emptied of this folk, this pious morn?
    And, little town, thy streets for evermore
Will silent be; and not a soul to tell
Why thou art desolate can e'er return.

At the outset of the poem, Keats moved quickly from addressing the urn to inspecting carefully the scene depicted on its decorative frieze. Here in the penultimate stanza, the poet has become so absorbed in this procession scene that he moves beyond the information offered by the urn to imagine the "green altar" where the procession is heading and the "little town" where these people—priest and celebrants—have come from. Neither altar nor town are visible on the urn; they exist in an imagined future and an imagined past bracketing the arrested present on the frieze. The altar is simply mentioned, but the imaginary town becomes a subject of speculation. The poet wonders where the town might have been located ("by river or sea shore,/ Or mountain . . ."), and then, quite marvelously, he enters the town by addressing it. Its empty streets, which will remain eternally silent—eternally nonexistent, we might add—become part of the larger unchanging realm of art, immune from the "burning forehead" and "parching tongue" of mortality. The urn as a work of art has not only teased us "out of thought," but transported us to a ghost town that exists in a kind of fourth dimension beyond the three-dimensional realm of the actual urn. If you ever looked at Edward Hopper's "Nighthawks" and wondered about the apartment where one of the figures at the counter must live, if you began to picture that apartment, imagined its wallpaper, then you were on the same wavelength as Keats.

"This Lime-Tree Bower My Prison," one of Coleridge's so-called "conversation poems," provides another kind of travel, an imaginative journey over a real and familiar landscape. Because of an accident—a pitcher of hot milk spilled by his wife on his foot—the poet has had to stay home while his house guests—among them, Charles Lamb—take a walk in the surrounding countryside.

> Well, they are gone, and here I must remain,
> This lime-tree bower my prison!

Confined to his garden, the poet is so familiar with the walk his friends are taking he is able to imagine where they must be on their journey at any given moment. By mentally following along, he recreates their journey in language and thus accompanies them on their walk. At one point, the little group, which also includes William and Dorothy Wordsworth, enters a

> . . . roaring dell, o'erwooded, narrow, deep,
> And only speckled by the mid-day sun . . .

. . . . and there my friends
Behold the dark green file of long lank weeds
That all at once (a most fantastic sight!)
Still nod and drip beneath the dripping edge
Of the blue clay-stone.

What the friends are experiencing is rendered with such vividness and excitement ("a few poor yellow leaves . . . tremble still,/ Fann'd by the water fall!) we might easily forget that Coleridge is back in his garden conjuring up these scenes by summoning up memories of previous walks. But that is where he has remained, timing the habitual procession of his friends over this terrain so that he and the reader can join them. The friends leave the enclosed dell and

                  emerge
Beneath the wide wide Heaven—and view again
The many-steepled tract magnificent
Of hilly fields and meadows, and the sea
With some fair bark, perhaps, whose sails light up
The slip of smooth clear blue betwixt two Isles
Of purple shadow! Yes! they wander on
In gladness all . . .

The poem alters the format of the romantic lyric in that the contact with Nature is not a past experience being remembered but rather one enacted in present time through an imaginative projection. Notice that Coleridge is careful to add "perhaps" because he is not sure if a ship will be visible to his friends at that point in their walk. The sea is a constant, the ship an accident, a kind of visual bonus. An additional novelty about the poem, which nicely complicates the reader's participation in it, is that here the poet manages to be in two places at once. During the time he has imagined the progress of his walking friends, he has also been aware of the more immediate delights of the garden where he has been sitting. Interestingly, he turns to this garden just at the point when he achieves and declares a union with his friends:

                  A delight
Comes sudden on my heart, and I am glad
As I myself were there! Nor in this bower,

> This little lime-tree bower, have I not mark'd
> Much that has sooth'd me.

Among the soothing sights have been the foliage of a walnut tree, some "ancient ivy," a line of elms, and even the minuscule phenomenon of a bee singing in a bean-flower. The speaker has taken the reader on two journeys that must be thought of as occurring simultaneously—an imagined walk over a landscape and a tour of the garden where the imagining is taking place. The poem is a unique mix of reality and unreality, alertness and daydream—both endorsed with equal enthusiasm. To the reader, the poem offers a complexity of locomotion.

Another example of the kinds of sudden imaginative travel—zone-shifting, if you will—that are part of the pleasure of poetry is a brief lyric by the Greek poet Yannis Ritsos titled "Miniature."

> The woman stood before the table. Her sad hands
> cut thin slices of lemon for tea
> like yellow wheels for a very small carriage
> in a child's fairy tale. The young officer across from her
> is sunk deep in the old armchair. He does not look at her,
> He lights his cigarette. His hand holding the match trembles,
> lighting up his tender chin and the teacup's handle. The clock
> for a moment holds its heartbeat. Something has been
>   postponed.
> The moment has gone. It is now too late. Let's drink our tea.
> Well then, is it possible for death to come in such a carriage?
> To pass by and disappear? Until only this carriage
> remains with its little yellow wheels of lemon
> halted for so many years on a side street with darkened lamps,
> and then a small song, a bit of mist, and then nothing?

[Yannis Ritsos, *Selected Poems 1938–88*, edited and translated by Kimon Friar
and Kostas Myrsiades (BOA Editions, 1989) p. 29.]

This poem leaves me blinking in wonderment. The first time I read it, the word "nothing" at the end of the poem made the rest of the poem vanish into thin air. The poem is a fine example of poetry's ability to address the mysterious. But the way Ritsos pulls this off is no mystery. The poem begins with a domestic scene, a room containing a woman, a soldier, a cigarette, an armchair, and a single simile. The slices of lemon are compared to the wheels of a carriage. The comparison is so visually apt, I cannot look at a lemon slice now without thinking of Ritsos's little carriage, just as every time I see a dogwood tree I think of Elizabeth's Bishop image of the tree's white petals looking as though they had been burned with the tip of a cigarette. Ritsos starts out his poem as a story, but it is interrupted midway by a series of abrupt, disturbing statements. ("Something has been postponed./The moment has gone. It is now too late.") Something unfathomable but irrevocable has occurred, and the resulting disequilibrium sets up the poem's key shift: the carriage, originally just the subordinate part of a simile, becomes real and replaces the original subject of the poem. The tenor (lemon) and vehicle (carriage) trade places, and by this bit of sleight of hand, the poet slips us into a purely literary dimension, yet one that seems as real as the poem's opening scene. The metaphor of the carriage becomes a kind of hologram that the reader can walk inside of. The carriage is promoted from an attendant simile to the new subject of the poem, as the poem becomes a meditation on death—a misty, dark side street where a little song is silenced and all that is left is nothing. The reader leaves the poem and enters the "child's fairy tale," only now it is also for adults.

In the maneuver I have described—not new with Ritsos, of course—the poem seems to develop a disproportionate and decisive interest in some aspect of itself (here, the carriage). This distraction, so to speak, causes the poem to re-focus. In the Ritsos poem, we watch the narrative progress go awry as the usual relationship of tenor and vehicle is destabilized and turned upside-down. In the resulting inversion, the poem loses its original subject. Of course, the ability of a poem to overcome the weight of its own subject and find a fresh direction is a well-known feature of contemporary poetry. Richard Hugo calls this the poem's movement from a "triggering" subject to a "generated" subject, the premise being that the poem does not know what its real interests are until it gets well underway. The poem's true subject is discovered, not preconceived.

To examine the maneuvers of a poem such as "Miniature"—to see how it manages to carry the reader to a new imaginative space—is to focus not on what the poem means, or what the poem is, but on what the poem *does:* specifically, how do the poem's various maneuvers register on the reader's mind. And one of the most pleasurable and unforeseeable experiences available to us as readers of poetry is to be carried off suddenly into a new conceptual zone, to be slipped through a secret passageway and into the extraordinary rooms of the imagination.

THE PLEASURE OF CONNECTING

For many readers, an ingredient of poetry almost as basic as rhyme and meter is the making of comparisons through simile and metaphor. To say that your love is similar to a red rose or to complain that you have been pricked by the thorns of love are assertions that seem especially to belong in the domain of poetry. When we think of some of the admirable poets, we often think of them in terms of their comparisons. Take Donne's famous use of a drawing compass to clarify his feelings about having to be absent from his beloved. Or Keats's portrayal of autumn as a woman asleep in a "half-reaped furrow." Or Dickinson's disturbing sense that her life is a loaded gun. An interesting exception to this busy making of comparisons is haiku or, by extension, haiku-spirited poems. In haiku, a thing is not like another thing—it is itself. A cherry tree is a cherry tree, and a frog is a frog. The Buddhist belief in the sufficiency of things leaves no room for the interfering enhancements of metaphor and simile. In much Chinese and Japanese poetry, we are asked simply to look at a thing or a scene: a jug of wine rests under a tree, a heron stands in a shallow water. But in the poetry of this culture, we are regularly asked to look away from the subject of a poem in order to understand it. It is impossible to look at love, the famous Burns poem implies, but if you look at that rose over there you will learn something about this ineffable emotion. The itch to compare, which is so prevalent in Western poetry, is a symptom of the deeper need to create order in a world where variety, if not chaos, prevails. By making connections between things, especially apparently unrelated things such as a pair of lovers and the points of that drawing compass, the poet creates a new linkage and establishes a reassuring affiliation. The poet who employs metaphor and simile is not unlike one of the ancient sky-watchers who connected the dots of the stars to form the intelligible shapes of animals and persons, thus making some sense out of what Yeats called the "disheveled" sky. The philosophical motive behind poetic comparisons is, then, to move the world closer to the condition of harmony, ultimately an absolute harmony in which all things are connected, a simile- and metaphor-riddled world where everything is like everything else. But how does the reader experience such comparisons, and how do they give pleasure? Here is Eamon Grennan speculating on what he must look like to his newborn daughter as he bends over his crib:

> My face
> floats down—a spiked cloud
> of flesh and freckles, a sphere
> of hairy thunder. My hand
> is a sea anemone
> in a pool of air, my crook'd finger
> a shy beast brushing something
> she can feel she feels.

["Circlings," from *Relations: New and Selected Poems* (Graywolf, 1998) p. 78.]

Hoping to get a glimpse of how a baby perceives the world, the poet deploys the metaphors of sphere, thunder, anemone, and beast—a wild array of vehicles that signals the difficulty of describing infant vision. For the reader, the claim that a man's face is like thunder with hair and that his hand is an undersea creature opens up fresh mental associations, and that is the essential effect of metaphor on the reader's mind. The shopworn claim that poets "see the world differently" rests largely on the reflexive poetic habit of drawing original lines of association. According to association psychology, which began with English empiricists such as John Locke and David Hume and was modified by gestalt theory, human consciousness is made up of a combination of sense impressions held in place by previous associations. And free association, as we know, is used in psychoanalysis to reveal deeply repressed connections that may lie at the root of a dysfunction. Let us see if associationism can shed some light on the experience of reading poetry.

When we read a poem, we are experiencing a set of verbal associations the poet is making. We are also associating the poem with our own past experience, which not infrequently can lead to irrelevant associations and, consequently, gross misinterpretations. But when we come across a fresh metaphor or simile, a new association is created in our minds. Suddenly, between two things that we have never previously connected, a new trail is blazed, a new channel is opened. To use Dr. Johnson's image, two widely disparate things are violently yoked together. When a metaphor strikes us powerfully with its originality and its aptness, we almost feel that a new neurological path has been created in us, that a previously dormant synapse has been activated. Insofar as such a metaphor rewires our way of perceiving, we experience a breakthrough in the usual categories of thought.

Sometimes a poetic comparison has the effect of throwing us suddenly from one context into another. Here are the first two stanzas of "The Zen of Housework" by Al Zolynas:

I look over my own shoulder
down my arms
to where they disappear under water
into hand inside pink rubber gloves
moiling among dinner dishes.

My hand lifts a wine glass,
holding it by the stem under the bowl.
It breaks the surface
like a chalice
rising from a medieval lake.

[Al Zolynas, *The New Physics* (Al Zolynas, 1979)]

The effect of the simile is to cast a very ordinary domestic scene into an exotic and faraway world: here, Arthurian romance with all its religious and chivalric resonance. The everyday is lifted without warning into the mythic. A line is drawn, possibly for the first time, between doing the dishes and medieval magic.

Since no comparison is absolute—since love is not exclusively like a rose—the poet may add an alternate or two as in the Grennan poem above and in the opening lines of W. S. Merwin's "Utterance."

Sitting over words
very late I have heard a kind of whispered sighing
not far
like a night wind in pines or like the sea in the dark . . .

[W.S. Merwin, *The Rain in the Trees* (Knopf, 1988)]

The reader who would want to tell Merwin to make up his mind is being insensitive to the provisional nature of metaphor and simile, the way that the wind or the sea can only approximate the sensation of listening to "everything that has ever/been spoken."

May Swenson's poem "Question," quoted here in full, begins by introducing three metaphors—house, horse, and dog—to describe the human body; the poem then proceeds to braid them together as if any one were insufficient to convey the mortal vulnerability of the flesh:

Body my house
my horse my hound
what will I do
when you are fallen

Where will I sleep
How will I ride
What will I hunt

Where can I go
without my mount
all eager and quick

How will I know
in thicket ahead
is danger or treasure
when Body my good
bright dog is dead

How will it be
to lie in the sky
without roof or door
and wind for an eye
With cloud for shift
how will I hide?

[May Swenson, *The Complete Poems to Solve* (Simon and Shuster, 1993)]

Sliding deftly from the language of horsemanship to that of venery and architecture, the poem keeps three metaphoric balls in the air at once, lifting the reader into a state of suspended animation.

Fresh and inventive comparisons alter the reader's consciousness by making new mental linkages. And they should remind us of the repetitive limits of our usual grid of associations. How dull to associate fork with knife when, as Charles Simic shows us, fork can be associated with a thing that "must have crept/Right out of hell./ It resembles a bird's foot/Worn around the cannibal's neck." [Charles Simic, *"Fork," Dismantling the Silence* (Braziller, 1971)]

How mundane to associate spider with fly when Whitman knows the spider is like the soul, always seeking to connect, like the maker of metaphors himself, with the universe around it:

A noiseless patient spider,
I mark'd where on a little promontory it stood isolated,
Mark'd how to explore the vacant, vast surrounding.
It launch'd forth filament, filament, filament, out of itself,
Ever reeling them, ever tirelessly speeding them.

And you O my soul where you stand,
Surrounded, detached in measureless oceans of space,
Ceaselessly musing, venturing, throwing, seeking the spheres to
    connect them,
Till the bridge you will need be form'd, till the ductile anchor
    hold,
Till the gossamer thread you fling catch somewhere, O my soul.

THE PLEASURE OF MEANING

Let us circle back to the original question of what happens to us when we read a poem, or, more pointedly, where does a poem take us? With many poems, the answers, unfortunately, are nothing and nowhere. But it is not exactly nothing we feel when we read a poem "deflective of entry," as Henry Taylor politely put it. The reader is made to feel excluded because he is not provided with the means and the sense of direction to enter the poem. Some poets seem to feel it is their artistic duty to ignore the reader lest the poem result in some sensible, bourgeois form of communication. True, most habitual readers of poetry do not simply want to be comforted. Ordinary logic is agreeably challenged if the poem manages to defamiliarize the reader by warping the glass in his everyday lenses. But the question is how to go about this while still maintaining the reader's attention. Stephen Dobyns is a poet who is unabashedly interested in engaging and maintaining the interest of the reader. In *Best Words, Best Order,* he makes the point that if the poet can get the reader to accept a small thing in the beginning of the poem, the reader will be more disposed to accept a larger thing later in the poem, perhaps a more complex or disturbing thing. Frost, of course, is the master of this strategy. A Frost poem may begin simply and literally—a man comes to a fork in the road—but after only a dozen or so lines the speaker is grappling with human issues of the utmost magnitude. So the problem lies in how to stage the poem. The poem that begins incomprehensibly and then continues inside its own turgid windings refuses to participate in the seduction of the reader. In these cases, the reader is reduced to lingering on the edges of the poem, even walking around it looking for a door, a window, a way to get in and at least have a look. The reader, eager to participate, is reduced to a disappointed or at best bemused spectator.

If asked for a simple way to distinguish poetry from prose, many readers would point to poetry's higher degree of difficulty. It's hard, sometimes impossible to understand, is a common complaint in the classrooms where poetry is taught. Poetry is a place where ambiguity, ambivalence, and the mysterious find a home. As Frost put it, poetry is the "clear expression of mixed feelings." It is also a place where language is used not simply as a system of communication, but for its own sake. So it follows that poetic meaning is not presented in the straightforward, sequential manner that we rely on in prose. Difficult poems become easier to accept if the reader in search of a paraphrasable meaning remembers that the poet is moving language into a realm apart from its ordinary uses. And in the best of all possible worlds of reading, dealing with difficulty can be listed among poetry's pleasures.

The first thing a reader experiences when he confronts a difficult poem is a resistance to the normal flow of reading. The comfortable relationship between eye and page is partially disrupted. Some readers will feel only frustration because the poem is denying them the instant gratification of comprehension that they are accustomed to. Many will put the poem aside and turn to more accessible work. Some will turn away from Poetry itself. But others will see the difficulty as a signal to slow down, to reduce the pace of their reading. These readers view difficult poetry as an invitation to participate in a more exacting level of reading that involves careful rereading and may involve looking up words, consulting reference books, perhaps reading critical commentary, even biographies. Such involvement is not for everyone, for it involves a pleasure that is received over time and only through willful and energetic participation. The relatively small audience for modern poetry may be the result of its obscurity, but its loyal readers view the element of difficulty as a challenge and derive from it a pleasure not unrelated to the pleasure that attends solving puzzles or riddles, doing crosswords and cryptography itself. Moreover, the ambiguity of poetic meaning, instead of being a source of confusion, can enrich the texture of the poem and create an exciting "open-endedness." Poetry's refusal to carry only one meaning is an invitation to the reader to participate more fully in the text. As Richard Alter puts it, literary language has the "teasing effect of simultaneously revealing and disguising meaning," which demands from readers a "special kind of attentiveness" and results in a sense of "pleasurable discovery." [Richard Alter, *The Pleasures of Reading in an Ideological Age* (Simon and Shuster, 1989)] What makes difficult poetry even more difficult for some readers is the failure to discriminate among the many kinds of poetic difficulty. In fact, each poet may be said to offer a separate species of difficulty, and taking this into account at least gives a reader a way to approach poetic problems. Let us take Hart Crane and John Ashbery as examples of two poets who make very distinctive kinds of demands on the reader. Here is Crane's short elegy "At Melville's Tomb":

Often beneath the wave, wide from this ledge
The dice of drowned men's bones he saw bequeath
An embassy. Their numbers as he watched,
Beat on the dusty shore and were obscured.

And wrecks passed without sound of bells,
The calyx of death's bounty giving back
A scattered chapter, livid hieroglyph,
The portent wound in corridors of shells.

Then in the circuit calm of one vast coil,
Its lashings charmed and malice reconciled,
Frosted eyes there were that lifted altars,
And silent answers crept across the stars.

Compass, quadrant and sextant contrive
No farther tides . . . High in the azure steeps
Monody shall not wake the mariner.
This fabulous shadow only the sea keeps.

[*The Poems of Hart Crane,* edited by Marc Simon (Liveright, 1986).]

Our first impression of these lines is that we have entered a thicket of meaning in which every word seems freighted with significance. Instead of following a linear development of meaning as with prose, here we feel surrounded by meaning, engulfed in the warp and woof of its design. If the linear act of reading the poem does not result in a grasp of its meaning, the reader may try to find a point of entry anywhere in the poem. Or he may look for local, but soluble difficulties. "Calyx" (a whorl of leaves) or "monody" (poem of lament) might send him to the dictionary, but no dictionary will explain the apparent illogic of "dusty shore," "frosted eyes" that lift altars, "livid hieroglyph," and "a corridor of shells." It is the kind of poem, as Williams complained about *The Waste Land*, that returns us to the classroom. Even Harriet Monroe, the founder of *Poetry*, in which the poem was to appear, had to ask Crane for an explanation. Fortunately, he responded by letter with a fairly full explication, which is why I chose this poem from the many available examples of modern knottiness. Crane explained to Moore that he imagined the bones of dead sailors being ground by the action of the sea into dice which would then roll up onto the shore, their numbers obliterated by the pounding of the waves. "Dice as a symbol of chance and circumstance," Crane writes, "is also implied." But this is a very elliptical usage that asks the reader to work backwards to arrive at the connection that occurred in Crane's mind between dice and the bones of drowned sailors. The calyx, Crane explains with equal obliqueness, is the vortex shape that a sinking boat would leave in the water and the "livid hieroglyph" and "scattered chapter" would be the rising flotsam that would be the final record of the boat's demise. [Philip Horton, *Hart Crane* (New York, 1937).]

That even Harriet Monroe needed assistance with this one might console some readers, and Crane's commentary is much more extensive than what is quoted above. The point here is not to offer a complete explication of the poem, but to see that the poem challenges us with a specific kind of difficulty. We see from Crane's response that many of the poem's words have exact equivalencies. The poem makes sense if we use the logic of the imagination or, as he called it, the "logic of metaphor." The reader of this poem is thus invited to discover a set of equivalencies: to figure out that the calyx is not a flower part but a metaphor for a watery vortex and that the altar in the poem wants to suggest, in Crane's words again, that man, unsure of god, "postulates a deity somehow and the altar of that deity is the very *action* of the eyes *lifted* in searching." This may be asking a lot of a reader, but the challenge can be better met if the reader knows that, indeed, equivalencies exist and that the game is to identify them. If the metaphoric words in Column A can be matched up with their real equivalents in Column B, the poem will become clear.

An example of a very different, but no less demanding kind of poetic game would be the first two stanzas of Ashbery's "The Pursuit of Happiness," one of the many four-quatrain poems that make up *Shadow Train:*

It came about that there was no way of passing
Between the twin partitions that presented
A unified facade, that of a suburban shopping mall
In April. One turned, as one does, to other interests

Such as the tides in the Bay of Fundy. Meanwhile there was one
Who all unseen came creeping at this scale of visions
Like the gigantic specter of a cat towering over tiny mice
About to adjourn the town meeting due to the shadow . . .

[John Ashbery, *Selected Poems* (Viking Penguin, 1985)]

As with many Ashbery poems, the speaker's attention seems to slide from one thing to another in such a seemingly unplanned way that it would be hard to say what the poem is about, if anything. We hear a lot of familiar phrases, especially transitional ones such as "as one does" and "Meanwhile." "It came about" starts the poem off on a mock-biblical note. Here, we are not surrounded by meaning but taken on a ride through a landscape of shifting postures and tones. We move through the lines expecting the unexpected. The difficulty here is lighter than the kind we faced in the Crane poem. For one thing, we are not tempted to find equivalencies because of the tone of casual arbitrariness. Instead of the Bay of Fundy, Ashbery could have cited the Colossus at Rhodes or some other marvel. Or how about a stack of dish towels? What keeps the poem from the purposeful encoding of Crane is irony and silliness, particularly evident is the cartoonish mice holding a meeting in some imagined Mousetown. Ashbery's poems are delightfully self-conscious. They seem to be appreciating their own strangeness and inviting the reader to do the same. The "difficulty" of the poem does not require the reader to play the game of equivalence or to translate the poem into more literal discourse as with Crane and often, I would add, with Stevens and Eliot. Instead, once the reader allows himself to flow with the tonal changes and playful shifts of the poem—to ride through its ironies—the difficulty actually disappears.

Understanding the kind and not just the degree of difficulty that some poems present gives the reader a means to enter the poem and cope with—even enjoy—its complications. But there is a deeper issue with regard to meaning in poetry and that is the dominance of interpretation over all the other pleasurable aspects of a poem. The usual classroom treatment of poetry puts the greatest emphasis on finding out what the poem means, because this is the most teachable aspect of poetry, the easiest to discuss, the most susceptible to testing. More broadly, what we might call "the interpretive fallacy" reveals the supremacy of reason in our culture, its dominance over the somatic and the sensory. Surely, you can enjoy a poem before you understand it. Just because a first-time reader of "At Melville's Tomb" may initially be confused by the poem does not mean that he cannot appreciate its music, its linguistic play, its wild originality. The grasping of a poem's meaning, however provisional it may be, is only one of the many pleasures that poetry offers. Putting meaning into this kind of hedonist perspective might help to remove the shadow of the poetry teacher from the page and allow the reader to indulge more fully in the cluster of poetry's imaginative and physical pleasures. It was with that hope that I wrote this poem:

INTRODUCTION TO POETRY

I ask them to take a poem
and hold it up to the light
like a color slide
or press an ear against its hive

I say drop a mouse into a poem
and watch him probe his way out,

or walk inside the poem's room
and feel the walls for a light switch.

I want them to water-ski
across the surface of a poem
waving at the author's name on the shore.

But all they want to do
is tie the poem to a chair with rope
and torture a confession out of it.

They begin beating it with a hose
to find out what it really means.

[Billy Collins, *The Apple That Astonished Paris* (University of Arkansas Press, 1988).]

THE PLEASURE OF COMPANIONSHIP

To what extent does literature influence us when we are not actually reading it? Sven Birkerts points out how common it is to ask of someone "What are you reading now?" even though that person does not have a book in his hand at the moment. This curious use of the present tense suggests to Birkerts that "in many vital ways [reading] is carried on—continued—when the reader is away from the page." [Sven Birkerts, *The Gutenberg Elegies* (Fawcett Columbine, 1994) p. 95] Bikerts is thinking about literary fiction when he goes on to say that a book has a "shadow life" that is sustained by means of our reading memory. And he doesn't simply mean that we sometimes think about a book we are reading when we are not actually holding it in our hands. For however many days or weeks it takes us to finish a novel, the book occupies us; we are "haunted," invaded by its life. [Birkerts, *Gutenberg Elegies*, p. 100–01].

Birkerts points out that much of what we retain from reading fiction is an assortment of odd scraps. We don't know why certain characters, scenes, or passages linger with us, but they form layers of information that become part of the way we think and perceive. Among the many burrs that have stuck to my memory are the scene in which Nick Carraway opens the huge closet containing Gatsby's shirts and the scene in which Miss Lonelyhearts nervously holds hands with the crippled Mr. Doyle. To some extent, the same is true of poetry. The "shadow life" of poetry is also made up of scraps—phrases, images, metaphors, titles, opening lines, and other bits of poems that the involuntary memory has retained. The more we read, the more poetic details accumulate and furnish our consciousness. Every time I put a match to a piece of rolled up newspaper in a woodstove I think of Dante's use of that image to describe rumor, the way the brown edge of the burning part precedes the actual flame as rumor spreads before the facts. And often when I spot a hawk in the sky, Hopkins's opening "I caught this morning morning's minion" springs to mind unbidden. These bits and pieces form a kind of grid of poetry parts that is laminated over our other patterns of association. Our reading becomes linked to our nonliterary experience and forms a pattern of connections that unite our life before the page and away from it.

But poems can also inhabit us in a more complete way because they are the easiest form of discourse to memorize. Poems written with end rhyme and regular meter are easiest to commit to memory, of course. Sometimes they seem to ask us to memorize them, especially if we remind ourselves that rhyme, meter and many other poetic features began as mnemonic devices. In oral, preliterate cultures that lacked a means for recording, poetry satisfied the need to store vital information. Basic to survival would be information about hunting, gathering, or planting. Basic to one's identity would be the names and exploits of ancestors. And basic to a sense of culture would be broader information about the past: the history of the tribe, its stories and myths. Strictly speaking, once literacy enters a culture, the practical need for poetry vanishes.

Because poetry is portable and can be easily concealed in the pockets of memory, it is able to survive in even the most inhospitable environments. Dictatorships and totalitarian regimes can destroy painting and sculpture. They can shut down the museums and the opera house and force the national symphony to play only the state's anthem, but they cannot wrest poetry from the recesses of the human memory. Stalin could exile Osip Mandelstam to one remote Siberian prison camp after another, but he was powerless to prevent the poet's wife Nadezhda from committing her husband's new poems to memory. The colonizing British could attempt systematically to repress the native Gaelic culture in Ireland, but poetry and folk tales continued to survive through memorization and repetition. It is good to remember that many of the features of poetry that now provide us with aural and rhymic pleasure are the very reasons for the survival of much poetry.

Tales can be memorized, of course, by storytellers, but not with the word-by-word precision of poetry. Indeed, storytellers in oral cultures were praised for their ability to enhance a well-known story by putting their own improvisational spin on it. In Ray Bradbury's novel *Fahrenheit 451* (the temperature at which paper combusts), a faceless and ruthless political regime has burned all the books. Certain people have taken on the impossible task of memorizing entire books so as to preserve them. In one of the "book camps," people are pictured pacing back and forth, muttering the book they have memorized over and over to keep it alive in their minds. "There's *Walden* over there," a visitor is told, "and that woman in the shawl is *Madame Bovary.*" We see an old man who has managed to memorize *Great Expectations* sitting next to a child reciting the novel, passing it on to the next generation.

But this is science fiction. We can all embellish a story or a joke as we tell it, but only poetry lends itself to being captured in the precise form in which it was originally written, syllable for syllable. William Matthews has written that the poet is never alone when he writes because he is always accompanied by all the lines of other poets that are stuck in his head. So memorized poetry influences future compositions, adding to the impression of a great conversation going on among poets of all times. Prose is resistant to memorization, but even poetry that lacks the regularity of end rhyme and meter can be memorized because it comes in lines that can be gotten one at a time. Memorized whole poems or passages offer the reader a kind of companionship, a set of other voices that can speak to us any time we are away from the page. Poems may lie within us ready to be activated whenever we need to call them forth. Whether you are undergoing the claustrophobia of an MRI—"The Lake Isle of Innisfree" helped me through mine—waiting in an airport, or asked to stand and recite a poem, as is common, I know, at social gatherings in Ireland, a memorized poem will see you through. The unique memorizability of poetry and song was neatly summed up by composer Sammy Cohn during a question and answer session at a college where he had lectured. A tactless student asked him if he had ever considered a more significant profession than song-writing, such as being a lawyer or an architect. Cohn shot back: "Ever hear of anyone walking down the street humming a building?"

To memorize a poem is to indulge in a particularly focused kind of reading. Repeating individual lines will remind us that the line is a unit of thought and a unit of composition. We may become more aware of the moving parts of the poem and the way it develops. Saying the words of the poem aloud, perhaps for the first time, we will hear resonances and patterns of sound we had been unaware of. And as we progress, we will actually experience the poem entering us as we bring more of it under the control of our memory. Memorizing is not only the best way to know a poem, it can actually replace other ways of knowing. Once we internalize a poem, we are become less objective in our judgment of it. To detract from a poem that is inside us is to wound a part of ourselves.

Add, then, to the array of poetry's pleasures—only some of which have been touched on here—the pleasure of taking on a poem as a companion by reading it over and over in such a way that it becomes inscribed on the mind, even though, revealingly, we like to call this kind of knowing a knowing "by heart."

What is a Poem?

Carol Muske

Roses are red
Violets are blue
Sugar is sweet
And so are you.

—ANONYMOUS

Well? Is "Roses are Red" a poem? It has elements of a poem—it has a rhythmic structure (dactylic or um-pah-pah) and also rhyme. It has images and a simile-like analogy ("you" are as sweet as "sugar").

"Roses are Red" instructs us as to the essential nature of things. Roses and violets are *naturally* the colors that they are, thus the "you" is naturally pleasing, being sweet like sugar. These obvious observations become, by the poem's own logic, praise for a loved one. "Roses are Red" is known by heart by one and all; we've all recited it at one time or another. It is completely anonymous—and completely boring.

Here is another anonymous poetic effort, first in its original English (from an early sixteenth-century manuscript) and then in a version more accessible to our contemporary gaze.

Westron wynde when wyll thow blow
the small rayne downe can rayne.
Chryst yf my love were in my armys
and I yn my bed agayne.

[Anonymous, c. 1500]

Then in modern spelling:

Western wind, when will thou blow,
The small rain down can rain?
Christ! if my love was in my arms,
And I in my bed again!

[Anonymous, c. 1500]

This poem also has rhythmic structure (mainly iambic, a regular three-stress line) and rhyme. Like "Roses are Red," it's a kind of love poem, though it is more a cry of longing and loss: a lyric. "Western Wind" provides much more information than "Roses are Red"— though not an excess of facts. It tells us that the speaker of the poem is pining for his sweetheart, epitomized by spring, which arrives on the continent on prevailing winds from the west, along with gentle rainfall. It tells us our poet is far away from home. (Perhaps he is an English soldier, an itinerant scholar, or student.)

"Western Wind" is a poem of yearning, of singular apostrophe, and it addresses the reluctant western wind as if it is a person, as if the wind could hear and react. The wind is animate, named— whereas the "you" in "Roses" is faceless, undefined. "Roses" gives us a highly generalized situation, unspecific references, and a waiting-for-the-other-shoe-to-fall tone. "Western Wind" gives us particulars and particular emotion that color the tone. Both poems represent universal dilemmas: the subject of "Roses" is gee-whiz sentimentality, the subject of "Western Wind" is raw sentiment.

A poem cannot live in the merely descriptive—the flatness and rigidity of the diction of "Roses are Red" are an example. The poem is made up of statements: nothing *happens* in the poem or in its language, mere observations are recorded. "Roses are Red" is all surface and cheerfully committed to surface: tail-wagging doggerel. By contrast, "Western Wind" is charged, dead serious, it grabs us by the lapels, stares into our eyes, *insists* on itself. "Christ!" is the tonal epitome—the conflation of expletive and prayer, of explosive frustration and importuning. We know who this soul is—across centuries, without name or face—we know him (yes, *him*, probably not a woman, unless she's in drag!) because of that tone, the living passion in that voice. That voice is as alive today as it was in 1500—just like the phrase "small rain" (not a hard rain or a downpour, just a small spring shower), as the sweet wind from the west brings the change of season. We can feel that wind beginning to blow gently, the slow drops falling softly on that fierce, weary face upturned to the sky. *Christ!*

So it's easy enough. "Roses are Red" is "Chopsticks." "Western Wind" is "Greensleeves." If a poem is, as W. H. Auden said, a verbal object, the first is a ping pong ball, the second a planet. Though "Roses are Red" need not be mocked—it is what it is—even if it stands as an example of how *not* to write. It is an expression, like "Western Wind," of a kind of collective memory—"Roses" survives because it reaffirms the simple fun of analogy, of rhyme. But let's face it, it isn't enough to have reiterative structure or even a simile or two—we need a bit more than that to make a poem. "Roses are Red," like a bad pun, doesn't bear repetition, unless one is very drunk—or very literal minded—or both. The reason "Western Wind" works so effectively is because its poetic expostulations sound like natural speech, which is part of the mystery of its power to haunt us and send us back to it again and again—it sounds like something someone in the grip of great emotion might actually *say*. Which is a definition Yeats gives of poetic speech: that it be *sayable*. (Yeats also remarked, "You can refute Hegel, but you cannot refute 'A Song of Sixpence.'")

Still, a poem is not like other speech. Poems are made up of words, and a poem's diction is no accident: the words must be precise and evocative and dance to a rhythm. The words used in "Western Wind" are as plain as those in "Roses," but they have jobs, they are active. From calling up the wind, to conjuring that "small" rain, to crying out for a lover—they keep the reader moving. The plaintive sounds of the long vowels in "thou" and "blow," the falling repetition of "a small rain down can rain" rhyming with "again," the alliteration of "w's" in "West" and "wind") all strike emotional chords in the reader. The words *sound* like the wind blowing, keening, the rain falling. And as the poem sings itself, we listen.

Generally, a poem requires at least two silences: the silence that precedes it and the silence following it. If a poem is bordered by silence then what is in between those silences insists on momentousness, makes us *attend*. After all, a poem (as D. H. Lawrence said) is *an act of attention*. Poetry is an art made of consciousness. The poet's timeless act of itself listening to itself, reverberates in the imagination of the reader—a bee in a flower, the eye of the beholder beheld.

ARCHAIC TORSO OF APOLLO

We cannot know his legendary head
with eyes like ripening fruit. And yet his torso
is still suffused with brilliance from the inside,
like a lamp, in which his gaze, now turned to low,

gleams in all its power. Otherwise
the curved breast could not dazzle you so, nor could
a smile run through the placid hips and thighs
to that dark center where procreation flared.

Otherwise this stone would seem defaced
beneath the translucent cascade of the shoulders
and would not glisten like a wild beast's fur:

would not, from all the borders of itself,
burst like a star: for here there is no place
that does not see you. You must change your life.

[Rainer Maria Rilke, Trans. Stephen Mitchell]

The attention of art is all-seeing: ". . . for here there is no place/that does not see you." The silent regard of what is *not there* and yet is imaginable (like the head of Apollo above the headless torso) gives reverberative power to what *is* seen and said. That unseen but imaginable world demands that we acknowledge it completely and honor it implicitly within the actual: *you must change your life.*

Going back to "Western Wind"—if an anonymous voice from the sixteenth century can still move us, make us feel now as the poet felt then—if the poem makes us see what is invisible (the homesick wanderer in the field, the sleeping lover across the Channel—and *ourselves* reading the poem), then we could argue that the quality of attention and the transcendent perspective that inform poetry, indeed, the poem itself, have not changed that much throughout history. The poem is, after all, and always has been *expressive,* capable of imparting experience that moves us beyond our present circumstance.

It avails not, time nor place—distance avails not.
I am with you, you men and women of a generation, or ever so

many generations hence,
Just as you feel when you look on the river and sky, so I felt.

[Walt Whitman, "Crossing Brooklyn Ferry"]

That "so I felt" keeps traveling through time. And Whitman's "I" travels especially well. But the kind of immediacy I'm talking about is not bound up only with the self of the poet—or what we think of as self-expression. Certainly a self is implicit in every poem; a poem is told, even in its most expository or experimental forms, through a subjective filter. Still, the self as we understand it is a fairly new presence in poems. Wordsworth and the Romantics put the self, the "I," at the center of the poem, gave the first-person perspective its primacy. And Whitman's self was a celebratory self—a monolithic ego that "stood in" for the nominative plural, the collective, all our selves. "Just as you feel . . . so I felt."

The self as we understand it (that is to say, in its *modern* sense—"a permanent subject of successive and varying states of consciousness," according to the Oxford English Dictionary) did not seem to emerge until around the seventeenth century. The ancient self was a character, a figure in the landscape of the epic, the disembodied "eyes" that recorded the world created by the imagination.

Homer and Virgil certainly used the word "I" ("Arms and the man I sing . . . .") That "I" understood time, measure, and unity. It understood expression, but it did not understand itself as a psychological construct. Nevertheless, that sensibility, that unifying and integrating principle in the poem—whether we call it a "self" or not—is inextricably bound up with what makes a poem a poem.

It's worth noting that in "Archaic Torso of Apollo," the "modern" sense of self is put in its place. If our sense of self has to do with the "permanent subject" of "states of consciousness," then Rilke imagines a *greater* consciousness, the consciousness of Art, which *sees* and instructs our own. This sense of self is (interestingly, because Rilke is, in a way, the first Modern poet, on the bridge between the nineteenth and twentieth centuries) closer to the original story-poem, the epic, the sense of a god-managed world than that of the new or ancient lyric. Whatever form the perspective of the "organizer" takes—singer, griot, skald, oracle, the chorus-strophe, haiku-master, Sufi dervish, masks of classical drama or of Robert Browning, the postmodern nonlinear, "subjectless" experiments of conceptual or

L = A = N = G = U = A = G = E poets—it is subjective. As Gertrude
Stein-as-Alice-Toklas says in *The Autobiography of Alice B. Toklas:*

> Gertrude Stein never corrects any detail of anybody's writing, She
> sticks strictly to general principles, the way of seeing what the writer
> chooses to see, and the relation between that vision and how it gets
> down. When the vision is not complete the words are flat, it is very
> simple, there can be no mistake about it, so she insists.
>
> p. 203, Stein, Selected Writings

"The way of seeing what the writer chooses to see" not only delin-
eates the profound attention a writer grants her subject but epitomizes
the attention a writer hopes for from the reader. "The way" of style
leads us through the Iliad, the Odyssey, the Aeniad, and into Greek
drama—through all the varieties of poetry: narrative, lyric, and dra-
matic. It is here, where ancient poetry divides into categories that we
still recognize in the twentieth century, that we begin to understand
how much poetry reflects that prior interpretation (or a priori logic)
that becomes schematized as self-expression through the ages. What
we think a poem is *now* is the result of the slowest of evolutions—what
we see as a manifestation of the intrinsic essence of a poem is in fact
several centuries of simply responding to the Greeks and Romans.

This is, alas, an unabashedly Western perspective. I'm certainly
aware that the great poems of the Chinese pre-dated the Greeks—the
shih, or song-poetry, existed long before Confucius held sway in the
fifth century B.C., and poetry and song are embedded in two prehis-
toric Japanese chronicles, the *Kojiki* and the *Nihongi.* The earliest
identified author in world literature is a woman, Enheduanna (ca.
2300 B.C.E.) who was (as Jane Hirschfield reports in *Women in Praise
of the Sacred*) the daughter of a Sumerian king. Her poem-hymns
were inscribed on cuneiform tablets, and her portrait was discovered
on limestone in the ancient city of Ur.

You roar,
You thunder in thunder,
Snort in rampaging winds.
Your feet are continually restless.
Carrying your harp of sighs,
You breathe out the music of mourning.

Enheduanna was a high priestess whose life revolved around serving the moon-god and goddess, Nanna and Inanna—not an easy life, it appeared, as she was cast into exile because of political intrigue, but was finally re-instated in her rightful position.

It was in your service
That I first
entered the holy temple.
I, Enheduanna,
The highest priestess.
I carried the ritual basket,
I chanted your praise.
Now I have been cast out
To the place of lepers.
Day comes,
And the brightness
Is hidden around me.
Shadows cover the light,
Drape it in sandstorms.
My beautiful mouth knows only confusion.
Even my sex is dust.

In most of the hymns she sees only the deity—who *she*, Enheduanna was, beyond the official voice of the flame-keeper, remains mysterious, hermetic, a self-evoked shadow. The lines about her "beautiful mouth" and her "sex" seem shockingly personal, yet re-examination of her poems allows us to see that the body of the high priestess is sanctified by the goddess, in the manner of a holy object. The description of the body is particularized, but not necessarily personal, as we understand the word.

Like the Zen koan, most ancient literatures and the poetry of the East remain fixed, nearly timeless. Writing about Basho, how he was influenced by Tu Fu, and the priestly tradition of Sogi and Saigyo, Robert Hass notes that the influence was in the realm of the temporal:

It added to, or imposed on, the ideas of cyclical time and linear time the no time of Zen Buddhism. . . .—the world really seen is the world; every moment is eternal; or every moment of time is all time; therefore time doesn't exist.

Hass, *The Essential Haiku*

What we see in "Western" poetry is an ongoing demonstration of perfectability or, more aptly, a belief in this perfectability, as if there is a poem that represents an absolute to which we aspire. Do we conflate this "absolute poem," this perfectable state, with timelessness? We can readily acknowledge the uses and the illusion of *time* in the poem. It is narrative time, the story, and it is also the layered, episodic time of dramatic verse.

I'd like to concentrate on the origins of "Western" poetry here for two reasons. First, because the forms and attitudes that we employ in English, still seem to be evolving from their Greek and Roman roots and because even the most ancient forms of the lyric poem strike me as outrageously similar to the lyric poem being written today.

The traditional genres are still in place. It is amazing to me that we write in the same thought constructs as the ancients, though the epic narrative is gone, replaced by a much more condensed, elliptical form of narrative. And dramatic verse has slipped the bonds of the strophic and morphed into startling new forms. Yet there is something cyclic in dramatic verse: traditions rise, fall, are satirized, return. Because the Elizabethans misunderstood an ancient poet, for example, we have Shakespeare's tragedies. Seneca, a first-century Roman philosopher and man of letters wrote nine Latin tragedies, modeled largely on the Greek tragedies of Euripides, which he intended to be recited, not read. He thought of them as oratorical poetry, soliloquies. Renaissance playwrights, both English and French, completely miscomprehended this cornerstone of Senecan configuration and produced (and reproduced their own versions of) his work, on the stage. Dana Goia, writing about Seneca praises his "magnificent language," how his "mixing of techniques of poetry and oratory could create dramatic verse of powerful eloquence." Seneca's language is also filled with epigrams and *stichomythia,* or dueling exchanges of aphorisms. This rhetorical swordplay and mercurial language were not lost on young Will Shakespeare, in his Latin school far from London. Seneca (and the precision and expansion of Latin) haunted his writing—we would not have Hamlet but for the way the English ear heard oratory—and but for the way the stubborn image-hungry English imagination insisted on "seeing" oratory as well. (Seneca, by the way, after disappearing again for a couple of centuries, is back in the twentieth. T. S. Eliot wrote two important essays on Seneca, and Seneca himself is experiencing a revival in translations and adaptations.)

Here is William Levitan: "At root, Senecan theatricality is the imposition of will on time, and it collaborates with its own heroic monsters—Atreus, Medea, the mad Hercules—to stage the impossible requirements of their desires: to stop time if necessary, turn back on itself if necessary, and make the world watch. We do watch, and we are stunned."

There's the goal again: *stop time*. But it is the lyric poem that lives in that tradition most passionately. The lyric, the expression of the "inexpressible," epitomized by the fleeing moment, as words sung on the wind, afloat on the echoing sound of the lyre, has always been outside of time. Outside of time and connected to a speaking voice, a living person.

There were ancient lyrical poets who provided an alternative "self," away from the expectations of traditional narrative and dramatic verse. Regarding these lyric poets, Renate Wood notes in an essay, "We can only appreciate them properly if we understand how hidden the Self still was at Homer's time, and what it took for these poets, all of whom knew Homer's work and were instructed by it, to move in the new direction they chose." The idea of a "hidden self" is so foreign to us that it is difficult for us to imagine the audacity of these "melic" poets, trained to sing their poems, accompanied by flute or lyre, in speaking freely, "from the heart." One of these poets was Sappho. (Also the Greek lyric poets Archilocus. Ibycus, and Anacreon.) Sappho shows us how, two thousand five hundred years ago, in the sixth century B.C.E., body and soul came together for her in a new way.

Page duBois, in her wonderful book, *Sappho is Burning,* delineates this moment and Sappho's place in it: "Sappho's poetry stands at a moment of transition, in which the specificity of the particular is still visible, in which a particular object, a headband, a field of flowers, exists in all its particularity. . . ." We approach Sappho as Rilke's ephebe approaches the archaic torso of Apollo—the experience is fragmented, but what is *there* comes together with such implicative force it stands for the mysterious nature of Art's inherent symbolism.

Sappho's work is an excellent example of how a poem is an act of attention that blooms into expression. Sappho invests (in the eerie way all great poets do) a natural portentousness in the speaking psyche. The great irony regarding this enormous presence—her lyric voice is closer to the voice of contemporary poetry in its immediacy than many others—is that only a couple of complete poems by Sappho have survived; the rest are fragments.

Her seven books were condemned to the fire and burned by religious zealots and invading hordes—most of her work was lost when the great library at Alexandria was torched—but nineteenth-century Egyptologists found papyrus strips stuffed into the mouths of mummified crocodiles in sarcophagi, and these strips turned out to be fragments of Sappho's poems. Though only a small portion of the body of her work remains, it is her perspective on the world that continues to engage us, as does the intensity of her attention.

Here are two translations of a poem that provides us with details, explosive emotion, and a keen perspective. In these lines, the self in love steps out of the enamored psyche and records, thrillingly, the drama of infatuation.

"HE IS MORE THAN A HERO" POEM #31

He is more than a hero
He is a god in my eyes—
the man who is allowed
to sit beside you—he

who listens intimately
to the sweet murmur of
your voice, the enticing

laughter that makes my own
heart beat fast. If I meet
you suddenly, I can't

speak—my tongue is broken;
a thin flame runs under
my skin; seeing nothing

hearing only my own ears
drumming, I drip with sweat;
trembling shakes my body

and I turn paler than
dry grass. At such times
death isn't far from me

[p. 331, *Western Literature in a World Context*
translated by Mary Barnard]

And another version:

POEM #31

To me he seems like a god
as he sits facing you and
hears you near as you speak
softly and laugh

in a sweet echo that jolts
the heart in my ribs. For now
as I look at you my voice
is empty and

can say nothing as my tongue
cracks and slender fire is quick
under my skin. My eyes are dead
to light, my ears

pound, and sweat pours over me.
I convulse, greener than grass,
and feel my mind slip as I
    go close to death.

[p. 108, Page duBois, translated by Willis Barnstone]

The reader will notice immediately how different translators handle
the "re-creation" of Sappho in English. The reader will decide which
translation is more effective (and knowledge of ancient Greek would
help immensely here!)—but Sappho's voice materializes, even in dif-
fering dictions. Look at the words the translators choose to carry the
brute immediacy of her energy: *beat fast, broken, drumming, jolt, pound,
convulse.* There is a studious effort in both versions to try and capture
the drive and the delight, the tumult and turmoil of Sappho's original
poem.

It is her spirit (a combination of energy and perspective) that seems
narrowly to elude both translators as it dances among the syllables.
This is what Ezra Pound called *logopoeia,* and it is most difficult
to reproduce in translation, because this spirit is poetry itself. (Pound,
who called poetry "the most concentrated form of verbal expression,"
set out three techniques for the neophyte poet to use to "charge
words with meaning": *phanopoeia, melopoeia,* and *logopoeia. Phanao-
poeia* meant using a word to cast a visual image on the reader's imag-

ination, *melopoeia* meant charging that word with sound, and *logopoeia* meant doing the same with groups of words—or *orchestrating* sight and sound and sense, mind and emotion.)

It's important to remember that Homer wrote the epic poems that underscore our sense of history and how we read history. (In fact, literature is our real history.) The ancient Greek poets and dramatists all employed particularity: they used images, they "painted" scenes. But just beyond them was the movement toward abstraction in thought: the speculation of the pre-Socratics, the metaphysics of Platonic dialogues, Aristotelian logic.

The "thin flame that runs under the skin" haunts us because it is so exact, so familiar, so strange. ("Just as you feel . . . so I felt.") Yet Greek critics ultimately were less interested in lyric or "melic" poetry like Sappho's than they were in verse that was moving toward abstraction. Sappho's famous meter (the Sapphic stanza is comprised of four lines, the first three containing eleven syllables and the last, five syllables) was considered nonepic, nondramatic (in the classical sense) and, thus, in some ways, unclassifiable. But the list of poetic qualities that we've accumulated so far: particularity, authentic emotion, act of attention—all add up as components of the lyric—and now we have read lyric poems that could only have been written by Sappho—and her voice is imprinted the way DNA codifies us in our genes.

Listen to a later (Roman) critic, the incomparable Longinus, on Sappho's poetry:

> Is it not wonderful? Are you not amazed how she summons, at the same time, soul body hearing tongue sight color, all as though they had wandered off apart from herself?

Longinus says that Sappho constructs of all these elements a *sunodos*: a meeting or a junction. This volatile cohesion doesn't frighten him at all. I cannot think of a better single-word description of what a poem does and is—or a more useful aesthetic definition of Self in the poem. In poetry, the self does not have to be the psychological tracking of consciousness that we are accustomed to living with and within. It can be different—a *crossroads*, a summoning place. Page duBois, in quoting Longinus, states that the poem is a "reassembly of the fragmented, disparate parts of the poetic 'I' that have 'wandered off apart from herself'." We are talking about her heart, her voice, her "broken" tongue, her skin, over which the flame races, her humming ears. Most mortals simply suffer through the self-fragmentation of infatuation; the poet, in writing the poem, brings the shattered world back together, piece by piece.

Emily Dickinson said she recognized a poem by the feeling that the top of her head was about to blow off. A violent coming-apart seems the exact balance of the equation that so gingerly engenders the *sunodos*, the juggling act that keeps the poem reassembled in air from the original explosion of the self. (Sappho's fragmented fate in history literally, ironically, approximates this.) When I write a poem, I find this cohesion and anti-hesion—or dispersion—exhilarating; the attempt to make the language hold still and yet dance is the part of the intoxication of creating a poem.

If a poem is an authentic voice, an act of attention, if it is expressive, if it is a sunodos *of poetic elements, if it is timeless and bordered by silence—then the self of the poem is a shape moving through certain inevitabilities of art. Or as Wallace Stevens says in "Of Modern Poetry," it is sounds moving through "sudden rightnesses."*

Still, some poets believe that the ancients have nothing to say to us about poetry. Since the great forces of cultural change from the Renaissance to the Romantic Age and thence to Modernism have swept, scattering sparks through the consciousness of poetry, our poetic lives seem far removed from, for example, what someone like Horace had to say about writing. Yet Horace, the indomitable Roman, influenced Petrarch and Pope, Johnson and Byron, Holderlin and even Donald Justice. In his "Ars Poetica" Horace has much to say about poetic style. He was very influenced, of course, by the Greeks, who gave him his sense of decorum or restraint, which he understood not as a rigidity or prescriptiveness, but rather a harmony of details (a *sunodos?*) He admired a poetry of limits and careful measures, but he had a large and satiric sense of what we call the universal human condition. "Let each style keep its place," he said—dwelling on what we would call "context" as it situates tone—in comedy and tragedy and domestic drama.

It's not enough that poems be exquisite.
Let empathy prevail and lead the listener's
Heart. A face will smile to see a smile,

Or weep at tears. If you would have me grieve,
Then first feel grief yourself.

["*The Art of Poetry*," trans. J. D. McClatchy, p. 183]

It is interesting that Horace chooses *empathy*, the ability of the self to identify with other selves, with universal human delight and suffering, as the the primary requirement of art. ("If you would have me grieve,/Then first feel grief yourself." Horace believes in life experience—and good readers.) In fact, what takes place in a poem is a kind of conversion process—the reader's attention approximates the attention enacted within the poem, the reader participates as witness, the reader finally "becomes" the voice speaking the poem. (As Mark Doty says in a recent essay, ". . . a great pressure of attention brought to bear on things reveals—magic!—not so much the things as the one who's paying the attention. What is bought, when attention is *paid*, is the self, the stamp of individuality.")

But what does Horace mean "It's not enough that a poem be exquisite?" Aren't poems supposed to be gorgeous? The notion of "being exquisite" carries a pejorative stain; there is a *too* self-conscious aspect implied. Can a work of art be too beautiful? Of course—who hasn't seen a grape-laden gilt rococo frame around a Fragonard? A mosaic of mirrors—an embarrassment of riches. Molti putti. Rococo. Over the top, "fin de siecle." The quality of "restraint" that Horace so honored is difficult to clarify since we often think of restraint as negative—a refusal to participate. But his idea of restraint is more a wise discipline, a thoughtfulness, a choice of *a shape of thought*. Here we are again at the idea of the *sunodos'*—Pound's "vessel" that holds the poem, Wallace Stevens speaks of the imagination finding "what will suffice" (as if there is a natural *weight* to the poem) in "the poem of the act of the mind," in "Of Modern Poetry."

It is easy to over-write, it is extremely difficult to write with symmetry. This poem by James Wright is about symmetry:

LYING IN A HAMMOCK AT WILLIAM DUFFY'S
FARM IN PINE ISLAND, MINNESOTA

Over my head, I see the bronze butterfly,
Asleep on the black trunk,

Blowing like a leaf in green shadow.
Down the ravine behind the empty house,
The cowbells follow one another
Into the distances of the afternoon.
To my right,
In a field of sunlight between two pines,
The droppings of last year's horses
Blaze up into golden stones.
I lean back, as the evening darkens and comes on.
A chicken hawk floats over, looking for home.
I have wasted my life.

"Lying in a Hammock" has a shape—and it is a shape of thought, geometric. It describes an arc, from the eye of the poet ("I") to the butterfly poised on the black trunk of the tree to the ravine and the "distances" of afternoon (then another arc, or completion of a circle) back into the "I." This shape, this moving symmetry, runs beneath the voice of the poem and underscores dramatically what the poem is saying.

Wright is also parodying here the importance of the self in poetry (as well as echoing Rilke). Wright releases the poem into a Zen-like abstraction at the end, the return to himself in the hammock is the perfect combination of climax and irony. "I have wasted my life." Robert Hass (again) in his introduction to Stephen Mitchell's translations of Rilke's poems allows his frustration with poetry's narcissistic tendencies to explode:

> It made me feel, on the one hand, that Rilke was a very great poet, that he had gone deeper than almost any poet of his age and stayed there longer, and I felt, on the other hand, a sudden restless revulsion from the whole tradition of nineteenth and early twentieth century poetry or maybe from lyric poetry as such, because it seemed finally, to have only one subject, the self . . .

But Wright's poem confronts this very notion and refutes it by being aware of it—and acutely, eloquently aware of the tradition from which the lyric springs.

Wright's poem is beautiful, even while gently parodying the art of apprehending beauty, the art that makes the poet's soul. The following poem by M. C. Richards, which I read as a very funny satire, is entirely "unbeautiful" in its confrontation with beauty—and sends up all the bad lyrical poetry ever written.

ECHO-LALIA

I am sitting in a lawn chair
in the late afternoon August sun
and suddenly I am covered with butterflies
kissing me with their tiny mouths
and their needle tools probing my pores for nectar.
Their wings are a subtle murmur, moving the air like fur.
Out of my fingers bloom Roses of Sharon,
and in the bush shines a face of deep amethyst.

Oh shining cattle
Oh grass matted and fish wet in our thighs
and pine branches tangled at Venus Mount,
the rocky ridges of our spines,
the caves of marrow.
Clay between our toes
and from our ears an untrimmed wick.
Oh feel your antlered skull,
your rage of ocean depths,
the harvest of night.

This grasshopper, green and heedless, blesses its destiny.
The geese of imagination fly north to nest and drowse.
Our skin is white water, fresh and porous.
The mammoth is our circus, the ibis our requiem.

We are a new species:
whose hands bloom
and whose spirit hovers like a water bird
whose tongue flashes fire
and who feeds like lichen on stone.

Both poems steep themselves in sensation and the responses of the senses—both poems sketch in a landscape (one stark, one excessive). Both poems situate the self within that landscape, then reach conclusions about the nature of life. Both poems have a seeming immediacy—the kind of immediacy also apparent in "Western Wind"

—and clearly both are acts of attention. The voices are passionate and specific. There are even images and motifs that echo each other—butterflies, cattle and cowbells, pines, sun, stone. One poem is masterful, the other dreadful—what saves the latter is self-knowledge of its awfulness.

The condition of "echolalia" has to do with the pathological repetition of other people's speech—and thus the title is a big clue as to what the poem is about. The poem is about bad poetry—and it has no self. The "self" in the poem attempts to define itself by the mindless repetition of terrible pseudo-poetic lines, borrowed at random, without awareness of the overall effect. The poem ends up without a *sunodos*, it does not come together, it's like a shattered ball of mercury, shining, sticky, ultimately unshapeable bits of substance—bouncing around in the reader's mind, where they try to cohere but do not cohere. (Remember Horace's instructions about "first feel grief," etc.) This is funny but also instructive. All beginning writers make mistakes like these—it's revelatory to see the accident happen on the page, right before your eyes. ("The mammoth is our circus/the ibis our requiem." *Yikes.*)

Tone carries the poem straightforwardly, ironically, doggedly, stridently. Failure of tone is common. Sappho sitting near her lover and the lonely wanderer in the field, Rilke and Bishop—we hear the emotion in all these voices. The reader can spot a counterfeit tone at forty paces. And a satire of counterfeit, writing-workshop-exercise-type rhetoric, at the same distance.

Perhaps going further with the idea of the "coming-togetherness" of a poem, I'd argue that almost every poem has an implied shape—by which I mean an engendering shape, a shape that is an idea—and some poems provide dramatic examples. Yeats's "The Second Coming" is a spiral, a *gyre:*

> Turning and turning in the widening gyre
> The falcon cannot hear the falconer;
> Things fall apart; the centre cannot hold;
> Mere anarchy is loosed upon the world,
> The blood-dimmer tide is loosed, and everywhere
> The ceremony of innocence is drowned;

The best lack all conviction, while the worst
Are full of passionate intensity.

Surely some revelation is at hand;
Surely the Second Coming is at hand.
The Second Coming! Hardly are those words out
When a vast image out of *Spiritus Mundi*
Troubles my sight: somewhere in the sands of the desert
A shape with lion body and the head of a man,
A gaze blank and pitiless as the sun,
Is moving its slow thighs, while all about it
Reel shadows of the indignant desert birds.
The darkness drops again; but now I know
That twenty centuries of stony sleep
Were vexed to nightmare by a rocking cradle,
And what rough beast, its hour come round at last,
Slouches toward Bethlehem to be born?

At the risk of over-literalizing this approach, I feel obligated to point out a few obvious examples. Elizabeth Bishop's "The Waiting Room" is an "o" that begins as small as mouth, then grows into a larger mouth, a monstrous gaping zero—then a whirling sphere that surrounds the earth. An excerpt:

Suddenly, from inside,
Came an oh! of pain
—Aunt Consuelo's voice—
Not very loud or long.
I wasn't at all surprised;
even then I knew she was
a foolish timid woman.
I might have been embarrassed,
but wasn't. What took me
completely by surprise
was that it was *me:*
my voice, in my mouth.
Without thinking at all
I was my foolish aunt,
I—we—were falling, falling,

our eyes glued to the cover
of the *National Geographic,*
February, 1918.

I said to myself: three days
and you'll be seven years old.
I was saying it to stop
the sensation of falling off
the round turning world
into cold, blue-black space.

Randall Jarrell, in a critical essay on Robert Frost's "Home Burial"
delineates shape after shape within the poem, as the young husband
and wife argue on a staircase—as he first looms threateningly over
her, then she rises, describing the way dirt "leapt" in the husband's
shovel as he dug the grave of their dead infant. In a later poem
(Frost's beautiful tribute to his wife, "Silken Tent"), the outwardly
radiating attention of the woman is symbolized by the tent's cone
shape and the tension of the tent's internal bonds. Here is an excerpt:

And its supporting central cedar pole,
That is its pinnacle to heavenward
And signifies the sureness of the soul,
Seems to owe naught to an single cord,
But strictly held by none, is loosely bound . . .

And in a much more contemporary postmodern, absurdly ironic
vein, Susan Wheeler's "He or She That's Got the Limb, That Holds
Me Out on It" is (it seems to me) in the shape of a shadow of a boat
lengthening or an arm outstretched, waving goodbye.

The girls are drifting in their ponytails
And their pig iron boat. So much for Sunday.
The dodo birds are making a racket
to beat the band. You could have come too.

The girls wave and throw their garters
from their pig iron boat. Why is this charming?
Where they were nailed on their knees
the garters all rip. You were expected.

The youngest sees a Fury in a Sentra
in a cloud. This is her intimation and she balks.
The boat begins rocking from the scourge
of the sunset. The youngest starts the song.

As Robert Hass has rather gleefully pointed out, this poem has an
antecedent in the first poem in Frost's 1915 book, *A Boy's Will:*

I'm going out to clean the pasture spring;
I'll only stop to rake the leaves away
(And wait to watch the water clear, I may);
I shan't be gone long.—You come too.

Or Rita Dove's topsy-turvy irreverent bird looking down on chim-
ing, rhyming, circling circles lengthening occasionally to bobbing
cylinders:

FREEDOM: BIRD'S EYE VIEW

The sun flies over the madrigals,
outsmarting the magisterial
wits, sad ducks
who imagine they matter.
What a parade! Wind tucks
a Dixie cup up its
sleeve, absconds with
a kid's bright chatter
while above, hawks
wheel as the magistrates circle
below, clutching their hats.

I'm not buying. To watch
the tops of 10,000
heads floating by on sticks
and not care if one of them
sees me (though it
would be a kick!)
—now, that's
what I'd call
freedom,

and justice,
and ice cream for all.

These are, as I mentioned, rather obvious shapes that guide our reading. But I also believe that every poem radiates from a "buried" shape. Poem shapes signify a poet's "foundation" thinking, the bottom line, the origin—the place where the poem originates as a morphous slouch toward Bethlehem—or image or sound-impression. Something gathering, gaining definition. Isomorphic. Cumulus. A person turning, laughing over her shoulder, a whirl of autumn leaves, upswept in an exhaust, the synchronized feet of a marching band. (To borrow two shapes from poems by Jorie Graham.) If the poet is lucky enough to discover a poem's inevitable shape, all the rest will fall into place.

To quote an earlier essay of my own: "Why does this dramatic action in language, why does the shape of a poem's journey within itself, argue beyond truth for its aesthetic inevitability? Perhaps because the abstract longs for a material manifestation like a soul for a body: for its object, action, shape?"

> *I'm four, maybe five. In the backyard of our newly built house on Pascal Street in St. Paul, there is a new red swing hung over a stretch of sand. I'm on that swing, tentatively pumping as my mother pushes me higher and higher into the air. As she pushes me, she recites a poem by Robert Louis Stevenson, "How Would You Like to Go Up in a Swing?"*
>
> *What stays with me is not just the rather ordinary diction of the poem ("How would you like to go up in a swing?/Up in the air so blue?) but the shape created by the words, by the question-answer tension. I remember the momentum caused by my mother's pushes and how my own sensations became fear as she flings me from her into space, then exhilaration at flying outward ("Up in the air and over the wall/Till I can see so wide . . .") Then, reaching a limit, I am pulled back into the field of the continuum.*
>
> from *Women and Poetry*

I understood that poem viscerally, bodily. I felt it move in two directions at once. I was moving outward on the poetic line and returning at its end. I was *swinging inside the poem itself . . .*

This experience of form and formulation, of tracking a poem's linaments, of swinging inside the poem itself—allows us to see that the more traditionally formal poems have similar constructs of thinking.

Each of the traditional sonnet types, for example, gives us insight into how its authors and earliest practictioners "built" the form around analytical and expressive patterns.
Many poem forms derived from dance or song. The sonnet's debt to these arts is not so evident (though the word "sonnet" comes from "sonneto" or "little song" in Italian), but it is there. Each sonnet form is choreographed and each has a shape that precedes the form. The Shakespearean sonnet, for example, is usually a progressive argument that I see as shape in the air: three quick spins and a sudden leap; that is to say, three quatrains and the final couplet. The rhyme scheme —abab, cdcd, efef, gg—reinforces this movement. In the following example, I have separated the quatrains to emphasize this progression.

Let me not to the marriage of true minds
Admit impediments. Love is not love
Which alters when it alteration finds,
Or bends with the remover to remove:

O no; it is an ever-fixed mark,
That looks on tempests, and is never shaken;
It is the star to every wandering bark,
Whose worth's unknown, although his height be taken.

Love's not Time's fool, though rosy lips and cheeks
Within his bending sickle's compass come;
Love alters not with his brief hours and weeks,
But bears it out even to the edge of doom.

If this be error, and upon me prov'd,
I never writ, nor no man ever loved.

[Shakespeare, Sonnet 116]

The Petrarchan sonnet, named for the fourteenth-century Italian poet, is made up of an octave and a sestet. Between those first eight lines and the six following is a psychological break, a turn. After laying out the subject of contemplation, the poem changes course rhythmically. The reader feels the quickening of expectation as the poem breaks in two.

On First Looking Into Chapman's Homer

Much have I traveled in the realms of gold,
  And many goodly states and kingdoms seen;

Round many western islands have I been
Which bards in fealty to Apollo hold.
Oft of one wide expanse have I been told
That deep-browed Homer ruled as his demesne;
Yet did I never breathe its pure serene
Till I heard Chapman speak out loud and bold;

Then felt I like some watcher of the skies
When a new planet swims into his ken;
Or like stout Cortez when with eagle eyes
He stared at the Pacific—and all his men
Looked at each other with wild surmise—
Silent, upon a peak in Darien.

[John Keats]

The last example of poem shape, the Spenserian sonnet, (named for
the sixteenth-century poet, Edmund Spenser) is a system of "envel-
opes" or linkages. The rhyme scheme is abab, bcbc, cdcd, ee—the qua-
trains are "stitched" together in "loops," the rhymes at the stanza ends
and beginnings "chime" off each other—pray/assay, likewise/devise
—and this linkage makes the isomorphic progression chain-like, a vi-
sual guide that underscores the continuity and triumph of expression.

Sonnet LXXV

One day I wrote her name upon the strand,
But came the waves and washed it away;
Again I wrote it with a second hand,
But came the tide and made my pains his prey.
"Vain man" said she, "that dost in vain assay
A mortal thing so to immortalize,
For I myself shall like to this decay,
And eke my name be wiped out likewise.
"Not so" quod I, "let baser things devise
To die in dust, but you shall live by fame;
My verse your virtues rare shall eternize
And in the heavens write your glorious name,
Where, whenas death shall all the world subdue,
Our love shall live, and life renew.

[Edmund Spenser]

Voice, tone, diction, *sunodos,* shape. In lyric, narrative, and dramatic poems, all these things come together. Beyond their technical manifestations, many of the elements are mysterious. Most mysterious of all is the last element I'll talk about—something to do with how the poem looks us in the eye.

At his early death, John Keats left behind some of the most beautiful poems in the English language and one haunting, disturbing fragment. Written out on a sheet of paper found with his other writings (around 1819 or so) was a kind of "margin note" in his hand. He had been working on "The Cap and Bells," a comic poem, at this time. Some scholars thought the fragment was meant to fit somewhere in that text, but given the poem's tone, this is unlikely. Others place it with "The Fall of Hyperion," and some think of it as a note to Fanny Brawne, whom he desperately, famously loved. I believe, as others do, that Keats jotted down these lines as a poem in and of itself—a frightening poem that came to him in the middle of other work—a vision of what a poem is, beyond the expressive and analytic: a third thing, an awful mystery.

This living hand, now warm and capable
Of earnest grasping, would, if it were cold
And in the icy silence of the tomb
So haunt thy days and chill thy dreaming nights
That thou would wish thine own heart dry of blood
So in my veins red life might stream again,
And thou be conscience-calmed. See here it is—
I hold it towards you.

It is a terrifying poem. Keats is saying that the poem has life beyond death, and life that can "haunt" and "chill" so much that the reader would long to give up her own life so that the poet could live again. It is a mortally wounded poem, a heartsick poem, the poem of a man about to die and utterly conscious of his incommutable sentence. He is so bitter that he wants the reader to feel guilty—to feel so guilty that she'd be willing to die in order to "calm" a bad conscience. It is a challenge to the reader: that hand reaches out to us, out of the page—*come on,* it dares us, *take it, take my hand.* Yes, it is a cry from a sad, sick, lonely young man—his despairing self lifts the hand and holds it out to us—but it is, to me, something beyond the gothic gesture, the disembodied hand stretching from the tomb.

That hand, that shape, that proffered grasp is poetry, *is the poem.*
This is what a poem does if it is working. It terrifies us, it makes us
feel like the top of our heads are coming off, it is bordered by silence,
it makes us see that we *(you) must change your life,* it cries *Christ!*
It is not a curse, it is an invitation to be conscious in the most
extraordinary way: it is *red life in the veins*—or nothing. Just as I feel,
every time I read those words, that I can see and *locate* Keats, sitting
in his lonely room—then getting up and staring at me, his gaze burn-
ing up the thin veils of years between us—I feel when I read a poem
that works. (*Just as you feel, so I felt . . .*) Thomas Hardy's "During
Wind and Rain," Sylvia Plath's "Death & Co.," Hopkins's "Dark Son-
nets," Gwendolyn Brooks's poem about her abortions, Tu Fu on the
vicissitudes of public life, Basho on the moon, Li Po on "The River
Merchant's Wife," Robert Burns turning up a mouse with the plough,
Shakespeare on festering lilies, Adrienne Rich and Wordsworth on
the dream of a common language, Wyatt on inconstancy, Anne Brad-
street on a burning house, Robert Lowell's "Skunk Hour," Cavafy,
James Merrill, Hart Crane on dreams, Lorca's "Sleepwalker's Ballad,"
Neruda's love poems, Gloria Fuertes's caustic songs, and Catullus
singing of his lady's sparrow's death.

Following is a poem that I wrote in response to Keats's proffered
hand. I tried to imagine Keats actually returning to life, entering the
twentieth century, and I tried to imagine him coming back as a
woman—in fact, a woman of slightly questionable character. Not ex-
actly a stripper, but a figure of the demi-monde named Kitty. I tried to
imagine how Keats would be treated if he returned in this altered
state, how many poets would recognize him. How many poets would
take his extended hand? How many contemporary poets, so con-
cerned with material life, as we all are, would grasp that hand?

OUR KITTY

She is swinging in a contraption above the heads
of the audience,
reflected in the glass lamps on the tables.

She sits in one of those fin-de-siecle gilded sleighs
hung from the ceiling
by braids of sparking hemp.

Here come all the poet-accountants pushing in
to talk about cate-
gories of experience. Wine, sex.

The ceiling is hammered tin, alight and jumping
with her shadow
        cast upward by the table lamps.

As she swings, she rubs herself, adjusts herself
in the seat so she
        can be seen through the see-through bottom.

Pink cheeks has Kitty. A pop-open camisole. Mother
is striking her
        name from the family bible. But

She has to eat, does Kitty. She is so petite & incautious
that all the poet-
        accountants are taking copious notes.

They can use: she may be the littlest
Whore of imagination.
        She might even be how they imagine

The twentieth-century's end: just like the end
of the last century,
        the dream of body parts floating

Above cigar smoke. In other words, *more war.*
Kitty inspires all
        of them to think about triage.

The end of the twentieth century: Artist or banker—
who should be saved?
        The artist in his same old tourniquet? The banker

With a dented skull? Try to guess. The poet-
accountants have
        already guessed. They know the price of

this ending. They've seen the banker and his surgeons,
the poet bleeding
        all over the sterile gauze. Who wants to be

John Keats? Well, the poems, yes—but not the death.
Now they hear Kitty
        coughing. I'm Keats, she gasps.

I'm John Fucking Keats returned in Kitty's body.
Forlorn she cries *forlorn*
        but they refuse to listen to her

As she swings, pale and beautiful, glittering, above them,
holding out her
>   *living hand, warm, capable*—as ever, untaken.

Well, yes, it's supposed to be a funny poem, but (like the
"Echolalia" poem) a little caustic as well. The poets in the poem may
have lost touch with *red life in the veins,* with the reasons why we
write poetry or the answer to the question, *What is a poem?*

There is, of course, no answer to this question. ("We do not teach
poetry," Theodore Roethke said, "we *insinuate* it.") We can see what
a poem insinuates about itself by recognizing what it sees in the mir-
ror. I sympathize with the revulsion and "restlessness" Robert Hass
describes in thinking of the self in premodern and modern poems
and throughout the lyric—but I believe that "Self" is other than the
tired phenomenon of ego—it is, in the best poems, what conscious-
ness can be if it imagines itself anew. It is possibility.

The real reason "Roses are Red" is not a poem is that it has no pos-
sibility, no self. It is truly anonymous. "Western Wind" may be
anonymous as well, but it still has a raging, keening, dreaming,
eccentric self, which means it has voice, tone, *sunodos,* shape. It is not
anonymous because it is our own experience, even if it is not, liter-
ally, ours: we feel what the poet felt. Yet it has mystery. Like Keats
offering his living hand, the homesick cry reaches out to us, familiar
and strange—as we remain to ourselves.

I was the world in which I walked, and what I saw
Or heard or felt came not from myself;
And there I found myself more truly and more strange.

["Tea at the Palaz of Hoon," *Palm,* Wallace Stevens]

As always, the poem itself says it best.

III

The Line/The Form/The Music

David Baker and Ann Townsend

We walk. We walk in order to go someplace. Walking has a practical function, taking people across a particular space and so across time. Through the eons, too, people have learned to speak. Speaking has a practical function, used to convey information, as in "I'm cold," or "Your softball team is terrible," or "Here come the dinosaurs and they look mighty hungry."

But sometimes we don't simply walk. We dance. And sometimes talking isn't good enough. Sometimes we throw back our heads, open our mouths, and sing.

Why do we need to enhance our practical expressions with more heightened, fancy, or artificial varieties? Why sing when we can talk, and why dance when we can walk? What is it about human beings that urges us to complicate or embellish the functional? Why paint our walls, decorate our forks and spoons, color our fingernails and eyelids?

We embellish out of exuberance, out of imaginative energy, and out of passion. Singing and dancing, for instance, are expressions of ecstasy: to be out of our stance, out of our heads, a touch crazed. That is the meaning of *ex stasis*. We embellish speaking into song when normalcy isn't sufficient to demonstrate our passions. Singing (like weeping) takes our speech into a more extreme dimension of communication. It is primitive, nonlogical, and expressive in ways that speaking cannot be, when our more typical syntax or pitch or demeanor can't measure the proportions of our lives. Dance, too, enhances and exaggerates the movements of walking. Dance makes movement strange again. It celebrates movement, studies it, draws our attention to what we typically take for granted. Our arts are *about* the more practical functions of our lives.

We write for many practical reasons, too. We write to retain information, to argue, to tell stories, to pass along knowledge. And sometimes we heighten our writing by further self-conscious gestures or formulations. Sometimes we turn to poetry to express, in writing, our most passionate experiences. Poetry is speech made artful, artificial, and self-aware. Like singing, poetry is a form of ecstasy: Poetry is writing out of our heads. And, as dancing is to walking, so poetry is more *about* writing than other kinds of writing may be.

Let's say that again. Of all the forms of writing, poetry is the most self-conscious and conspicuous, the most aware of itself *as writing*. Poets employ a myriad of techniques to slow the movement of the text, to draw a reader's attention to the poem's method as well as to its message. The method becomes part of the message.

Some may disagree with a judgment that poetry desires to heighten our awareness of its methods. William Stafford, for instance, often argued for simplicity or naturalness of style. "First thought, best thought!" he urged. He wanted to take the academic self-consciousness out of poetry. The Deep Image poets of the 1960s and 1970s, too, wanted to make their language "transparent," to allow the reader to look *through* the language, and through the poem's form and technique, to find something like psychic depth, emotional purity. In a comment from the time, W. S. Merwin says that "to recur in its purest form, poetry seems to have to keep reverting to its naked condition." This stance derives from Carl Jung's claim about language and the psyche that "if we hide our nakedness ... by putting on gorgeous robes and trappings ... we are essentially lying about our own history." Robert Bly is more adamant about the tyranny of technique: "All technical essays [about poetry and form] are attempts to construct poetry machines, so that even people with no imagination can write it." To Bly, we "descend" whenever we talk about technique, since the "[s]tudy of technique cannot help us to write an intense poem." He continues: "I refuse to say anything at all about prosody. What an ugly word it is!" Making poetry self-conscious about its "naked" tactics would seem antithetical to some poets' desire to probe a poem's (or poet's or reader's) subconscious.

Our own opinion is that all poetry is always, in fundamental ways, *about* its own form and tactic. Even the Deep Image poem is proud of its humility and asks readers to appreciate the eloquence of its "plain" strategies. We may be drawn to John Keats's assertion in his famous 1818 letter to his publisher, John Taylor, that "if Poetry comes not as naturally as Leaves to a tree it had better not come at all." But Richard Lanham, in *The Motives of Eloquence,* more fully clarifies the artist's paradox: "The way to naturalness lies through artifice, not around it." It is fundamental to our belief that the more a poet (and reader) knows about technique and the variety of effects of poetic style and technique, the more flexibility and command the poet will exercise. David Ferry, one of our age's finest poetry translators, confirms this opinion: "our vivid consciousness of the artifice of [poetry's] forms makes us vividly, radiantly, conscious of our experience of its meanings." Perhaps the most accurate synthesis of this paradox—the collision of natural ease and self-conscious labor—is found in William Butler Yeats's great "Adam's Curse":

> "A line will take us hours maybe,
> Yet if it does not seem a moment's thought
> Our stitching and unstitching has been naught.
> Better go down upon your marrow bones
> And scrub a kitchen pavement, or break stones
> Like an old pauper in all kinds of weather;
> For to articulate sweet sounds together
> Is to work harder than all these and yet
> Be thought an idler by the noisy set
> Of bankers, schoolmasters, and clergymen
> The martyrs call the world."

From the very beginning of this venture, we want to acknowledge the arguable nature of the subject. It's hard to think of a topic that makes poets more defensive, nervous, or possessive than the subject of technique and form. We hope to present many things here, to represent varieties of reading poetry, and to suggest different kinds of writing strategies. But let there be no doubt: We are writing our opinions, what works for us, what we believe as readers and do as writers of poetry.

Exercises

1. Read some of the famous Deep Image poetry from the '60s. Try Robert Bly's book *Silence in the Snowy Fields*, W. S. Merwin's *The Lice* or *The Carrier of Ladders*, James Wright's *The Branch Will Not Break*.

2. Read the more self-referential poetry of Robert Hass in *Praise* or *Sun Under Wood*, Jorie Graham's *The End of Beauty* or *Materialism*.

3. Consider (or write a journal entry about) the different desires, achievements, and insufficiencies of the Deep Image, with its desire to be "transparent," its need to locate the *sub*-conscious. Compare this to the capabilities and limitations of a more *self*-conscious poetry that wants to expose, to self-analyze, its own tactics.

4. Write a plain poem, seeking to make your techniques hidden; write another, full of eloquence and literary wit, whose tactics are obvious and self-aware.

We have been married for fourteen years, and embark on this adventure in technique and style with the same collective attention that we try to embody in our daily lives. We are both poets, critics, and teachers of literature and writing, who work in the same small English department. We are also both trained musicians and like to play together. Ann, the singer, specializes in Modernist art songs and contemporary jazz, and David, who taught guitar for six years, has worked with many jazz, rock, and country bands. When we cook, one of us cuts the herbs as the other heats the oil; one pours the wine, while the other sautés the garlic; one drinks the wine, while the other . . . well, you get the picture. Giving our young daughter a bath is a similar handing-back-and-forth of soap and socks and towels and toys. We write this chapter with a shared pen (and computer), though we have some different opinions and interests regarding the details of our subject.

We also know when to ask for advice. Here it is natural to turn for help first to our friends, the poets, as we try to determine the rules, at least the working definitions, for creating poetry by attending to issues of form and structure. What exactly *are* the technical characteristics of poetry that can help us understand, and create, the art? Stephen Minot has written a well-known textbook for creative writers entitled *Three Genres*. "There are," he says, "five fundamental qualities that distinguish poetry from prose: concern for the line as opposed to the sentence, greater attention to the *sound* of language, development of rhythms, a heightened use of images, and a tendency to create density by implying far more than is stated directly."

Minot's first three elements—line, sound, and rhythm—are some of our chapter's important characters. Elsewhere in this book, Yusef Komunyakaa discusses imagery, as Carol Muske examines issues of density and implication. But wait: As attractive as Minot's definition is, we sense some arguable points, too. Isn't good prose interested in sound? Doesn't all fine syntax have precise rhythmic structure? Could any text be more dense and implicative than, say, James Joyce's *Finnegan's Wake*, that grand, layered, 700-page novel? Notice how Minot uses qualifiers like *greater* attention and *heightened* use to suggest that poetry uses what all good writing uses, only more intensely.

That's the point. Poetry makes more intense use, more self-aware use, of the elements of good writing.

WHAT'S MY LINE?

Then what elements do establish the meaningful differences between poetry and other forms of writing? Robert Wallace, whose *Writing Poetry* is one of the most successful college writing texts, makes a simple, intrepid assertion when he says that "[i]t is the unit of line that distinguishes verse from prose or speech." That's short and sweet. In his splendid study *Free Verse: An Essay On Prosody*, Charles O. Hartman issues a compatible opinion: "*Verse is language in lines. This distinguishes it from prose.*"*

---

*Realize even here the arguable nature of things. Lewis Turco is the author of the useful reference for poets, *The New Book of Forms*. Responding directly to Wallace's assertion that the line distinguishes poetry from prose or speech, he says with certainty: "Not so. Much more than merely the existence of 'lines' in the genre of 'poetry' distinguishes verse from prose, which are the only *modes* of language in which any *genre* (fiction, drama, poetry) may be written. . . . Prose is *unmetered* language; verse is *metered* language." To Turco

The line is the fundamental formal unit of poetry, along with, of course, the sentence. The appearance of lines, the look of the poem on the page, often compels a reader's expectations even before the reader has actually started to read a poem. You know what we mean. You pick up a book, open a page, and if all the lines break before arriving at the right margin—that is, if the lines look like poetry— then you put certain expectations into play and suppress others. If it looks like a poem, then you read it like a poem. The line tells you it's a poem. Starting to write a poem is, for us, often largely an issue of finding the right line: the right line length, the right line density, the right line rhythm, the right number of lines in a stanza.

In the next section of this chapter, we will talk about the several ways we count and measure lines, as well as the larger ways to formulate the shape of a whole poem and a poem's argument. But before we venture into measurement, we want to explore more about the poetic line—its effects, its elements, its movement. The line is a device to control the pace of a poem, to defer its descent. The line also creates the border of the poem, the *out*line of its features. It is the poem's cameo. David once wrote the following passage to describe the dynamic effects of a poem's line as compared to the movement of prose: "A poem's inexorable bearing is downward, to the bottom of the page, to its end, to stillness. Prose is more languid, drifting laterally, with leisure, nudged downward only by a right-hand margin. It spreads like water over wide earth, looking for small cracks. A poem is a waterfall, tumbling. But to defer or delay its downward-falling fate, a poem may construct and then usurp any number of impediments—from lengthened or heavily end-stopped lines, stanza breaks, or rhyme to the more rhetorical techniques of meditation, speculation, or song. The story, we know, the narrative, is already written in the poem's descent."

With the sentence, the line provides a dynamic force to organize the idea and music of one's mind into order and visual delight. In

---

the line may provide a visible shape for things, but meter, and only meter— which is audible rather than visual—is the necessary ingredient to make verse. Hartman says that "we can tell verse from prose on sight," but to Turco an unmetered free-verse poem is essentially prose. If you want to pursue this debate further, see David's book *Meter in English*, where this exchange occurs.

fact, the line's relationship to the sentence is one of poetry's basic points of tension and power:

> Look how
> this sentence, prosaic and ungraceful
> though it may be,
> derives some power and some anxiety, merely
> from the break of the sentence
> into these irregular lines.

Or, let's try it another way, for different effects:

> Look how this sentence, prosaic and ungraceful
> Though it may be, derives some power
> And some anxiety, merely from the break
> Of the sentence into these irregular lines.

See how it is more poised or regular, with a kind of traditional coherence, merely by the placement of the line breaks? We can make the same text much more harried, or fragmented, by audacious line-breaking:

> Look how this
> sentence, prosaic and ungraceful though it
> may be, derives some power and
>   some
> anxiety, merely from the
> break of
> the sentence into
>   these
> irregular
> lines.

That's sort of awful, isn't it? Especially those lines ending with prepositions, conjunctions, and articles may seem unthoughtful and sloppy to many readers, and the interruption of phrases—cracking those phrases into pieces—seems also unfortunate. Of course, the text itself isn't evocative either. Perhaps a more interesting visual display lends a touch of stylistic chutzpah to the language. There are times when this type of disjunctive lineation might be just the right effect, when a poet wants to create anxiety or to suggest the incomplete or imperfect, the broken: when a poet wants to argue against the conventional beauty (or tyranny, as some would say) of a regular line. It depends on the effect desired. What do you want your poem to do?

Exercises

1. Let's extend this thought a bit more. Before you go further, you might try this simple exercise. We have removed the line breaks and stanza breaks from these three poems. Now, you put them back in; retype each poem, and break the lines where you think they ought to be, based on your sense of pacing, based on the poem's syntax or punctuation or any other formalizing factors.

2. The first is a short, light poem by John Updike, called "Upon Shaving Off One's Beard."

> *The scissors cut the long-grown hair; the razor scrapes the remnant fuzz. Small-jawed, weak-chinned, bug-eyed, I stare at the forgotten boy I was.*

3. Try another short poem. Linda Pastan's "Caroline" has a different kind of tone and pace from Updike's.

> *She wore her coming death as gracefully as if it were a coat she'd learned to sew. When it grew cold enough she'd simply button it and go.*

4. Finally, one more. "The Lamb" by William Heyen is a slightly longer lyric, presenting you more choices regarding lining and stanzas. Try a few different versions to see how it works best.

> *Both hindlegs wrapped with rope, Wenzel's chosen lamb hung head down from a branch of one of his elms. Its throat slashed, the lamb drained, its nose and neckwool dripping, lawn soaking up the bright blood. Once skinned, once emptied of its blue and yellow organs, its translucent strings of intestines, and though its eyes still bulged, the lamb rose like steam from the pail of its*

> *guts, toward stray shafts of sunlight filtering through the trees.*
> *Until it came to pass: I forgot my knees, and entered the deep*
> *kingdom of death.*
>
> **5.** There is no real right answer to this task, but the actual poems, as structured by the poets, will appear later in this chapter. We will talk then about what choices the poets made. Another suggestion: when you revise your own poems, feel this kind of liberty to line and reline.

In the three versions of lining "Look how this sentence," above, you probably noticed the different effects produced by the locations of the line breaks. But what all three versions share is a persistently *enjambed* line. Enjambment is the alternative to the *end-stopped* line. An enjambed line produces a line break without accompanying punctuation, as in "Look how/this sentence." The end-stopped line, however, intensifies or heightens the turn of the line by breaking at the point of punctuation, as in "though it may be,/derives some power." It's as though two pieces of punctuation exist at the end of the line. Look at Shakespeare's great sonnets, and you will discover the persistent regularity of his lines. Nearly every line is end-stopped, producing a distinct and measured pause; very many of the quatrains stop with a period or semicolon, making an even more dramatic pause than a comma's; nearly every line completes a phrase or clause, and thus completes a thought. Shakespeare's lines have a distinct unity and balance, a formalized, regular weight. In fact, the end-stopped line is the normative line throughout the history of English poetry.

Let's examine another, very beautiful poem:

When you are old and gray and full of sleep,
And nodding by the fire, take down this book,
And slowly read, and dream of the soft look
Your eyes had once, and of their shadows deep;

How many loved your moments of glad grace,
And loved your beauty with love false or true;
But one man loved the pilgrim soul in you,
And loved the sorrows of your changing face.

And bending down beside the glowing bars
Murmur, a little sadly, how love fled
And paced upon the mountains overhead
And hid his face amid a crowd of stars.

Perhaps the most significant point in any poetic line is the final word. After all, that word stays fresh in the mind while the eyes travel back to the starting point of the next line. Notice how you can scan the ends of these lines and have a basic sense of the poem's narrative and theme. Yeats is thinking hard about his terminal words. Their importance is further emphasized by Yeats's lovely, perfect envelope rhymes.

"When You Are Old" is the first poem we memorized together, sixteen years ago. It is a brilliantly paced lyric, measured in careful degrees. The first stanza is slow, deliberate as the aged lover, as she relaxes by the fire, as she moves, as she reads; and the line breaks emphasize the unhurried pace, her measured breath. In the end-stopped lines, in fact, notice how the line break reemphasizes the punctuation, making the break more significant. Then notice how the pace quickens in the next stanzas, as time passes with more haste. The lines in stanza two move fast, without internal punctuation, then pause at line's end; and by the final stanza, the only punctuation comes in line two, as the lines, enjambed, rapidly descend. The syntax is actually quite similar throughout—lots of clauses and compound verbs connected by so many *and*'s—but in the last stanza Yeats has removed the ultimate commas, and so the poem flies away, into the sky. It's as though the lover cannot halt the passing and hastening of time, as she cannot prevent her own aging. But the poet possesses the power to measure time. Yeats is proud of that power. He's rubbing it in a little, in fact, as though to say, "See, now it's too late. I am gone into the eternity of art and you have only books to love you."

To complement his measured lines, Yeats writes with the fluid syntax of a song. There's a kind of rhetorical agreement or purity to this poem. All systems seem to be working toward a singular end: a kind of quickening, inevitable logic. The long line seems especially capable of this kind of graceful, sustained pace. Visually, the long line is closer to prose than the short line, and its rhythms are more capable of the fluidity of prose. Some say the long line is best suited for narrative poems; such lines can contain the fuller breadth of a story. Some say the long line has the best capacity for meditation and argument, to sustain a stream of thought.

Here is an entire draft of one of David's poems, written early in his career. It's scary to show, so publicly, one's more flawed work. This draft is a fairly late draft, the result of more than two dozen revisions over a couple of hot summer months. You can notice David's desire for a fluid or sustained syntax and tone. He tried to write long sentences, relatively unbroken by punctuation. Notice as well the poem's meditative impulse:

Every night for weeks, from the lilac's deep heart,
a catbird has softly sung through my sleep,
the same one always quietly calling when I come home
or when I bend beneath it in the garden. This morning
I listened until the bulbs I planted seemed
like teardrops and I put them in the ground sadly.

Every night it has sung through my sleep
until now, as I lie here restless, alone, tugged
from the slow wash of night not by light
or any noise, but by a silence dark and choking.
I do not know whether the bird has flown away or what
has happened. It is too dark to see anything

from the window except the wind wasting away
in the near leaves and a few stars, high, faint.
How strange to feel such loss as small absences.
I wish I could reach out and touch the song
where it floats, to keep it from the darkness.
I wish I heard it singing softly, safe now, saved.

It's a decent draft, with some lovely phrases, but there are also plenty of awkward or unremarkable gestures. We're going to come back to this poem, this draft, later. Believe us, this is not how the poem ends up. For now:

Exercises

1. Do some reading of poems in long lines to determine for yourself the potential effects. Look at C. K. Williams, who may write the longest lines in recent poetry. Notice his clear narrative and journalistic impulses, those prose virtues. Look at T. R.

Hummer, Rodney Jones, Campbell McGrath, or Brigit Pegeen Kelly, for other recent poets who have mastered the long line. Read, of course, Walt Whitman, whose long, prose-like lines derive less from earlier poetry and more from the Bible, from the expansive rhetoric of opera, and from oratory.

2. Try these effects yourself in a poem, or at least in some opening lines of a poem. That is, write in a relatively unbroken or flowing syntax. Pay close attention to the line breaks. Write a series of lines with end-stopped, punctuated lines; write some with enjambment. Consider the differing effects (or write about that in a journal entry).

3. Write a new poem in long lines, perhaps very long lines.

Then what of the short line? If the long line may be more suited to the needs of narrative and meditation, then perhaps the shorter line is suited to a kind of heightened focus, since it tends to magnify its smaller portion of material. The short line is perhaps better suited to fragment, too, to a more anxious or purposely halting movement. Of course the short line also falls quicker down the page. Maybe such anxiety is what William Carlos Williams meant by his assertion in *I Wanted to Write a Poem:* "I found I could not use the long line because of my nervous nature." Williams is being funny, of course, but he is also quite aware of the strength of his own short lines, so taut and restless. Let's look at a poem in short lines. Like the draft of the poem about the vanished catbird, this is another of David's poems-in-progress. He wrote this during the same months as the other poem:

> Once there was beauty
> in the wreck we made
> of the world. The quarry lake
> was waveless and freckled
>
> under the evening's early
> moon. The piles
> of low rubble rocks
> shone along the shore

bare in the last light.
Who could blame us
as we stepped from
our clothes and dove

to the deep heart
of water? Who could
see there, like a dim
and floating stone

in the still sheen,
the ball of cottonmouths
simmer? There was
nothing to do.

We stood back
on the glistening bank
and watched as she drifted.
She had found their secret.

They must have been
on her, mouths like
white flowers, her mouth
open as if to call or

sing, yet silent, perhaps
already choked with water.
Or did she really smile,
as it seemed to us

who were too far to see
her fear, as she floated
among them that evening,
waving to us on shore?

Again, this is only a draft. It has its good moments, and is driven
by a compelling and dramatic narrative—the story of the drowned
friend—but it is also full of missteps and rough, flat gestures. If you
retyped into prose both this poem and the poem about the catbird,
you'd see that they are nearly the same length. But this one, with its
much shorter lines, has a different pace and effect. Where the catbird
poem seems to read smoothly, where its lines seem to spread laterally
across the page, like water on a flat surface, this poem is notable for

its momentum downward, water falling. Few of the lines end-stop, and that adds to the feeling that gravity pulls the narrative downward. There's a grimmer sense of fate to it.

David observes a good rule-of-thumb regarding the short line here: Notice how, even in the shortest lines, he places one or two significant anchors in every line, something to hold the line down. Look, though, at the lightness of the following invented lines:

See how these lines
are rather
light-weighted,
and as if
they were simply
about to fly away?

Lines two and four are especially weak lines, with no focus, no weight, hardly even a metrical beat. Lines five and six are also relatively weak, with little to anchor them. David's short lines earlier, though, seem balanced, well weighted despite their brevity.

Exercises

1. Read the work of poets who frequently work in the short line. Look at William Carlos Williams, and compare his lines' "nervous nature" to the short lines of Robert Creeley, a master of tiny narratives. Remember Emily Dickinson with her relatively short but dramatic lines; maybe there has never been a poet more capable of anxiety, of short-lined drama, than Dickinson.

2. Take a draft of a new poem, and type it out two different ways. First arrange it in long lines, and think about the lateral momentum of the line and poem. Then, type it in short lines, remembering to give each line an anchor; notice, and try to emphasize, the way the poem wants to move downward rather than sideways.

3. Write a poem in very short lines. Experiment with the length of the sentences, from short to long; experiment as well with the placement of punctuation, in end-stopped or enjambed lines.

Now, let's look at one last poem in short lines. Earlier we asked you to put into lines Linda Pastan's poem, "Caroline." Here is Pastan's arrangement:

She wore
her coming death
as gracefully
as if it were a coat
she'd learned to sew.
When it grew cold enough
she'd simply button it
and go.

What a clean, lovely little lyric. We admire the sheer simplicity of the metaphor. The whole poem fulfills that metaphor: Her coming death is like a coat. The trope of the garment is familiar, isn't it? Remember the Naked Poets earlier in this chapter, their desire to strip language of its "robes and trappings" in order to "revert to [language's] naked condition." Pastan flips that impulse on its head. The character accepts the inevitability of her death, and wears it like a familiar, even protective, garment. She connects, with rhyme, the actions of to "sew" and to "go." She puts on, rather than takes off, the transcendental garment.

But let's look further at the poem's technique. Pastan employs the enjambed line fully, and though the lines are very short, they are also quite coherent and complete. Each line focuses on a single, central image or notion. See how the lines get subtly longer, then are reined in quickly at the end? The last line, a single iambic foot (like the first line), seems like a hasty fate, bitten off too quickly, like her life. In fact, the whole poem is iambic, with a clear echo of the anthem meter—to say nothing of the familiar, homely death scene—of Emily Dickinson. The double quatrain is a Dickinson specialty, but Pastan adapts this structure beautifully to her own usage.

How did you do it in your own version? Where did you break the lines, and what effects did your line breaks have? Did you notice the iambic rhythms? Did your version move across the page or down? Did each of your individual lines have an integrity of its own, a coherent thought or image, at least one anchoring element?

Exercises

1. Read poems in lines of unequal length. You might begin with Galway Kinnell's long poem *The Book of Nightmares*. Thomas Lux writes wonderful poems whose lines fluctuate widely, and Sharon Olds, too, writes with a flexible line length and often with a risky sense of line-ending and enjambment. What are the effects of a poem whose lines vary significantly, compared to the effects of a poem whose lines are all long or all short?

2. Write a poem of your own in which the line length varies widely. Try for different effects: a closed line, a continuous line, long and short sentences.

Whatever the length of one's poetic lines, those lines operate in partnership with the other primary form of meaning, the sentence. The line argues with the sentence, it disrupts the momentum of the sentence, but it also can heighten the interior meanings of a sentence. The line focuses on and magnifies the phrase, the piece, the fragment. The line can also give a sense of multiplicity to a sentence, as the new line adjusts our thinking from the previous line.

See the way this line break works?

I kissed Tommy and Jane
got mad.

First I seemed to have kissed both Tommy and Jane; then we understand that I kissed only Tommy, while Jane responded angrily. The line break provides irony, complexity, perhaps humor. The line break can be a means by which one line undermines another, a means by which the poet can add or adjust information, enrich an irony, or complete a paradox, surprising the reader into further alertness.

Here are the opening lines to one of Ann's poems, "After the End." The first passage seems descriptive, rich yet clearly focused, as Ann depicts a dead hawk on the lawn. But notice her steady enjambment in these long sentences, and especially the way the meaning or implication of each descriptive sentence often changes, line by line, as the enjambed phrase or word is revised by its own continuing syntax:

Because I left him there so you could see
his body, broken by the fall, the hawk's

small relatives hopped from higher branches
and called a kind of glee that he was dead.

By afternoon, the ground around him dusted

with feathers and gravel kicked up, he looked
like a bundle of rags tossed

from a car and tumbled there, but still
graceful, neck flung back in the moss and dirt,
and the yellow claws curled to question marks.

Then the trees were quiet, the other voices
gone . . .

In line two, the phrase "the hawk's" seems to point back to "his body," but as the sentence continues past its enjambment we see the whole phrase focus into "the hawk's small relatives." At the end of line five, "dusted" works like a verb until after the line break, when we reread the word as a participle. Then "he looked" seems like an action the hawk performed, though we find out in the next line that it reflects his static appearance, not his action. And, even more dramatic, line eight provides a delightful irony. Does "still" describe the hawk's composure, by modifying "he," as in the "still hawk?" We see that it actually modifies the subsequent adjective "graceful," which itself describes how he appeared. And in the final lines quoted, see how Ann so gently silences the scene further? First we imagine those "other voices." Then we imagine them "gone."

Exercises

1. Write a journal entry about the relationship of line to sentence. Write a poem in which your sentence length varies greatly, from long to short, and where perhaps your line length varies, too.

2. Look at the book *Song* by Brigit Pegeen Kelly. Notice the tense relationship between her fairly sizable lines and her often extremely short sentences and sentence fragments.

3. Look at David Wagoner's poetry for an example of a poet who can write massive sentences; often his poems are only one sentence long, and absolutely clear. Read A. R. Ammons's *Garbage*, a brilliant book-length poem made of only a handful of sentences.

Now, let's regard one last poem to bring together many of our individual points so far. Earlier we invited you to put into lines a poem called "The Lamb" by William Heyen. Heyen's own version is a little masterpiece of construction, in which his regular lines nonetheless are capable of very important fluctuations in pace and effect. He moves with calculation from the end-stopped to the enjambed line, and also varies his syntax significantly to coordinate with the poem's literal narrative. But let's look at the poem first:

Both hindlegs wrapped with rope,
Wenzel's chosen lamb hung head down
from a branch of one of his elms.

Its throat slashed, the lamb drained,
its nose and neckwool dripping,
lawn soaking up the bright blood.

Once skinned, once emptied of its blue
and yellow organs, its translucent
strings of intestines, and though its eyes

still bulged, the lamb rose
like steam from the pail of its guts,
toward stray shafts of sunlight

filtering through the trees. Until
it came to pass: I forgot my knees,
and entered the deep kingdom of death.

Form and content seem married in a wonderfully compelling way, don't they? This story of the slaughtered farm animal is redolent with biblical suggestions. But literally, of course, farmers regularly butcher their livestock. Here a young speaker observes his neighbor,

Wenzel, doing just that, and at first the speaker's account is clear-headed, rendered like an objective, journalistic report. Notice how coherent and measured the first lines are. Five of the first six lines are end-stopped, with a deliberate pace and formality much like Yeats's in the opening stanza of "When You Are Old." Each line is a logical, closed portion of information, and each of the first two stanzas, likewise, gives us one sentence, one equally measured observation: clear, coherent, in control. But something happens as the poem and story proceed. Heyen announces a serious change in the third stanza, an adjustment marked by the style of the line and sentence as well as by the speaker's changing emotional and mental state. The lamb seems to be staring at him: The visual images of those "blue" and "translucent" innards are emphasized by line breaks, and an even more insistent visual image—"though its eyes"—comes at the break of the third line and the stanza. That enjambed phrase catches us. It fixes us, and the speaker, wide eyed. But different from the earlier stanzas, here the sentence continues for many more lines, through and past even the next stanza. This requires a much longer breath, more breath than we can hold. What is happening? The narrative picks up speed through those enjambed lines and stanzas, until the speaker finally "forgets" his knees—that is, until he faints. He doesn't just report, but personally experiences a kind of dying, just like the lamb, and those long sentences imitate his loss of reason, his breathless wonder at the scene he witnesses. See how line and syntax work together, and how Heyen manipulates them to suit their effects to his narrative?

Fainting becomes a figure for dying, as the lamb is a figure of a Christian martyrdom and resurrection. Certainly that's the result of Heyen's breaking a line with "the lamb rose." We hear the clear biblical intonation again, later, emphasized by another significant line break: "Until/it came to pass." We might even backtrack now, to suggest that the elm tree from which the lamb hangs is parallel to the wooden cross of the crucifixion. The sacrifice of the farmer's lamb reenacts to the speaker the archetypal biblical story. He is its witness, and, in seeing, he participates in a similar narrative. He dies for a moment; he passes out, even as the lamb's death "came to pass."

It's a masterful lyric. Notice how fully Heyen has attended to issues of both line and syntax, telling his story—and acting it out—as much through his technique as through his literal narrative. This may be free verse, but Heyen brilliantly employs many kinds of *formal* tactics.

We have discussed some of the important effects and variations of the poetic line, as we read and as we write. We will explore in the next section of this chapter some of the means of determining or measuring the length of one's lines. For now, we'll invite you to some further reading and consideration:

Exercises

1. The more traditional notions of the line are brought into the most thorough critique by the Language Poets. Poets like Susan Howe, Lyn Hejinian, and Ron Padgett are more likely to doubt the integrity of the formal line, pursuing the effects of disruption more often than of coherence. Howe, in fact, experiments with notions of depth in the line, as though we can look not only left and right, up and down, but *into* the line as a kind of historical or geological marker. Each line bears the partial memory of the language and forms that came before it. Look at her *Singularities.*

2. Write a poem in which the linear tactics of fragment, disruption, or rupture preside, or where the more Romantic notion of a single speaker is rejected in favor of the impersonal, historical, or collective voice. Use the bibliography of this chapter to locate some sources for other Language and postmodern poetic texts.

3. For discussion of the ideology, the politics, of poetic form, look at James Scully's book *Line Break: Poetry as Social Practice.* In it he argues that "Aesthetic questions are political questions," and so every point in our present discussion of technique and form can be read as political and ideological. Anthony Easthope's *Poetry as Discourse* is another fine critical book for those who wish to pursue this "line" of poetics. Contrast these Marxist principles with the more Romantic poetic articulated by John Hollander in *The Work of Poetry.* Hollander envalues the virtues of aesthetics over ideology, originality over history, visionary and individual genius over the collective.

4. Formulate your own theory about the relationship of art to politics. How does your literary and cultural inheritance determine your individual taste, your poetic style, your beliefs? And how did your literary and cultural inheritance come to be?

TO BE IN ANY FORM, WHAT IS THAT?

The title of this section is a question Walt Whitman asks in "Song of Myself." Whitman, the transcendentalist, wants to rise beyond the body, to abandon the body's physical imperfections and temporal constraints. This spiritual ideal suggests formlessness, a soul with no need of a body, an "oversoul" (as Emerson calls it), which can float ethereal and pure, timeless, beyond substance. Mere form, he seems to suggest, is inconsequential. One irony of Whitman's question is that it comes in section 27 of "Song of Myself"—that is, almost in the perfect middle of the body of that great poem, where the muscular heart is. Only deep within the body can Whitman utter such out-of-body statements. And he knows it. After all, as he says in "Crossing Brooklyn Ferry":

> I too had receiv'd identity by my body,
> That I was I knew was of my body, and what I should be I knew
> I should be of my body.

Or, as if to counter the question from "Song of Myself," he asks this in "Crossing Brooklyn Ferry":

> What gods can exceed these that clasp me by the hand, and with
> voices I love call me promptly and loudly by my nighest
> name as I approach?

In other words, to be in any form is *everything*.

All poem are formal creatures. They have a physical body made of words, lines, sentences. Yet poets fight about such things. Some declare form to be obsolete, a quaint expression from an earlier time; or they insist that form is tantamount to tyranny—whether that be the tyranny of politics or gender, race or nationality. Others claim that form is coherence, a time-proven methodology, a necessary discipline for the intellect and the spirit. We think that whenever one chooses to write a poem, one makes a formal choice. *All poetry is formal poetry.* Now, what kind of form? That's the fascinating question. By form, we know that some people mean traditional form: rhyme and meter. And of course, then, the attending debates are serious and important. For instance, Whitman's free verse is a radical, audacious argument against the metrical, measured forms of European poetry. He wanted to write, as Margaret Fuller and Ralph Waldo Emerson prescribed, a distinctly American poetry to reflect a distinctly American experience. He wanted a form to reflect the voice and style of the common, democratic citizen. Nearly all debates about poetic form are debates about tradition: who possesses the power of the word, who steers (or commandeers) the continuities of memory, of history. Again, in these debates form usually means traditional form.

But that's not what we mean by form, or that's not what we mean only. We mean shape. All poems have a shape; thus, form. The search for a poem, to us, is a search for the best form, be that a form we have inherited, invented, or adapted. To our practice and thinking, there are not one but three central kinds of form in poetry. In other words, every poem is not just in "a" form, but every poem has several forms at once.

Don't be alarmed. Having a full, curious knowledge of form, of the *forms,* will enhance your abilities as a poet. The more you know, the more you can enjoy and the more you can do. Weight-lifters don't work on just one muscle; they'd teeter and fall from the imbalance! Instead, they work on different muscles groups, trying to build a coherent body. That's what we're urging: a coherent, flexible body of work capable of growing. We often notice that our students become proficient at one or two kinds of poems, and then grow too contented with repeating that form: one or two big muscles in an otherwise undeveloped body.

We call our first category of poetic form *linear or metrical form.* These are, simply, the ways to measure or determine the length of the individual poetic line. Paul Celan, the great twentieth-century Romanian poet, wrote that the poet's task is "measuring off the area of the given and the possible." In fact, the word meter implies just that. In Greek, a *metron* is any thing by which one measures. Anne Carson asserts in her *Economy of the Unlost* that the first poetry "written to be read [as] literature," was written by the Greek poet Simonides in the fifth century B.C., and his need to measure poetry was both practical and exacting. Simonides made his lucrative living by providing inscriptional verse for graves of the wealthy and powerful, so "Simonides' poem [had] to fit on the stone bought for it." How's that for a form?

There are five ways to make a line of poetry.

1. *Syllabic.* Poets can construct their lines according to the number of syllables in those lines. Remember your textbook definition of a syllable. It is the basic, the smallest unit of verbal rhythm. It is a single pulse of sound. Syllabics—that is, counting the number of syllables in a line—is a way of determining line length. Syllabics provides a visual shape to a poem. Some argue that syllabics also provides an audible shape, though we find that harder to believe. Richard Wilbur says he thinks it's possible to hear the syllabics of relatively short lines, as in haiku, though he agrees that longer syllabic lines may be "a discipline for the poet, perhaps, but [are] not audible for the reader."

There are two kinds of syllabic lines, *normative* syllabics and *quantitative* syllabics, and both can provide you with a discipline and a structure. In the normative syllabic poem, each line contains the same number of syllables. Here are the opening lines of a draft of one of David's recent poems, "That Moon." He wanted a regular and coherent line, so wrote the poem in decasyllabic or ten syllable lines:

> They are halfway between here and dying,
> our Canada geese, as this evening we
> pick down the pine path. They are so hungry,
> landing, they howl as rowdy as birddogs.
> First, they're a dozen gathering on the
> lake muck where we go—then more melting down,
> wide on their wings, wild from the flight, hitting
> hard, flat stone, splashing . . .

Count them. David used the strategy of normative syllabics through the whole poem, which runs for about forty lines. The syllabic line provided him—like Simonides' stone—a very concrete formal measurement. But David wasn't pleased. Some of the line breaks seem capricious or ugly, and several of the lines crack poorly, right in the middle. It's just not a graceful pace. He tinkered for days with syntax but finally decided the lines themselves were too long (or wrong) for the kinds of sentences he'd written, or, more accurately, the sentences and phrases needed a more spacious but deliberate sense of lineation. So he tried again, this time in quantitative syllabics:

> They are halfway
> between here
> and dying,
>
> our Canada geese,
>
> as this evening
> we pick down
> the pine path.
>
> They are so hungry,
>
> landing, they howl
> as rowdy
> as birddogs.
>
> First they're a dozen
>
> gathering on
> the lake muck
> where we go—
>
> then more melting down,
>
> wide on their wings,
> wild from the
> flight, hitting
>
> hard, flat stone, splashing.

Can you define quantitative syllabics from the lines above? While the lines in each stanza may contain differing numbers of syllables, each corresponding line in each stanza has the same number. That is, each first line has four syllables, each second and third lines have three, and each isolated line has five syllables. The movement down the page is more congruent with David's sense of the poem's drama and its syntax; it unpacks more carefully, and seems richer for the frequent line breaks, the indented lines, the isolated lines. The quantitative syllabic provides a form and pattern for those tactics. Each stanza is shaped, sculpted, like each other, like a fractal, self-replicating. Alice Fulton and Paul Lake have written, separately, about applying the trope of fractal physics to poetic prosody. And of course, no poet has expressed a deeper genius for syllabics, especially quantitative syllabics, than the wonderful Marianne Moore.

Exercises

1. Read Fulton's *Feeling as a Foreign Language*, especially the chapters "Of Formal, Free, and Fractal Verse" and "Fractal Amplifications"; and Lake's essays "Disorderly Orders: Free Verse, Chaos, and the Tradition" published in the autumn 1998 *Southern Review* and his "The Shape of Poetry" in the 2nd edition of Robert McDowell's book *Poetry after Modernism*.

2. Read Marianne Moore's poems, and count her syllabic lines.

3. Try your own poems; try both varieties of syllabics.

Syllabics is a favorite prosodic tactic of David's. Many of the poems in his recent book, *The Truth about Small Towns*, are syllabic, and nearly every poem in his new collection, *Changeable Thunder*, is syllabic—sometimes normative, sometimes quantitative. The beauty of the syllabic line is its rhythmic flexibility. Syllabics may provide for a regular measurement of syllables, but the actual rhythm of the line and sentence is not prescribed.

So here is a related tip regarding syllabics. We've found that writing in syllabics is a great bridge from free verse to accentual-syllabic poetry. That is, if you always write free verse but want to write in, say, iambic pentameter, first try a poem in syllabics. It's a great means for the transition. Syllabics will help you measure your line but doesn't demand all the rhythmic discipline of iambic pentameter. This will begin to teach you to count. Likewise, if you write in meter but find yourself sometimes too "sing-songy," or want to free your regular rhythm but can't seem to get away from it, try syllabics first, before you try free verse. In his *Shelf Life*, the poet Thom Gunn concurs: "[Syllabics] were a way of getting iambics out of my ears."

Remember, syllabics isn't a rhythm (can you *hear* it?) as much as it is a form of compositional measure. If you're still having trouble getting away from the drum-beat of regular meter, write in quantitative-syllabic stanzas (thus making your lines different lengths); or write in uneven-numbered syllabics (say, a seven- or eleven-syllable line), and consciously work to make your numbers of beats different line by line.

Beats: That leads us to our second form of linear or metrical form.

2. *Accentual.* Instead of counting the number of syllables in a line, we count the numbers of stressed or accented syllables in those lines: the beats. This form of measurement comes closer to providing an audible structure to your line. You can hear the rhythm of stresses, whereas you probably can't hear the rhythm of syllables. In this regard, accentuals is probably closer than syllabics to what we mean when we refer to a "meter," especially if meter means a poetic structure that is both audible and predictive. Can you hear syllabics? Can you predict the rhythm of yet-unwritten lines in syllabics? No. Can you hear a line of accentuals and predict the rhythm of any subsequent lines? Maybe yes, though some would still argue no.

How many accents do you hear in the first couple of lines of Yeats's "When You Are Old"?

When you are old and gray and full of sleep,
And nodding by the fire, take down this book . . .

Say it out loud. We hear five hard beats in each line. We'll mark those beats here with the diacritical mark called an *ictus* ´.

When you are old and gray and full of sleep,
And nodding by the fire, take down this book . . .

Do you hear how regular the first line's rhythm is? Then notice how the second line fluctuates a bit when Yeats stresses with two hard beats his imperative to TAKE DOWN the book.

Before we go further, let's try an experiment to check more fully your ability to scan a poem for its linear measurement. Here is another of David's recent poems, "Graveyard":

Heat in the short field and dust scuffed up, glare
off the guard-tower glass where the three pickets

lean on their guns. The score is one to one.
Everybody's nervous but the inmates,
who joke around—they jostle, they hassle
the team of boys in trouble and their dads.
It's all in sport. The warden is the ump.
The flat bleachers are dotted with guards; no
one can recall the last time they got one
over the wall. The cons play hard, then lose.
And the warden springs for drinks all around—
something he calls *graveyard,* which is five kinds
of soda pop poured over ice into
each one's cup, until the cup overflows.

What can you determine about the prosody? If you say accentuals, then you need to listen harder. If you say syllabics, you counted pretty well. Here is a funny thing about the poem. David wanted the poem to be in normative syllabics, and every line here is decasyllabic except for line two, which has eleven syllables. But David heard that line in ten syllables, too, for his Missouri pronunciation of "tow-er" is more like "tahr": one syllable! When Ann pointed that out to him, he decided to keep the line as is, with its one potentially extra syllable as a remnant. He could easily have cut the little syllable "the" before the "three pickets" without losing much, but he liked the slight regional nod. Slight regional flaw, says Ann.

"Graveyard" is a kind of sonnet, or recalls the form of the sonnet, with its fourteen lines, its rhetorical shift or turn after the eighth line, and a summarizing capture in the last two-and-a-half lines. It's a poem about power and powerlessness, too, among the different kinds of teams: the boys against their fathers, the cons against the guards and warden, the boys and the cons against the law, the baseball team of boys against the team of cons. Everybody's watching everybody, nervously guarding, though the whole game is fraudulent since the warden seems to have commanded the cons to lose from the very beginning. The warden's gesture of pouring the soda pop so abundantly also seems fraudulent or at least ironic: The irony comes in providing so much, too quickly, to those who usually have so little. The game itself, of course, has its own strict rules, as the syllabic line exacts a formal strictness, good behavior.

But here was the fun thing. The syllabic line produces a form of regular measurement. But David wanted to exert a clear argument against that regularity. We both believe that a poem must embody a powerful sense of pressure or tension in some aspects. To counter the regular syllabic, David worked hard to construct lines with irregular numbers of beats or accents: arrhythmia in the heartbeat. Notice in line one how heavy and slow the rhythm is, with at least six, perhaps seven hard beats (do you stress "up"?). Then count the beats in line four: three, perhaps four. Do you hear how rapidly that line runs? EV'rybody's NERvous but the INmates. Just like the many other forms of competition in the poem—the power struggles—those regular syllables argue with those very irregular beats. Attending to accentuals sometimes means making unequal rather than equal lines.

To write the poem in regular accentuals, we might come up with these first lines:

> Heat in the short field and dust
> scuffed up, glare off the guard-tower
> glass where the three pickets lean
> on their guns. The score is one to one.
> Everybody's nervous but the inmates . . .

In this version, the lines have a much more balanced rhythm, and that balance is something a reader senses whether or not the reader is counting beats. That's one of the hidden strengths of a poet like Philip Levine, one of our favorites. Often described as a free-verse poet, Levine frequently sculpts his lines into equally stressed arrangements, as these opening lines of his recent "Coming Close":

> Take this quiet woman, she has been
> standing before a polishing wheel
> for over three hours, and she lacks
> twenty minutes before she can take
> a lunch break? Is she a woman?

In addition to Levine's strong voice and clean syntax, the lines seem tight and equal. They are about the same length, we might say. But what does that mean? They all have eight or nine syllables, they look equivalent, and indeed there are probably four accents in each line, giving them a kind of mirror rhythm. If you read the rest of the poem, you'll see that Levine does vary the lines a bit more, especially in numbers of syllables, but they seem to average out in a four-beat accentual.

3. *Accentual-syllabic.* This is the dominant form of traditional poetry in English. When your teacher used to say that "Frost's poem is in iambic pentameter," your teacher was describing an accentual-syllabic form. This combines the previous two forms by counting both the numbers of syllables and the numbers of beats; further, this technique prescribes the placement of those beats within those syllables. This is also what people usually mean when they say a poem is in "meter." Accentual-syllabics is both audible and predictive—that is, you can hear the rhythmic pattern, loud and soft, and can predict what that pattern will produce in forthcoming lines.

The meter of accentual-syllabics is marked with two diacritical marks, *ictus* ´ and *breve* ˘.

When you are old and gray and full of sleep,

And nodding by the fire, take down this book . . .

We're using a two-stress system to scan poems, a heavy and a light beat, though we put the stress over "by" in parenthesis to indicate a slightly less heavy beat; it's more than a weak beat, less than a hard one. In part, "by" receives some accent because of its relative position between two other, even lighter, syllables. Some metrists argue that a four-stress system works to mark more subtle variations. We know a linguist-metrist who can determine up to seventeen degrees of stress in a poem. Can you imagine trying to write a poem, given such a blueprint to follow? In Yeats's poem, we've noted that the rhythm of line two isn't entirely regular. Yeats makes some *metrical substitutions*. In a substitution, a poet alters the metrical norm of a line, replacing one kind of foot with another, for any one of a variety of purposes—to emphasize, to surprise, to relieve a rhythmic monotony. In *Meter in English,* Robert Wallace argues that the only real meter in English is accentual-syllabic meter with a normative iambic rhythm. Others in that book argue vociferously with Wallace, wishing to maintain an equal metrical status for other rhythmic feet. The basic rhythmic feet are:

iambic ˘ ´   trochaic ´ ˘   (double rhythms, or a foot with two syllables)

anapestic ˘ ˘ ´ dactylic ´ ˘ ˘ (triple rhythms, a foot with three syllables)

Poets will also often employ a spondaic foot (´ ´) for added emphasis. "Whose woods these are I think I know," Mr. Frost famously wrote, starting with a strong opening foot. Marianne Moore advised poets always to begin their poems with strong stresses. There are many other metrical varieties, especially deriving from classical prosody— the amphibrach and cretic, the bacchic and antibacchic, and many more—but they are essentially meaningless in English practice.

Why is it hard to apply some of the classical meters to modern English, and why can't English accommodate quantities? We suspect that recent English is such a mongrel language, produced by the influences of so many other languages and cultures, that its relative impurity prevents its replication of purer prosodies. You can't eat your stew as though it were broth.

Exercises

1. Read the great formal poets: Shakespeare, Pope, Dickinson, Frost. You have your own list of favorites. See if you can determine the metrical structure of your favorite poems.

2. Write a poem in accentual-syllabics. Try it in iambic rhythm, then try it in trochaic. Notice how the iambic is smooth, while the trochaic is more manic, insistent. No wonder Shakespeare's witches say "Double, double, toil and trouble./Fire burn, and cauldron bubble." No wonder Poe begins with "Once upon a midnight dreary . . . ." Hear the crazed trochees?

3. What other observations can you make? Does anapestic seem light-footed, fast, to you? Do you notice that dactylic meter is poetry's version of waltz time? Try them.

Being able to determine the rhythm of a line or foot is one part of accentual-syllabic poetry. Measuring the length of the line is the other. Each rhythmic unit, each repeating group of syllables, is called a foot. In traditional poetry, then, poets construct their lines of equal numbers of feet. In progressive order, those lines are called monometer, dimeter, trimeter, tetrameter, pentameter, hexameter, heptameter, and octameter. So if you now want to try your hand at dactylic trimeter, you know your line's rhythm and length will be ´ ˇ ˇ ´ ˇ ˇ ´ ˇ ˇ. And if you recall our assignment earlier to reline John Updike's "Upon Shaving Off One's Beard," you will know what Updike did when we tell you his version is a quatrain in iambic tetrameter; you don't even need to see it here to understand that structure.

4. *Quantitative.* Here is a fascinating form of linear measurement. Unfortunately—or perhaps fortunately—it's not really a viable construction in English! Quantitative prosody is a feature of classical Greek and Latin poetry, but we think poets should know the meaning of a form even if we don't or can't write the form. Rather than counting the numbers of beats of certain syllables, a quantitative poet measures a duration, the amount of time it takes to say or sing those syllables.

Greek poetry was sung long before it was written. Singers, then and now, exaggerate syllables for the melody's sake. Say the word "amazing." You hear the harder beat of the second syllable. Still, that syllable requires about the same amount of time to say as the other two syllables. Now sing the first line of "Amazing Grace." It sounds like "a MAAAY zing grace, how swEEt the sound, that SAAved a wretch like MEEEEE." Those emphasized syllables each receive a very long note, don't they? They require a much more sustained quantity of time to sing. In fact, Greek poets used the pitch of vowels and syllables, as well as their duration, to denote quantities. Latin poets, whose work was far more likely to be written, made quantities of duration only, not pitch.

So quantitative meter is a measurement of long and short syllables, rather than hard and soft ones. We see the remnant of quantitative measurement in our designation of short vowel sounds, as in bit, and long vowel sounds, as in bite. Still, both of those syllables would be considered short in quantitative poetry. A long quantity must be an unstopped vowel sound, as in buy, the sound bī.That's a long syllabic quantity.

Can you imagine trying to write a poem whose scansion might be – ˘ – ˘ ˘ – ˘? A few poets have tried to make English work that way. William Cowper's "Lines Written in a Period of Insanity" is one example, as Robert Hass argues in his essay in *Meter in English.* And in *Patterns of Poetry,* Miller Williams provides a fine discussion of quantities, then brilliantly scans the quantitative construction of Robert Bridges's "Johannes Milton, Senex."

Exercises

1. Go ahead. Give it a try. Write a few lines in which you think hard about emphasizing the duration of your syllables, in a pattern. Try to find open or unstopped syllables to emphasize the longer time it takes to say them.

5. *Free verse.* The final way to measure or make lines in poetry we define as much by what it isn't as by what it is. In free verse, we do not count. But don't be misled: In free verse, many things count.

In free verse, we *don't* count syllables or beats or seconds or any traditional rhythmic pattern. Free verse, then, can't be described by using the terms of formal prosody, except in negation. Free verse does not use the regular patterns of formal verse. Free verse exploits and heightens the rhythms of prose. That makes the other formalizing factors of free verse more urgent, especially lines and line endings. If there is no particular given measurement, no governing or determining principle, to the line, then how do you know when to break that line? The tactics of end-stopping and enjambing become much more important, and the structures of the line and stanza, while fluid, become more flexible. Some people hate this. Robert Frost used to complain that free verse is like playing tennis without a net. "Where's the challenge?" he'd mutter. And remember Lewis Turco's argument that free verse, because it is unmetered language, is nothing more than prose broken into lines. *Bad* free verse is prose broken into lines, we think. Oh, about that complaint of Frost's, here's how we'd answer: "Sure, Mr. Frost, but I play the game as if the net were there."

Memory is thus a fundamental element in free verse. Some free-verse poetry recalls the structure of traditional poetry by finding its form in lines of equal visual lengths. Here are the opening lines of Ann's "Sorrow":

> It's in the air between us
> as the next true moment
> after I yell, tear sheets away,
> spring from bed and you, faster,
> grapple, wrestle me back
> from the bedroom door.

The lines have varying numbers of syllables, varying accents, yet visually bear the memory of formality. Some free-verse poetry remembers its formal past by taking shape in regular stanzas. In these opening lines of her lovely, frightening "In a Moment," Ann is again not metering, but her shaped and regular stanzas provide a formal memory within the contemporary scene:

> She drives alone and quickly
> on a snow-blasted highway—
> no cars, only the salt kiss
> of the semis as they steam by.

> Jazz on the radio, in and out
> with the storm's static fuzz,
> and through the night haze
> the searchlights of the auto mall

> scrape the sky in wild arcs.
> In the hospital where she left

her daughter finally sleeping
in her crib, nurses whisper
behind a high desk and hurry
to monitors buzzing, the sound of emergency . . .

As we said before, free verse abandons some of the tactics of traditional poetry, so that makes its remaining effects and unique devices even more important. Much of what we think about as we write free verse is the line and syntax; but we won't reiterate here what we discussed earlier in this chapter. And much of what we think about are language's musical effects, which we'll talk more about in the next section of this chapter. Tone, voice, and personality also may become centralized in free verse.

Exercises

1. Read Stanley Plumly's essay "The Prose Lyric" for discussion of tone and personality in poetry. The essay appeared in two installments in *American Poetry Review*, 1977–78.

Partly, free verse wants to forget the rules. That is its heritage, in fact. Free verse in English intended to be a radical erasure of European prosodies. Free verse was a kind of poetic declaration of independence, a revolt against the staid, the privileged, the formal. Democracy versus aristocracy—at least that was the presumption. To be sure, part of the daring and danger of Walt Whitman was his enthusiastic rejection of many elements of formal prosody. But what began as radical experiment has become orthodoxy. Most poets today write in free verse, and sometimes formal verse seems, in comparison, daring or cutting-edge. Or, more fairly, we are living in a wonderful time for poetry when the old stereotypes about free verse (that it is necessarily dangerous or experimental) and formal verse (that it is always privileged or tidy) are just not accurate. Poets can write any kind of poetry for any kind of purpose—radical or conservative. One of the most daring poets we know, Marilyn Hacker, writes sonnets, villanelles, and perfect metrics; but while she maintains the outer prosodic forms exactly, she often dismantles their traditional rhetorical forms or standards from the inside, like a spy! Some of the poets who bore us most write "experimental" free verse. So do some of the most exciting.

There is much more to think and say about free verse. But again, look back at the section on line and ahead to our discussions of rhetorical form and musical effects, for those are of primary import to the crafting of free verse. It's not an oversight that no one has written a satisfactory prosody of free verse. Free verse *isn't* a prosody in the way that these other four linear forms are.

Exercises

1. There are so many potential challenges we might issue here that we won't even try to be inclusive. The basic possibilities are obvious anyway, right? Write a poem in one rhythm, then try another draft in a different rhythm to see which best suits the poem's narrative and desire. Or, subtly shift your rhythm in one poem from one meter to another, again for tonal effect.

2. Rewrite a formal poem into free verse; recast a free verse piece into meter. We do this over and over again as we draft our poems. The search for a poem is a search for its best forms.

3. Write a journal entry on the differences, to you, between free verse and metrical verse. Are there particular subjects, occasions, tones that you feel better suited by one prosody than other? Why?

We call our second category of form *fixed or inherited form*. Here we are not interested in the shape of individual lines but rather in the form or shape of a whole poem or parts of a poem. This discussion could be book length, if we tried to present and analyze all the available fixed forms. But that's what handbooks are for, as we indicate in the bibliography. We're going to refer to several fixed forms, hoping you will look further in the *New Princeton Encyclopedia of Poetry and Poetics*, in Turco's *The New Book of Forms*, and elsewhere.

Form is more than the vessel into which to pour one's ideas. Form *is* one's ideas, the shape and nature and history of those ideas. Form can enable those ideas. We think, in fact, a fixed form can answer questions, can help you write the poem, not only shaping but suggesting what you have to say. Poems are as much about *how* you say as what you say. Forms are a discipline and a means.

Let's think about fixed forms in three different categories. First, there are prescribed forms for the *shape of whole poems*. Here are some of those primary forms and their countries or regions of origin: sonnet (Italy for Petrarch's sonnets; England for Shakespeare's variety), haiku (Japan), villanelle (France), canzone (Italy), sestina (Provence), rondeau and rondel (France), ballade (France). There are many more. In these cases, the whole form and length of the poem is prescribed by the definition. All sestinas are thirty-nine lines long, with a pattern of repeated end-words and with a final three-line envoi. All villanelles have nineteen lines, with five three-line stanzas and a final four-line stanza, with a very rigid pattern of linear rhyme and repetition.

Of these forms, we both most often return to the sonnet, though we have written in all of the above forms. Perhaps the sonnet has been the most adaptable and popular lyric form for poetry in English throughout the last 500 years. Why? We will propose an answer to that in the next section, when we talk about rhetoric. Not only have we written many sonnets, but we have written many poems varying the sonnet form: poems in stanzas of thirteen to fifteen lines, poems that make the requisite turns and counter-turns, poems that, as we said before about free verse, remember the sonnet.

This is a sonnet variation of David's, "Sonnet for a Separation." The traditional sonnet is patterned in iambic pentameter, but David wanted a much more severe line to go with his severe story. So he set the poem in the perilously strict monometer:

Where have
you gone,
my love?
Moon on
our wet
street burns
without
you.
    When,
dear soul,
did we

live so
purely,
no shame
or blame?

The failing lovers are represented in gaunt, two-syllable lines. The poem splits in half, in two voices, and ends with a very telling couplet. The rhyme scheme was particularly challenging to construct, with little room to maneuver.

Exercises

1. Study one of the fixed forms above. Write a pure or exact version. Write another poem, using one of the forms but adapting it.

There are other kinds of fixed forms that don't prescribe whole poems but rather *parts of poems or stanzas.* Some of them are the ghazal (Persia), pantoum (Malaysia), terza rima (Italy), ballad stanza (untraceable), heroic sestet (Sicily), Spenserian stanza (England), hymnal or common measure (England), sapphics (Greece). A poet can write these stanza-forms in poems of any length; Dante's entire *Divine Comedy* is in terza rima, for instance, though a terza-rima poem may also be a single page. The form prescribes the stanza—its length and/or pattern of rhyme and meter—but that pattern may continue as long as the poet desires.

Ann had never written a ghazal until she met Agha Shahid Ali at the Bread Loaf Writers' Conference in 1998. A splendid poet who writes primarily in English himself, Shahid also translates ghazals from the Persian. "You must write them!" he urged Ann. This is one of her results, entitled "Ghazal of the Winter Storm":

The fire's out. I wish you would come home.
Moonlight calms the gate where you stumbled. Come home.

When rations are lifted we'll cook all day
and never mind the heat that out of hell comes home.

The plates, piled high with meat, the tumblers
we pull from shelves, the table, all call come home.

Pie will fill your mouth, toothsome apple I plucked
from the tree which each fall comes home.

Even the dog misses you, that you kicked
until he bled, and sends his humble come home.

I never meant to send you into snow that day.
One step away's the fire's anvil: come home.

Ghazals written in Persian are self-contained couplets with certain key repetitions. We'll quote John Hollander's concise explanation in *Rhyme's Reason:* "Both lines of the first couplet, and the second lines of all the following ones, end with a repeated refrain (Radif) and, just before that, a rhyming word (Qafia). The poet signs his name pseudonymously in the final ghazal." So Ann's ghazal repeats the phrase "come home," and embeds a rhyme just prior to that phrase (in this case, lots of slant rhymes: stumbled, hell, call, fall, humble, anvil). As these self-contained couplets progressed, the poem grew into its narrative—of cruelty, perhaps of war. It was a hard task for Ann, who works mostly in free verse and syllabics, but finally very satisfying and exciting. Did you notice how she sneaked her name in the word "anvil" in the last line of the poem?

It is both a discipline and a liberty to write in the forms above. Learning the forms is an end in itself, and writing each form can be a completely rewarding act. But further, you can learn particular skills in particular forms, skills that you can hone and then transfer to other kinds of poems. Haiku, for example, compels you to sharpen your ability and honesty with an individual image, and clear imagery will improve all of your poetic efforts. Likewise, working with the villanelle can educate your ear for better handling of repetition and refrain, for recurrences of phrases and ideas; the sonnet will require your more careful custody of the shape, timing, and turning of your story and your argument. Each form has its own special concentrations, but those concentrations can transfer from form to form, poem to poem, as your skill deepens and widens.

So let's suggest one final poetic form to you: the *nonce form.* A nonce form is one invented by the poet for one poem, a form that doesn't exist elsewhere. All poetic forms must have originated as nonce forms. Here is David's poem "Home":

Again the time has come to take our morning walk.
Look beneath the heavy cedars, little dear.
Deer have strayed here overnight. Their hooves
have left some telltale moons and hearts in
innocent dry sands along our bending creek.
Creatures of many hungers say we're near.
Hear them call our human name. Like your mother,
her voice floating down the distant air
where we have come awhile, they sing us back
because they fear our straying out too far,
farther than the deep woods reach. Because we
went without her knowing we'd be gone, hear
her sweet voice cry above the others come back in.
In time we'll let it lead us home again.

Again, you'll notice that the poem is based on the sonnet. But it does not follow a strict iambic pentameter meter, it does not rhyme in either the Petrarchan or Shakespearean pattern, it does not turn the story or rhetoric after the eighth line, nor does it employ a concluding couplet. It is in fourteen lines, though, and does approximate an iambic rhythm. But it was the rhyme that David focused on. The poem is about our daughter, Katie, and David taking a walk without telling Ann, who called and called for them. David wanted to suggest the echo that rang through the woods. None of the lines employs a terminal rhyme; rather, look at how the final syllable of each line suggests the first syllable's sound in the next line. It's definitely not a rhyme you see, but clearly something you hear, a voice that accompanies, and carries over, and finally calls you home. Look at the way the last line returns you to the beginning of the poem, a circuit, the path back.

Here's a more amazing nonce poem, probably also based on the form of the sonnet. It uses the echo to a remarkable effect. This is "Narcissus and Echo" by Fred Chappell:

Shall the water not remember   *Ember*
my hand's slow gesture, tracing above   *of*
its mirror my half-imaginary   *airy*
portrait? My only belonging   *longing,*
is my beauty, which I take   *ache*
away and then return, as love   *of*

teasing playfully the one being   *unbeing.*
whose gratitude I treasure   *Is your*
moves me. I live apart   *heart*
from myself, yet cannot   *not*
live apart. In the water's tone   *stone?*
that brilliant silence, a flower   *Hour,*
whispers my name with such slight   *light,*
moment, it seems filament of air,   *fare*
the world become cloudswell.   *well.*

How brilliantly has Chappell invented a form to coincide with his narrative! It's actually three poems in one: what Narcissus says, what Echo says in response (in italics), and the two voices together. See how Echo echoes each of Narcissus' last sounds in each line? Her voice is his voice, and that is their doom, separately and together. Narcissus, the egotist, may not even know that Echo is calling (he thinks the flower is talking!), and he is consumed by the waters in which he gazes at himself. Echo is well aware of Narcissus' [Addopostrapher] self-absorption, however, and she realizes with great grief the impossibility of her love. Chappell has adapted the possibilities of poetic form to suit, precisely, the myth-narrative he inherits and the tone he desires.

Forms do not constrain; they permit. And individual poets do not need to limit themselves to one kind of poetry—whether sonnets, free verse, or metered lines—though some poets are only interested in limited possibilities. W. S. Merwin, one of the great poets of our age, has had a long career marked by books of extreme formality—whole books in syllabics or metrics, whole books in fixed forms. And he has written books in extremely open forms. Some poems have followed the strictest syntactic patterns of eloquence, and others have explored a severe plainness of expression, even forsaking punctuation and capitalization. Perhaps it's no coincidence that he is also one of the greatest recent translators of poetry, having worked in languages from around the world, in forms used throughout thousands of years of literary history. Merwin's pursuit is beautiful and tireless, as though he were seeking to find the language and form to last for all time. Otherwise, as he warns in his tiny poem, "Witness," the limits of our abilities will be our doom:

I want to tell what the forests
were like

I will have to speak
in a forgotten language

Exercises

1. Study how other poets adapt the forms. People often remark on the experimentalism of E. E. Cummings. But look (and listen) more closely. There are 775 poems in his *Complete Poems.* About 225 of them are radical varieties of the sonnet! Cummings, also a painter, wholly revisualized the sonnet's form.

2. Read early, middle, and recent books of Adrienne Rich or W. S. Merwin to see how they have formed and reformed their poetry.

3. Invent a form. Adapt pieces of other forms. Entirely reimagine a poetic shape. Write new poems accordingly.

Our third and final category of forms is *rhetorical form.* Just as poems have shapes or outer forms, so do they have inner shapes. *All poems are rhetorical constructions.* Sometimes people don't want to acknowledge that fact, preferring to see poems as pure, untainted by the more coercive designs of language. And it's true: A poem is not an advertisement or sermon or political speech; it does not want you to give up your money, it won't convince you to change your faith, and it won't seek your vote. Rather, a poem wants to *give* you some kinds of power rather than ask for your obedience. But make no mistake: All language argues, whether overtly or under cover.

Poems may narrate, sing, muse with wonder, or quarrel. All of those kinds of rhetorical modes (the narrative, lyric, meditative, and speculative) have definite shapes. In fact, each mode itself contains a myriad of possible shapes. To us, this is one of the most fascinating kinds of poetic forms: the shape and pattern of the thinking itself. A primary reason for the failure of a poem is that it hasn't come to grips with the argument, the shape, and destination of its rhetoric: It hasn't decided what it wants to do. Rather, it meanders from image to image, one impulse to another, the way we may speak. Poetry is not mere speaking. It is speech shaped. Part of what is shaped is story or argument.

We mentioned earlier that we had a theory to explain the long, adaptable life of the sonnet. Perhaps no other Western form has been applied, and adapted, so fully. Why? Because the sonnet actually prescribes all three kinds of poetic form: linear, fixed, and rhetorical. Does any other form have such durability or formal flexibility? As Robert Hass writes, "We speak of the sonnet as 'a form,' when no two sonnets, however similar their structures, have the same form." A traditional sonnet requires an iambic pentameter line. Both Petrarchan and Shakespearean sonnets prescribe particular rhyme schemes. And rhetorically, the sonnet suggests a clear pattern to the argument or narrative, with shifts after the eighth and twelfth lines. It requires a stance, a complicating turn, and a capture or summary of the idea.

But this three-stepped rhetoric is not new to the sonnet, nor limited to the sonnet. Miller Williams describes the ancient Pindaric ode's rhetorical pattern as "in three parts: the turn, or *strophe;* the counterturn, or *antistrophe;* and the stand, or *epode."* Nearly all seventeenth- and eighteenth-century Puritan sermons were based on significant biblical passages: In the Puritan sermon, the preacher first offers an *observation* of the biblical passage by locating its literal context; then an *explication* of the meaning, analyzing its significance as allegory and belief; and finally suggests an *application* of the text, how to use the text, for the congregation's daily life. And isn't a legal debate composed of an argument, rebuttal, and summary? That pattern seems to be a fundamental design, at least to some Western traditions of thinking.

Exercises

1. Write a poem based on the three-part structure, above, but write the poem in free verse.

2. Now look at your past poems. Maybe you already have employed that rhetorical pattern without realizing it! There's a good chance.

3. Read Marilyn Hacker, who, as we said before, often uses the outer forms of traditional prosody yet rewrites the rhetorical possibilities of those forms from the inside.

Among the significant modes of rhetoric in classical poetry, we will single out these as among the fundamental forms: the ode, with its elevated language and subject; the pastoral; the related forms of the eclogue and georgic; the complaint; the elegy; the love poem; the praise poem. These are viable forms for today. They *are* the forms for today, among others, whether we want to acknowledge that or not. As we've said before, the present chapter doesn't intend to replace your good handbooks and encyclopedias, but rather traces our personal practices: what we think and do when we read and write. Therefore, refer to your handbooks and anthologies for definitions and examples. Greek and Latin lyrics are typically rather pure examples of the rhetorical forms.

Exercises

1. Locate an interesting classical rhetoric. Example: read the definition of a georgic in the *Princeton Encyclopedia*, then read Hesiod's *Works and Days*. Find contemporary examples: Wendell Berry's poetry, or Maxine Kumin's. Study the complaint; read the work of June Jordan or Carolyn Forché.

2. Write one.

The Renaissance provides another historical period when poetry developed, quickly, some remarkable rhetorical forms. The Renaissance poets added plentifully to the store of fixed forms, too. The sonnet, for instance, fits both categories. But more deeply, the Renaissance mind changed poetry, not just by inventing the sonnet but by complicating the actual problem-solving tactics a poem might undertake. There is a plainness or purity to the classical lyric, a singleness of intent. In her essay "Ben Jonson and the Loathed Word," Linda Gregerson is wonderfully lucid about the further complexity of the Renaissance lyric: "Process . . . is the chief contribution the Renaissance lyric has made to our tradition. Visible process: a way of getting in conceptual or figurative or syntactical trouble (carried away with metaphorical vehicles, for instance, or with branching modifiers) and needing to invent a way out." Gregerson calls this a "specific lyric *shape*, an instinct for crux which the poem must discover and without which the poem is merely a series of verses." The Renaissance lyric poets deepened the crisis of the poem. Through complex conceits, eloquent syntax, or more intensely turning narratives, these lyrics began to articulate a modern, even scientific mind, and poets today still take much influence from the Renaissance. This is one of Ann's most abundant sources of inspiration. Here is the opening of her "A Trick of the Eye":

I have no imagination but what I steal.
    I think of it when I walk past
the strangely fashioned chair
    in the furniture store window,

whose back is shaped and painted
    like a shocking red poppy,
green stem upright
    where the spine might press back,

black heart where the shoulders would yield—
    how the painted chair looks best
behind shop glass, how I want to make
    that shapeliness myself,

with small brushes and held breath,
    how my shaky hand fails the design,
my inventions and patterns
    only incomplete hieroglyphs,

how surprised I am, just the same.
    Someone else can always do it better.

For this contemporary scene, Ann borrowed a complex thought and design from the Renaissance. She's fascinated by the way that Renaissance poetry can develop a metaphor and sustain it, or transform one metaphor into another, thus extending the *conceit* of the poem. Here she foregrounds the artificial nature of the imagination, its complicity with theft or counterfeit devices, when she says "I have no imagination but what I steal." The triggering image that demonstrates this idea is the chair, itself an artificial, or made, object. In this instance, its design makes it even stranger. Intended to look "natural," the chair is painted like "a shocking red poppy." It's not simply a chair anymore but a quasi-art object, which looks best when it's framed "behind shop glass," separated from its function as a useful object. Ann further complicates the metaphor by internalizing it, taking it into the body and into the imagination ("I want to make/that shapeliness myself"). Sustained, this metaphoric transformation enriches both the object under scrutiny and the imagination itself.

Exercises

1. Compare the lyrics of contemporary to Renaissance poets: Louise Gluck to George Herbert; Jorie Graham to John Donne; Albert Goldbarth to Edward Taylor.

The nineteenth-century Romantics, in turn, can provide your poetry with important models and forms. David frequently turns to the Romantics for their tropes and rhetorical shapes. Wordsworth and Whitman both "invent" the poetry of the common person by pursuing the rhetoric and voice of speech. This Romantic trope continues into much of today's poetry, even as it provides for its own antithesis in the form of the Poststructuralists' critique of the "common speech" of poetry. The Romantic lyric also shows a more inner landscape, as poets purposely explored the psychology, the cognitive processes, of a speaker (perhaps following the brilliant innovations of Shakespeare's great plays). This development leads directly to the Modernist stream-of-consciousness, and anticipates Freud and confessional poetry.

The transcendentalist impulse provides a further pattern within the rhetoric of Romanticism. The transcendentalist desires connection with a wider spiritual and natural sense of things, beyond the individual body's experience. Can you think of ways in which this impulse describes a rhetorical strategy? A formal pattern? Here is one of David's shorter lyrics, "Mercy":

Small flames afloat in a blue duskfall, beneath trees
anonymous and hooded, the solemn trees—by ones
and twos and threes we go down to the water's level edge

with our candles cupped and melted onto little pie-tins
to set our newest loss free. Everyone is here.
Everyone is wholly quiet in the river's hush and appropriate
    dark.
The tenuous fires slip from our palms and seem to settle
in the stilling water, but then float, ever so slowly,
in a loose string like a necklace's pearls spilled,
down the river barely as wide as a dusty road.

No one is singing, and no one leaves—we stand back
beneath the grieving trees on both banks, bowed but watching,
as our tiny boats pass like a long history of moons
reflected, or like notes in an elder's hymn, or like us,
death after death, around the far, awakening bend.

David wanted a quiet, prayer-like tone and a continuous syntax, like
that important river, to provide a rhetorical context for the family
wake. The ceremony is secular and naturalistic, rather than churchly,
though the behavior is strict, even ritualized or "holy." The plural
point of view provides a sense of the larger collective—the "long his-
tory" of the living and dead—and the tender gesture of sending
those candle boats down the river is, somehow, more familiar than
odd. The grief is so fully shared that the speaker projects that human
sensation onto the accompanying natural elements (a risky gesture,
easily sentimentalized). Finally, the rhetorical pattern suggests the
concluding act of sending off the body, like those candles, down the
fluid passage of time. That's the primary transcendental rhetoric, to
undertake such a journey. Here, while the people don't ever see the
body's destination, they see its illumination around that "awaken-
ing" bend. What a fortunate, rich word is "awakening," connecting
the ceremony, the flutter of water, and a sense of being wakened to a
continuing life. David's application of a transcendentalist impulse
provides the poem its formal structures—in tone, setting, detail,
point of view, and narrative.

So what of the modern and contemporary poets? Here rhetorical
strategies of fragment and rupture underscore the power of Eliot's
The Waste Land, and redescribe the century's aesthetic forms. The
broken vessel suggests not only the form of the poem but also the
psyche of its speaker. Consider further the effect of Freud and psy-
choanalysis, the multiple and repressed minds, as a model for a

poem's voice and its physical form. How does a poet's authority change when we factor in the notion of the subconscious? How has Einstein's relativity, or the uncertainty principle of quantum physics, recast the rhetoric of language and our basic notions of time and story? Recent poets have developed the rhetorical modes of the confessional, the personal lyric, the anti-poem, the editorial, the palimpsest. And we still have at our fingertips the rhetorical gifts of earlier poets.

Or do we? It is fascinating to note what we don't or can't have. While the praise-poem was a fundamental lyric form of the Greek and Latin poets, perhaps best articulated by Simonides, the contemporary poet seldom seems driven to, or capable of, such degrees of cultural praise. Anne Carson is on point: "It would be an understatement to say the function of praise is denied to the modern poet. Not only because all epistemological authority to define a boundary between blameworthy and praiseworthy action has been withdrawn from him, but because the justice and health of his community are regarded as beyond redemption." Do you agree?

Exercises

1. What rhetorical patterns have we maintained from antiquity? What have we lost? Are there patterns we have newly discovered? Again, think of the advances is physics, mathematics, psychology, and try to apply the formal structures of those disciplines to the forms of poetry.

2. Write a poem in the narrative mode, then recast it as a meditative or speculative poem. Does each mode have lyric sensibilities? Read Ellen Bryant Voigt's essay "The Regenerate Lyric" for more discussion of the relationship of these lyric modes.

3. Read Jonathan Holden's *The Rhetoric of the Contemporary Lyric* in which he envalues a coherence of voice and personality in recent poetry. Compare Holden's integrated vision with Marjorie Perloff's in *Radical Artifice* or Charles Bernstein's *A Poetics*, both of which deconstruct the Romantic notions favored by Holden.

Can you cast farther afield for other forms? What disciplines and activities are you accomplished in? Can you use their forms and rhetoric? David has written poems whose formal and rhetorical models are based on herb gardens, rock-and-roll songs, maps, sermons. Speaking of casting "afield": One poem, "Cardinals in Spring," uses the nine-inning, two-team structure of baseball to provide the form; and David further applies the seventh-inning stretch, an introduction of the players, and other ball game strategies, to shape his poem. Further, the poem is an argument, a competition, between the rhetoric and tropes of Whitman's transcendental optimism and the more pessimistic gestures of the semiologists and deconstructionists. No kidding. Here is the whole fifth section of the poem, to give you a taste. The young speaker's Uncle Buster has just held out his hand to reveal a "baseball signed by the entire team," so the speaker exhorts, in an enthusiastic Whitman-like catalogue:

it is [so] incredible; and now I think
it is the pure/seamy duality of rewritten lives crossing, forever
stitched in red, the yin and yang of postmodern expression,
and nothing less; and now the hatching egg of hope;
and he looks at me, and now I think it is

an antique opaque eyeball, a foggy crystal ball
through which even cliché transcends itself and so signifies
our inarticulate, collective excitement that nothing
in particular, always already, is happening with sensational
    urgency
. . . and now he's giving it to me . . .

The stanzas are a tangle of allusions: Emerson's transparent eyeball, Derrida's notion of the "always-already" belatedness of language, Whitman's sense of eternal reincarnation, a semiologist's deconstruction of game theory. All this in a simple description of the baseball.

It is one thing to begin a pattern in poetry, a technical pattern or a rhetorical pattern. That is important. It is another thing to know how to finish. A poem can finish by completing or closing or resolving its pattern; or it can reject closure in favor of opening out, expanding. One of our basic notions has been that all poems have a shape, an inherent argument. We like to think about how these shapes and strategies work. In a wonderful essay about formal choices, "Verse and Voice," Charles O. Hartman says:

> The point about verse, by now, is not contention between free and metrical verse. That choice is important for each poet, vital for each poem; but it is not a choice between formlessness and form, or fresh and trite form, or the old and the new, or responsibility and anarchy. The point about verse is prosody, in a sense—not a particular prosodic choice, but the presence, for both poet and reader, of a fully imagined shape in time.

His phrase "a shape in time" is suggestive for two reasons. First, it helps us see that the poem occupies *space,* is a shapely, organic entity. Second, it suggests that the poem is *heading* somewhere ("in time"), ultimately toward some type of closure. We are intensely interested in how poems end, in how writers choose to finish their poems. At the most basic level, we see two types of closure: determinate and indeterminate. Poems can be compact, brief, self-enclosed. Or they can range widely, asking questions, changing direction, gathering ideas and letting them float. In tomato growing (another of our shared obsessions!), "determinate" plants grow to a certain size, produce fruit, and quit. They are the miniatures, the orderly citizens of the tomato world. "Indeterminate" tomatoes, by far the largest variety, are the ones that, given a chance, will never stop growing: They reach their vines to the sky and fling tomatoes all around. They are the cause of tomato glut, late in summer. In poetry, there are poems that announce their endings, and poems where ending seems not to be the point.

Emily Dickinson's poem #1540 and William Carlos Williams's "Love Song" are very different, brief lyrics, but they make the same determinate gesture toward closure, one worth looking at as we ponder how poems end. They conclude when the poems' subjects walk away, into the future. Ending, in these two cases, is a matter of saying goodbye. Here are the two poems:

#1540

As imperceptibly as Grief
The Summer lapsed away—
Too imperceptible at last
To seem like Perfidy—

A Quietness distilled
As Twilight long begun,
Or Nature spending with herself
Sequestered Afternoon—
The Dusk drew earlier in—
The Morning foreign shone—
A courteous, yet harrowing Grace,
As Guest, that would be gone—
And thus, without a Wing
Or service of a Keel
Our Summer made her light escape
Into the Beautiful.

LOVE SONG

I lie here thinking of you: —

the stain of love
is upon the world!
Yellow, yellow, yellow
it eats into the leaves,
smears with saffron
the horned branches that lean
heavily
against a smooth purple sky!
There is no light
only a honey-thick stain
that drips from leaf to leaf
and limb to limb
spoiling the colors
of the whole world—

you far off there under
the wine-red selvage of the west!

Good poems! And at the end of each, a figure makes "her light escape/into the Beautiful." As in a movie, in which the hero walks off into the sunset, toward the future, toward that place unreachable by the narrator of the poem, these poems present us with a resonant final image. In these endings, the poets' images shift from the concrete or specific to the general. As we dwell on the final image, we see the action of the poem as both finished and enlarged.

There are poems that end by announcing their larger scope or idea, or by giving us an image to linger over, as the poems by Williams and Dickinson do. If we continue to think in terms of photography or film, we might usefully imagine these endings as akin to panorama shots. They feel a little like departures. Other poems announce, in their ending lines, an arrival instead. Most sonnets of the seventeenth century are of this variety. In other words, these "arrival" poems have a rhetorical destination. At the end, a reader reaches a new place, a home; she opens a slip of paper on which truth is revealed. Tess Gallagher's poem "Wake" demonstrates this sort of ending:

> Three nights you lay in our house.
> Three nights in the chill of the body.
> Did I want to prove how surely
> I'd been left behind? In the room's great dark
> I climbed up beside you onto our high bed, bed
> we'd loved in and slept in, married
> and unmarried.
>
> There was a halo of cold around you
> as if the body's messages carry further
> in death, my own warmth taking on the silver-white
> of a voice sent unbroken across snow just to hear
> itself in its clarity of calling. We were dead
> a little while together then, serene
> and afloat on the strange broad canopy
> of the abandoned world.

This poem asks a question ("Did I want to prove how surely / I'd been left behind?") and answers it ("We were dead/a little while together then. . . ."). The poem's answer is also its ending, afloat and abandoned in a place of mourning, like a destination the narrator has been searching for and found.

Some poems close by opening up. "Open-ended" or "indeterminate" poems have in common an emphasis not on closure or stasis but on the creation of language as a dynamic, organic process. Many of Jane Hirshfield's works feel open-ended, leading us not toward answers but toward other questions. In her brief poem "Abundant Heart," we see the connection between each named thing, but we also see there's an unanswered mystery at the heart of these connections, which the poem will not divulge to us:

Because the pelicans circle and dive, the fish

Because the cows are fat, the rains

Because the tree is heavy with pears, the earth

Because the woman grows thin, the heart

Some poets reject the notion of closure altogether. Lyn Hejinian takes this more open-ended position in her construction of a poetry of "perpetual beginning." This stance is fundamental in the work of the Language poets, whose aesthetic denies strategies of traditional closure and fixed form. Why? Because, they say, closure itself is a fiction, dishonest to the way the world really is. In her essay "The Rejection of Closure," Hejinian says "the world [is] vast and overwhelming; each moment stands under an enormous vertical and horizontal pressure of information, potent with ambiguity, meaning-full, unfixed, and certainly incomplete." Language poetry claims this unfixed territory and tries to describe the flux of the world's condition by using strategies of writing like pastiche, collage, and improvisation. These strategies work to undercut a coherent narrative line, to highlight the gaps between moments or between words. The poem's meaning, Hejinian says, "is always in flux, always in the process of being created. Repetition, and the rewriting that repetition becomes, make a perpetual beginning . . . ; they postpone completion indefinitely."

Good poets show us that they are headed somewhere, with a goal or a destination, even (maybe especially) if that destination is the open space of the unknown. Poems may end by repeating patterns of sound introduced earlier or even by depicting other kinds of endings (night, death, seasonal changes, for instance). Poems may conclude by answering questions, by posing new ones, by dwelling on a single resonant image, or by walking us toward the future.

To conclude this long section on form, we'll show you a shortened version of a semester-long assignment that we have developed for advanced students. (It's a task we gladly undertake ourselves, often, when we want to start a new poem.) We call this our Poetry Encyclopedia, but it's really a kind of recipe for building a poem, as well as for understanding many kinds of poems. We ask our students to research four sets of formal categories. Each category or chapter takes two weeks to compile. For each chapter, one student chooses one term, then he or she writes and distributes to the class a thorough entry on that term. Entries must include a definition, a history, a list of poets who prominently employ that term, a summary of the evolution or recent use of that term, and one or two poems to represent the entry. Here are the chapters with ten of the various entries we suggest:

1. Fixed forms: curtal sonnet, Shakespearean sonnet, Petrarchan sonnet, villanelle, sestina, canzone, triolet, rondeau, ballade, and limerick

2. Stanza and line techniques: enjambment and end-stopped lines, partial/slant rhyme, sapphics, syllabics and accentuals, terza rima, ghazal, caesura, internal rhyme, alcaics, *vers libre*/free verse

3. Tropes: metaphor and simile, metonymy and synecdoche, image and Imagism, allegory, catachesis, paradox, allusion, periphrasis, personification and the pathetic fallacy, and irony (classical and modern)

4. Rhetorical forms: ode, elegy, complaint, narrative, flashback, confession, eclogue and georgic, meditation, satire, and dramatic monologue

You can imagine many other entries in each category. You can also imagine the moans and groans! But over the course of the semester, the students research their entries and compose wonderful chapters, resulting in a class-made handbook.

But here is the final part of the assignment: the payoff. For the fifth chapter, each student must write a new poem, and each poem must make thorough use of—must represent—one term in each of the four chapters. Example: Judy writes a curtal sonnet in slant rhyme, built around a single paradox, and memorializing a dead loved one. The students groan louder; and nearly always write the best poem of their lives. Do one yourself. Do more; mix and match. Try to write the same poem in different forms or using different tactics. Is it the same poem?

SONG REPLYING TO SONG

In Eclogue VII of Virgil's great sequence of eclogues, two Arcadian shepherds, Corydon and Thyrsis, relax in a pasture while their flocks graze. To pass the time, they play songs to each other, but their playing quickly becomes a kind of poetic contest. Each in turn, Virgil says, they are "ready to compete/With song replying to song replying to song." What a wonderful trope for the accumulating histories of the lyric poem. Harold Bloom has constructed an entire literary theory based on this notion. He calls it the "agon" of literature, referring to the competition that any one serious literary text undertakes with all related texts that have previously existed. The new poem must somehow defeat or silence the powerful strength exerted by a prior great poem. It must win the shepherd's challenge. T. S. Eliot issues a similar formula in his important essay, "Tradition and the Individual Talent": "[W]hat happens when a new work of art is created is something that happens simultaneously to all the works of art which preceded it."

Poetry comes from music and returns us to music. The first lyric poems were songs accompanied by the lyre, and the texture of a poem still (and always) derives from its blending of sound and sense, music and meaning. As Robert Hass writes: "The form of a poem exists in the relation between its music and its seeing; form is not the number or kind of restrictions, conscious or unconscious, many or few, with which a piece of writing begins." Hass describes the tension, the field of energy, between a poem's sonic sense and its visual sense. Remember, to see is to visualize *and* to comprehend.

Exercises

1. Explore Hass's "music" and "seeing," by considering the influence of music and painting in poetry. Read poets who seem to be musical: Yeats, Dickinson. Read poets who seem painterly: Cummings, John Ashbery, the Language poets. Is our suspicion true that music-based poetry is often more traditionally formal, while visual poetry is often more formally experimental?

When a poet makes a choice about form, whether to write in traditional modes or free verse, in long lines or short, in plain or baroque style, that choice will affect the song of the poem, and, ultimately, its story as well. That seems an obvious proposition. But most beginning writers aren't thinking about music as they write. There are so many things to think about! Part of the joy and terror of writing poetry is juggling all the different possibilities—image, metaphor, form, lineation, tone, story, where to begin and end. But we return again to music, in our own work and in the work of writers we treasure. Without an awareness of the musical strategies a poet might bring to bear, readers come to poetry with earplugs on, and can only respond to the poem's "statement," its theme. Music, as we find it visually in line break or aurally in rhyme or other sound effects, sets poetic language apart from prose.

Ann remembers her senses coming alive when she first read Eliot's "Prufrock," then the *Four Quartets,* as a college freshman—the strangeness of a music that could sound like this: "Let us go then, you and I,/when the evening is spread out against the sky/like a patient, etherized upon a table." Etherized: cool! she said to herself, as her roommate turned up the volume of her Peter Frampton album. All that languid sadness, those open vowels. Then, much later, when we were falling in love, we memorized Yeats's love poem "When You Are Old." How easy it is to memorize a love poem when you are in love! What is primary in all the poems we admire is a devotion to sound texture, to phrasing and musical composition. When we say that someone's poetry is "musical," what we often mean is that we notice its phrasing, its way of linking language and story to elements of timing and its use of rhyming or nonrhyming sound techniques. Listen to Edgar Allen Poe: "It is in music, perhaps, that the soul most nearly attains the great end for which, when inspired by the poetic sentiment, it struggles. . . . To recapitulate, then: I would define, in brief, the poetry of words as the rhythmical creation of beauty."

When you have the urge to write a poem, isn't your mind singing to you? Don't you aspire to make a certain kind of sound as well as a meaning? You may hear chords, you may want to be soothing or raucous, you may imagine the modulation of phrase into phrase or tone into tone. The correlation between music and poetry is age-old, and their histories are twins. Consider the intense harmonies and counterpoint of the baroque fugue as music's version of a dense, metaphysical conceit. Reread these lines by Emily Dickinson as you hum, in Protestant anthem-meter, "Amazing Grace": "Because I could not stop for Death—/He kindly stopped for me—/The Carriage held but just Ourselves—/and Immortality." Langston Hughes and others from the Harlem Renaissance developed a new style of poetry at just the time when Dixieland music was evolving into jazz, and you can hear it in the verse. David based his twenty-page poem, "Sweet Home, Saturday Night," on the Lynyrd Skynyrd song "Sweet Home Alabama"; the poem duplicates the form of the song, with its harmonies and solos, its verses and choruses, and screeching voices and cacophonous chords. What are your musical analogues? What makes you sing and dance? Can you do that in a poem? Can you make your poem contain all the instruments as well as the words?

When Ann writes poems, she often starts with a much more particular musical impulse: sound, a single phrase that gets in her head. But that phrasing is often intrinsically linked to a narrative, since her poems are usually driven by narrative. It's hard to say which comes first, the story or the method of telling. Here is the beginning of a story and the poem that grew out of it.

We were eating lunch at a roadside restaurant outside of Sandusky, Ohio, on our way home from a week at a Lake Erie beach house. We were sand-covered, sunburned, already tired in anticipation of the journey home in a car crowded with suitcases, souvenirs, and a faded bouquet of Queen Ann's lace and chicory we couldn't bring ourselves to leave behind. The restaurant specialized in breakfast, and all around us the patrons consumed plates of eggs, sausage gravy, biscuits that dripped with honey. Across the dining room sat a woman who wasn't eating, but who was accompanied by a man who seemed famished. In fact, his evident hunger prevented him from speaking to her at all, and she sat perched on her chair in a pool of silence. She was so still, so blonde, dressed so differently from the others in her ornate white lace dress, that she created her own light. She looked fragile.

Re-imagining the details of this place, and the people who inhabited it, helped Ann begin this poem. But what she focused on at the same time was the *sound* of hunger, the emphatic way everyone was eating. She wasn't sure whose story she would tell until later in the poem. Writing the poem created the story, not the other way around. Beginning poets often try to place theme or idea into a poem first. In fact, the ideas in the poem, such as they are, emerge directly from the music. The story doesn't exist without the music that generates it. Here's how she started:

So we're munching down on the farm cooking
in that methodical way you adopt
when food is fuel and your surroundings

have hardened to a watery glaze
of crockery and animal prints
lining all the walls—hey,

my husband says to me, you're staring—
and like a sheep who's grazed too long
on rich fodder I come out of it,

taste my food, and transfer my eyes
away from the woman in the last booth.
It's her manner, a kind of crazy

shabbiness, an outlandish calling-of-attention
to herself, that I can't resist.

That first sentence is pretty long. Why? Because Ann takes her time
with the initial scene, and, more important, makes the poem sound
full of food, noise, chewing, the greed of hunger. At first, she uses
heavily enjambed lines and repetitions that suggest the chewiness of
this language (lots of "ing" words like 'munching,' 'cooking,' 'lining,'
'surroundings,' 'staring'). Later, she relies on alliteration, to slow
down and look hard (like 'taste' and 'transfer') and open vowels (the
'a' sounds in 'taste,' 'away,' 'crazy'). The strong stresses in the first
stanza—the chewy sounds we referred to earlier—combined with the
alliteration (munching/methodical, farm/food/fuel) creates the ini-
tial tone of the poem. Now that she has created a sound pattern, Ann
is bound to it, if only loosely, and any reader of this poem has the right
to assume this kind of sound will continue. That's often one of the
basic contractual agreements free-verse poets make with their audi-
ence, in the absence of meter or other regular repetitions.

Serious poets pay attention to matters of sound by educating
themselves first of all. They read other poets. They find the music
that satisfies them. One strategy that often works well is to focus on
a poem's musical strategies (rather than its ideas or images) and try
to duplicate those strategies in a poem of your own. By this we don't
mean the often-repeated advice to writers, to imitate the writers you
love. What we suggest isn't imitation, exactly. It is homage, and tran-
scription, and the creation of a new sound. Gerard Manley Hopkins's

intensity, original sound textures, and dense compression have inspired the attention of many contemporary poets. Lynne McMahon's poem "In the American Grain" begins:

> I caught this evening evening's genie,
> epoxyed to the chrome in light-
> sensitive fluorescent script
> repeating in each headlight's sweep
> *No Fat Chicks. No Fat Chicks,*
> unegged, unknifed, not yet set aflame
> or painted out, a crud anomalous
> even in the sixties when I saw it first
> and felt along the viscera
> what seventeen was going to mean.

While she takes her title from William Carlos Williams's book of that same title, we quickly and more fully hear the echo of the Hopkins poem "The Windhover," which begins "I caught this morning morning's minion, king-/dom of daylight's dauphin, dapple-dawn-drawn Falcon, in his riding/of the rolling level underneath him steady air. . . ." The neat reversal of morning into evening, minion into genie, is one strategy McMahon relies upon for re-hearing and re-energizing the music of Hopkins's language. In an even more interesting strategy, her next lines transform what is initially homage into critique. Instead of the terrifying, natural falcon who rides the air, McMahon sees a chaotic, fluorescent script, which lights up its insult each time headlights pass: "No Fat Chicks." We hear the dense alliteration of Hopkins throughout these lines, but we see an urban landscape, a wrecked place. It's a wonderful mix of old and new, homage and play. What we hear first, even as we read for the "meaning," is sound itself, the music of the mind.

Exercises

1. Who are your favorite poets, and what kinds of musical effects do they favor? Write a journal entry exploring this. Then, write a poem in which you employ another poet's identifying musical style.

> **2.** What are your own musical tendencies? Are you soft, loud, reverent, bluesy? Find a poet who values a different music from yours, study that poet, and then write a new "song of yourself."
>
> **3.** Read H. T. Kirby-Smith's new book *The Celestial Twins: Poetry and Music Through the Ages.*

We have written, earlier, about the ways that meter creates musical effect. When we hear meter, we hear the ebb and flow of sound as it departs from and returns to a normative pattern. Robert Hass has called this sense of return one of the fundamental beauties of poetry. He says, in *Twentieth Century Pleasures,* "the first fact of the world is that it repeats itself." This repetition, he says, helps us feel the inherent "shapeliness in things." We would argue that many poets write poems to discover or impose order upon chaotic emotions and events. We write poems to make sense of ideas, to narrate stories, to explore feelings, or to create music. What these impulses have in common is the desire to place language into an ordered form, in which something difficult may be clarified. Beyond meter, which we discussed earlier, there are many kinds of repetition in poetry, and these all serve to heighten our sense that we are finding a new version of order. We can start by focusing on sound repetitions.

Every poem is an experiment in theme and variation, repetition and renewal. Human beings like repetition because it makes us feel at home in the world. We like variation because we love to be surprised. Here's an example. Three days a week, Ann drives to a stable where she rides a 16-hand gray gelding named Selway. She is learning dressage—as close as riding comes to poetry—a disciplined and choreographed collaboration between rider and horse. Selway is beautiful, big-moving, graceful, athletic. Ann and Selway practice in an outdoor ring in summer, inside an arena in winter. Each day they ride circles, serpentines, practice their gaits and transitions. Ann loves the discipline of this repetition, the gradual flexing and ease she feels working at these exercises day after day. And yet, no day is the same. Why?

Because even in the repetition of these school figures are variations, missteps, improvements, failures in communication. And also, because Selway is chicken-hearted: alarmed at rustles in the grass, a truck parked in the wrong place on the berm, a wheelbarrow full of gravel next to the arena. He has been known to dislike a certain corner of the ring for weeks at a time. He fears dragonflies. Ann's challenge is to calm him and guide him without getting tossed off his back. That's where the element of surprise comes in. With his combination of random jumpiness and athletic grace, he keeps her alert, so her days are pleasure mixed with a little tension. Too much surprise, and she hyperventilates. She doesn't sleep well. Too much sameness, and they're both bored.

The music of poetry operates on this merging of chaos and shapeliness. Ezra Pound says "verse consists of a constant and a variant," and that sense of return and continuity, coupled with the surprise of the variant, is what makes each good song new. Listen to the shift and change in the opening lines of Galway Kinnell's *The Book of Nightmares*:

> On the path,
> by this wet site
> of old fires—
> black ashes, black stones, where tramps
> must have squatted down,
> gnawing on stream water,
> unhouseling themselves on cursed bread,
> failing to get warm at a twigfire—
>
> I stop,
> gather wet wood,
> cut dry shavings, and for her,
> whose face
> I held in my hands
> a few hours, whom I gave back
> only to keep holding the space where she was,
> I light
> a small fire in the rain.

There aren't large variations in voice or tone here, but subtle, smart ones. The poem's tone shifts from the rough, narrative observations of the first stanza to a modulation into tenderness in the second stanza as the speaker recalls his daughter's birth. That's only the beginning of the pleasure and surprise in this poem. In three short stanzas, Kinnell reveals many images that will become central to *The Book of Nightmares*, and the sounds he uses complement and intensify these images.

In the opening stanza, we see a barren landscape made up of "cursed bread," the cold, the ash of old fires. At this dark campsite, Kinnell's words are equally harsh: "black ashes, black stones, where tramps / must have squatted down, / gnawing on stream water. . . ." You can hear the percussive 'b' and 't' repeating in these lines, and so the poem begins with these verbal stresses, as well as with the brevity and march-step of many single-syllable words. These sounds recur throughout the poem, and match the dramatic subject, but they are coupled with a tenderness of tone that the second and third stanzas introduce. In these lines, we hear more open vowel sounds, and though the monosyllabic words continue here, the sound has changed, matching its song to the tenderness of its subject: "and for her, / whose face / I held in my hands / a few hours . . . / I light / a small fire in the rain." That tenderness creates surprise in the poem: Beauty might emerge in this forsaken place.

Exercises

1. Do your poems make tonal changes, like complex songs, or are they more pure, like Gregorian chants, one note, one tone? Try to vary your tones, and coordinate those changes with the movement of your narrative or idea, as they develop.

2. For such tonal developments, look at the poetry of Eavan Boland, Robert Hayden, or William Wordsworth.

Now let's discuss the particulars of sound effects. So far we have tried to articulate the primacy of music in poetic language. We have talked about becoming aware of our own use of sound devices in poetry, and we have explored shapeliness of sound in a poem's repetition and renewal. All of these discussions help us think about why well-written poems make us *feel* something. Though we haven't said so, what we've really been discussing all along is *rhyme* itself. While rhyme is usually thought of as something quite particular (the repetition of final sounds at the end of lines of poetry, like *muse* and *hues*), we think all the varieties of sound repetitions are versions of rhyme. We don't believe rhyme is only a line-ending strategy, though it is also that. What we hear in free verse or formal poems are different rhyming strategies: true rhyme, slant rhyme, alliteration, assonance, consonance, onomatopoeia. There are also larger strategies for highlighting patterns of sound repetition, such as anaphora, catalog, epistrophe, and chiasmus. Rhyme is a mnemonic device. It helps us keep the poem in memory. Bits and pieces of rhyming poems appear in our minds as we go about our day, as we shower, as we sleep. Rhyme exaggerates the song, and tells us, in fact, that we are reading or listening to something specifically musical. In its most traditional use, at the end of a line, rhyme helps to keep the tone of the poem consistent, and announces the arrival of the end of a line. We like rhyming poems that surprise us with their rhyme, that don't allow us to anticipate what comes next. We have all read doggerel (or limericks) that is so predictably rhyming that we can fill in the blanks ourselves: "There once was a man from Mars/Who drove around in speedy red—." You know what comes next. Cars. We don't take this seriously as poetry, in part because it lacks this element of inventive surprise.

Here is an excerpt from Marilyn Hacker's poem "Cancer Winter" that makes more complex choices in rhyme. In this section of the sonnet cycle, the speaker wakes from surgery, a mastectomy, and the language of this awakening reflects the haze of anesthesia, the confusion of people in the room, her thirst, her fear:

> At noon, an orderly wheeled me upstairs
> via an elevator hung with Season's
> Greetings streamers, bright and false as treason.
> The single room the surgeon let us share
> the night before the knife was scrubbed and bare
> except for blush-pink roses in a vase on
> the dresser. Veering through a morphine haze on
> the cranked bed, I was avidly aware
> of my own breathing, my thirst, that it was over—
> the week that ended on this New Year's Eve.
> A known hand held, while I sipped, icewater,
> afloat between ache, sleep, lover and lover.
> The one who stayed would stay; the one would leave.
> The hand that held the cup next was my daughter's.

This is a Petrarchan sonnet (rhyming ABBA ABBA CDE CDE), and Hacker mixes what we would call "true" or exact rhymes with "slant" or inexact rhymes. For instance, at the end of the poem, we find the rhymes "over" and "lover," "eve" and "leave," and "icewater" and "daughter's." "Eve" and "leave" make identical sounds, and so may be called *true rhyme;* the other two rhymes are not exact (though they are very close to being exact), and so may be called *slant rhymes.* But Hacker uses other strategies that highlight or undercut the rhyme itself. The choices she makes concerning line break will either help us hear the rhyme clearly, or hide it from us. Her end-stopped lines make us pause at the rhyming words, and that brief pause will let us dwell, if only for a moment, on the last word of the line. That pause helps us hear the rhyme more clearly. The last six lines of this sonnet are end-stopped. Compare them to the previous eight, most of which are heavily enjambed. Enjambed lines mask the rhyming words because our eye moves past them more quickly, as we reach, syntactically, for the line that follows. Interestingly, Hacker's "true" rhymes are to be found in the most enjambed lines. Slant rhyme, in combination with enjambed lines, can create a very subtle music. We may not even recognize it as rhyme at first: The poem is like a tapestry, in which the repetition of the pattern is woven so fully into the fabric that it deceives the eye. Hacker's use of rhyme works this way, helping us feel an undercurrent of pain, the wound asserting itself beneath the anaesthetic hush of the poem.

When we repeat sounds *inside* a line of poetry, we still rely on rhyming strategies, for many of the same reasons we might choose to employ end rhyme in a formal or metered poem. Strategies like *assonance, consonance,* and *alliteration* are at work in all poems, whether they are formal verse or free verse. At this more microcosmic level, a line of poetry is a balancing act between vowels and consonants. Which of these elements gets more emphasis will determine the particular quality of the music in that line. If vowels get more play in a line, we hear a more melodious sound. If the line relies heavily on consonants, we hear a more heavily stressed music. Here are two highly alliterative final lines from Gerard Manley Hopkins's poem "God's Grandeur":

Because the Holy Ghost over the bent
World broods with warm breast and with ah! bright wings.

The plosive "b" in these lines intensifies the emotion of Hopkins's devotional lyric. The insistent sound of the alliteration is allied to the theme of the poem, that the Holy Ghost is an inexorable presence even in a debased world. The heavy, pounding use of consonants here creates an intensified music. What else contributes to the overall effect of the poem? Hopkins likes monosyllabic words here and throughout the poem, and that choice helps us feel that the poem is packed full, densely compressed, and charged with emotion. Whether our lines feel loosely musical or sharply percussive arises from a multitude of choices, not least among them whether we emphasize vowels or consonants in a line. Consonants themselves can be loud or soft, as can vowels. We like the romantic ease, the nostalgia of D. H. Lawrence's poem "Piano" for that reason. Listen to these lines:

Softly, in the dusk, a woman is singing to me;
Taking me back down the vista of years, till I see
A child sitting under the piano, in the boom of the tingling
    strings
And pressing the small, poised feet of a mother who smiles as
    she sings.

In spite of myself, the insidious mastery of song
Betrays me back, till the heart of me weeps to belong
To the old Sunday evenings at home, with winter outside
And hymns in the cozy parlour, the tinkling piano our guide.

When Lawrence's open vowel sounds are combined with softer or fricative consonants like "f" and "v," they create a feeling of ease, of memory. The soft syllables and strongly sibilant alliteration make a softer, more "romantic"-sounding diction than, for instance, the opening lines of Rodney Jones's poem, "On the Bearing of Waitresses." Here we see lots of closed vowel sounds combined with strong alliteration, and the poem consequently has a hard-hitting precision and humor:

Always I thought they suffered, the way they huffed
through the Benzedrine light of waffle houses,
hustling trays of omelets, gossiping by the grill,
or pruning passes like the too prodigal buds of roses,
and I imagined each come home to a trailer court,
the yard of bricked-in violets, the younger sister
pregnant and petulant at her manicure, the mother
with her white Bible, the father sullen in his corner.

Jones's closed vowel sounds (in words like "suffered," "grill," "buds," "pregnant," and "corner") create a grim, tightened world, a world of tiny steps and bad luck. Combine this with the harder consonants of the poem ("Benzedrine," "pruning passes") and you have a sharp, emphatic picture. Further, you may want to combine these strategies, to show a change in tone or mood. This is what Eavan Boland does in many poems. As the mood of the poem modulates, so does her handling of sound. In the final stanzas of "The Glass King," Boland shifts from closed vowel sounds that describe the insane king, to the open sounds of the last stanza, which correspond with the portrait of the wife's vulnerable, open face:

> My prince, demented
>
> in a crystal past, a lost France, I elect you emblem
> and ancestor of our lyric: it fits you like a glove—
> doesn't it?—the part; untouchable, outlandish,
> esoteric, inarticulate and out of reach
>
> of human love: studied every day by your wife,
> an ordinary, honest woman out of place
> in all this, wanting nothing more than the man
> she married, all her sorrows in her stolid face.

All poets mix sound strategies, using them to suit the occasion, as Boland does here. What Boland achieves is a flexible music, one that varies as the poem's focus turns from the baroque king to his more simple wife.

Exercises

1. For splendid discussions of poetic rhyme, read Timothy Steele's chapter "Rhyme" in *All the Fun's in How You Say a Thing* and Anthony Hecht's essay, "On Rhyme," *Yale Review* (fall 1997).

We have looked at the building blocks poets use to create musical effect. Beyond these minute elements, we think sound may carry broadly across the body of the poem. Some of the strategies a poet might use with a larger, symphonic shape in mind include such rhetorical devices as *anaphora, epistrophe,* and *catalog.* All of these intensify our experience of repetition, just as rhyme and other sound devices do. For instance, when a poet decides to write a catalog, or list of items, in her poem, she is making use of a time-tested device found in biblical and epic poetry. One effect of catalog is the sense of bounty such a list might suggest. In ancient texts, catalog helped a reader see the vastness of the thing being described or the event being explained. In *The Aeneid,* lists of the dead appear amidst the narrative, the names a recitation of disaster. After epic battles, names of conquered cities magnify the victory at hand. Catalog helps to slow down the momentum, lends drama to the scene being described, and enlarges the experience of the poem. In this regard, it affects the entire scope of the poem. We think of Walt Whitman or Allen Ginsberg, modern poets who admire and use catalog. Other poets who use this device include Gwendolyn Brooks, Jorie Graham, and Charles Olson, among many others. Olson, in an excerpt from the *Maximus Poems,* uses catalog to show us the multitudes embedded in a single person, and by extension, poetry itself:

one loves only form,
and form only comes
into existence when
the thing is born

        born of yourself, born
        of hay and cotton struts,
        of street-pickings, wharves, weeds
        you carry in, my bird

                of a bone of a fish
                of a straw, or will
                of a color, of a bell
                of yourself, torn. . . .

Anaphora is another widely used strategy of repetition that carries across the body of the poem. Here, a word or phrase is repeated at the beginning of several lines of poetry (another strategy, closely linked, called epistrophe, is the strategy of repeating a word or phrase at the *end* of the line). You can think of anaphora as a kind of rhyme at the beginning of a line. Like catalog, this strategy uses repetitions intensely to create an intense tone. Additionally, it creates parallel structures that help us see connections between the ideas of the poem. Like litany, anaphora is used most fully in the Bible, and the connections between these strategies remind us of the ritual, prayerful quality of this language. At the end of Galway Kinnell's *The Book of Nightmares*, we hear the elemental emotions rising from these insistent lines, the raw love of the father for his child:

I have heard you tell
the sun, *don't go down,* I have stood by
as you told the flower, *don't grow old,*
don't die. Little Maud,

I would blow the flame out of your silver cup,
I would suck the rot from your fingernail,
I would brush your sprouting hair of the dying light,
I would scrape the rust off your ivory bones,
I would help death alchemize the ashes of your cradle back into
    wood,
I would let nothing of you go, ever. . . .

The poem says "I love you" in each of these final six lines. At the same time, it also reminds us that love and mortality are part of the same body, the same song.

Let's explore one last tactic involving the musical effects of poetry. But this time let's attend to the largest of the musical effects—the point/counterpoint of an overall narrative, its whole symphonic structure—as well as to the note-by-note melody. Remember those two drafts that David wrote several years ago, the ones from earlier in this chapter? Turn back to them for a moment, and reread, then turn back here. They are on pages 71 and 72–3.

David worked on those poems during the same long summer months many years ago. They are each the product of many revisions. One recounts the drama of the skinny-dippers, the old quarry and snakes, and the bitten or drowned friend. The other is much less eventful, more quiet, meditative, and haunting. They are both full of good moments as well as uncertain, ungraceful ones.

In working on those poems, David developed a tactic that has led to many other poems. Here is what he began to see and hear: many similar phrases in both poems (the recurrent heart, the flower, the settling darkness, the voice or song, especially the voice or song *missing*, and more); a similar mournful tone; the same approximate length of both drafts, though the lines and stanzas are very different. In other words, he saw he was writing two poems with similar impulses. He was singing versions of the same song.

So, he thought, why not make one poem? In his next draft, David relined the quarry poem to make it look like the catbird poem—three stanzas with six long, fluid lines. It worked. Then he arranged the poems into two numbered parts, the quarry poem first, catbird poem second, and called the poem "Silence." That haunting absence of sound deeply unites the pieces.

That was the first wonderful discovery, and it produced a deeper sense of understanding in the poem: The reason why the man in the catbird poem is awakened so violently may *not* be because the bird is gone but because the friend is gone. The vanished bird-song haunts him, reminding some part of his mind of the vanished friend's voice. "Aha!" David thought: the connection, the metaphor. One moment haunts the other.

That version was a big improvement, combining the different poems, making the leap. But it wasn't enough. It also seemed a touch calculated or contrived, a neat "before and after" picture. If the two drafts really were one poem, then why not make them one poem, fusing them rather than merely attaching them as a numbered sequence?

What David did to finish the poem was to apply virtually every formal tactic this chapter has examined. Rather than put the stories next to each other, he buried one inside the other, as memories are buried but active inside our present lives. He examined the lines, and preferred the fluid, connective longer line over the short, halting line; he balanced the numbers of accents to five and six beats per line; he recombined the stanzas into larger, fuller ones; he fused the rhetorical impulses of lyric and narrative, dramatic and meditative, elegiac and confessional, collective and personal. In making the poem more complex, he made the voice more coherent or singular. He further balanced the large and small musical effects: interior rhyming and repetition, the echo of phrases with the echo of events, a kind of narrative counterpointing, a large tonal and narrative resolution in the final stanza. He tried to do what we have talked about all chapter long:

THE ANNIVERSARY OF SILENCE

Every night for weeks, from the lilac's deep heart,
a catbird has softly sung through my sleep,
the same one always quietly mewing when I come home
or when I bend beneath it in the garden. This morning
I listened until the bulbs I planted seemed
like teardrops and I put them in the ground sadly.
Once there was a beauty even in the wreckage
men made of the world. The old quarry lake
lay waveless as it freckled under that evening's
early moon, and the low piles of rubble-rock
shone along the shore bare in the failing light.
Who could blame us as we stepped out of our clothes

and dove into the green heart of water? Who
could have seen there, like a dim, floating stone
in the still sheen, the ball of cottonmouths simmering?
There was nothing we could do. We stood back
on the glistening bank and watched as she just drifted.
She had found their black secret, so they must have been
on her, mouths blossoming like white flowers,
her mouth open as if to call or sing, yet oddly silent,
perhaps already choked with water. Or perhaps she really
smiled, as it seemed to us who were too far to see
the details of fear, as she floated among them
in the lovely evening, waving to us on shore.

Every night it has sung softly through my sleep.
Now I lie here restless, alone, tugged
from the slow wash of slumber not by light
or any noise, but by a silence dark and choking.
I do not know whether the bird has flown away or what
has happened. It is too dark to see anything
from the window, except the late wind wasting away
in the nearest leaves and a few stars high, faint.
How strange to feel such loss as this small
absence. I wish I could reach out and touch her

hand where she floats, and pull her from the darkness.
I wish I heard her singing softly, safe now, saved.

So, in this final version, the poem starts at the more current moment and ends there, and within that "present" comes the more distant, but vivid, memory. If a metaphor compares two images or ideas, then perhaps in a larger sense the whole poem is a figurative combination of the two episodes. David also rewrote many small parts of the poem. Go back now to the earlier drafts: Compare the details in phrase, syntax, and image. Do you see the many improvements and adjustments throughout? But the magic is strongest at the beginning of the final stanza, isn't it? When "it" sings, we don't know whether "it" is the imagined voice of the friend or the song of the vanished bird. Rather, "it" is both, at once, concurrently. It is guilt and loss and mourning. The last stanza blends the two scenarios completely; subsequently, the poem becomes a third, larger narrative. The whole poem becomes larger than both of the individual stories.

What did he do? He took two separate drafts and made one poem. We both have learned to wait when we write now, sometimes gathering notes and drafts from three, four, five separate impulses to make one poem. This is a wonderful, large tactic, which produces surprise and connection, and which can provide history, context, and meaning. That's the "form" and the metaphor—to find likeness and unlikeliness. And that's the magic.

Now, try your own.

FURTHER READING

Here is a short list of some useful books regarding poetry's forms and techniques. We don't intend this list to be complete or exclusive; it is representative at best, but will help you on your way. For a more complete bibliography of books on metrics and prosody, find the bibliography in *Meter in English*, listed below.

There are many wonderful anthologies of poetry, new and old, but their editors have assembled these anthologies to focus on specific formal, technical, or aesthetic issues:

Berg, Stephen and Robert Mezey. *Naked Poetry* and *The New Naked Poetry*. Indianapolis: Bobbs-Merrill. These two anthologies represent the best of the Deep Image free-verse poetry of the 1960s and 70s. Each selection includes an aesthetic statement, often about prosody and technique, by the poet.

Dacey, Philip and David Jauss, eds. *Strong Measures: Contemporary American Poetry in Traditional Forms.* New York: HarperCollins. This is a wonderful triple play: an abundant collection of poems, all in traditional forms; a clear dictionary of those forms; a cross-referenced index, matching poems with their forms and definitions. Very useful.

Hoover, Paul. *Postmodern American Poetry: A Norton Anthology.* New York: Norton. A representative collection of recent experimental poetry, mainly identified as postmodern or post-structuralist, from the Beats and Projectivists to more recent Language and performance poets. Also includes a section of poetic statements by several of the important poets.

Jarman, Mark and David Mason. *Rebel Angels: 25 Poets of the New Formalism.* Brownsville, OR: Story Line. Anthology representing the contemporary traditionalist school known as New Formalism, dedicated to writing in meter and rhyme.

Richman, Robert. *The Direction of Poetry: An Anthology of Rhymed and Metered Verse Written in the English Language Since 1975.* Boston: Houghton Mifflin. A good collection. The subtitle says it all.

Rothenberg, Jerome and Pierre Joris, eds. *Poems for the Millennium: The University of California Book of Modern and Postmodern Poetry.* Berkeley: University of California. This huge two-volume anthology presents a wide range of experimental poetries. Volume one is subtitled *From Fin-de-Siecle to Negritude* and volume two is *From Postwar to Millennium.* Together they provide a complete view of the non-traditional and non-formalist aesthetics running through the 20th century.

For reference and resource books on poetic form and technique, try:

Beyers, Chris. *A History of Free Verse.* Fayetteville: University of Arkansas. Interesting new study of the "genres" of free verse.

Corn, Alfred. *The Poem's Heartbeat: A Manual of Prosody.* Brownsville, OR: Story Line. A good introductory tour.

Hirsch, Edward. *How to Read a Poem and Fall in Love with Poetry.* New York: Harcourt Brace. This new book about the pleasures of poetry features an excellent glossary of poetic and prosodic terms and techniques.

Hollander, John. *Rhyme's Reason: A Guide to English Verse.* New Haven: Yale University. Concise, precise, and very enjoyable.

Kinzie, Mary. *A Poet's Guide to Poetry.* Chicago: University of Chicago. This fine new book features a large dictionary and chapters on form, rhetoric, rhythm, and content.

Preminger, Alex and T. V. F. Brogan. *The New Princeton Encyclopedia of Poetry and Poetics.* Princeton: Princeton University. An essential resource for poets, with entries on virtually every aspect of poetry and poetics from the technical and historical to the aesthetic. At nearly 1,400 pages, this is an important book for a poet's desk.

Turco, Lewis. *The New Book of Forms: A Handbook of Poetics.* Hanover, NH: University Presses of New England. An excellent encyclopedia of versification.

Williams, Miller. *Patterns of Poetry: An Encyclopedia of Forms.* Baton Rouge: Louisiana State University. A very instructive manual of prosody, with definitions and many illustrative poems.

For critical studies of prosody, form, and technique, try:

Attridge, Derek. *Poetic Rhythm: An Introduction.* Cambridge: Cambridge University. Attridge's discussion of rhythm is based on his linguistic approach to stress, metrics, and syntax.

Baker, David, ed. *Meter in English: A Critical Engagement.* Fayetteville: University of Arkansas. A lively (sometimes contentious) symposium on the elements of meter and scansion, centered around a long essay by Robert Wallace, with responding essays by fourteen other poet-critics. You can see the specifics of prosody in practice and in debate.

Bernstein, Charles. *A Poetics.* Cambridge: Harvard University. Bernstein's book is both a poetic text and a critical discussion of the politics and prosody of Language poetry.

Cooper, G. Burns. *Mysterious Music: Rhythm and Free Verse.* Stanford: Stanford University. This new book presents a sophisticated, linguistics-based discussion of rhythm and music at the "molecular" level.

DuPlessis, Rachel Blau. *The Pink Guitar: Writing as Feminist Practice.* New York: Routledge. One of the smartest discussions of post-structural feminist poetics, with significant discussion of the meaning of form in relation to gender and ideology.

Finch, Annie. *The Ghost of Meter: Culture and Prosody in American Free Verse.* Ann Arbor: University of Michigan. This is an interesting study of the (often hidden or oblique) metrical bases of free verse since the mid-19th century.

Frank, Robert and Henry Sayre, eds. *The Line in Postmodern Poetry.* Urbana: University of Illinois. A gathering of critical essays on theories of lineation in free verse, formal verse, and Language poetry.

Fulton, Alice. *Feeling as a Foreign Language: The Good Strangeness of Poetry.* St. Paul: Graywolf. The second section features Fulton's discussion of poetic form and the science of fractals.

Hartman, Charles O. *Free Verse: An Essay on Prosody.* Princeton: Princeton University. An excellent introduction to the history, aesthetics, and practice of free verse. A new edition is available from Northwestern University.

Kirby-Smith, H. T. *The Celestial Twins: Poetry and Music through the Ages.* Amherst: University of Massachusetts.

Kirby-Smith, H. T. *The Origins of Free Verse.* Ann Arbor: University of Michigan. A full, clear history of the development and evolution of free verse poetics.

Mariani, Paul and George Murphy. *Poetics: Essays on the Art of Poetry.* Issued as both a special issue of *Tendril* magazine and a book from Tendril Press, this out-of-print essay collection features several extremely good pieces on poetics, metaphor, line, and rhythm, among other subjects.

McCorkle, James, ed. *Conversant Essays: Contemporary Poets on Poetry.* Detroit: Wayne State University. This essay anthology features a chapter on "Questions of Form," with representative comments from a wide range of political and aesthetic schools.

Scully, James. *Line Break: Poetry as Social Practice.* Seattle: Bay Press. Sometimes hard to find, this is a fascinating study of poetic form in relation to political action and the avant-garde.

Steele, Timothy. *All the Fun's in How You Say a Thing.* Athens: Ohio University. This new book is one of the most engaging works of scholarship on the nature of versification ever written. Steele's splendid discussions are lessons in both the historical evolution and the present application of such entities as rhyme, stanza forms, and metrics.

Steele, Timothy. *Missing Measures: Modern Poetry and the Revolt against Meter.* Fayetteville: University of Arkansas. This fine scholarly work traces the aesthetic and historical reasons beyond the Modernist rejection of traditional prosody.

These three older texts are classics for good reason. They are useful and clear, among the best in the field:

Fussell, Paul. *Poetic Meter and Poetic Form.* New York: Random House. One of the most intelligent and precise discussions of prosody written in the last fifty years. A new revised edition is available from McGraw Hill.

Nims, John Frederick. *Western Wind: An Introduction to Poetry.* New York: Random House. This important text features excellent discussions and applications of poetic form and style.

Perrine, Laurence. *Sound and Sense: An Introduction to Poetry.* New York: Harcourt Brace. Thomas Arp has updated and reissued this classic creative writing text, first published in 1956.

IV

Kit & Caboodle

Yusef Komunyakaa

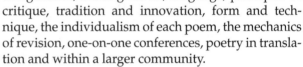

The ideal poetry workshop becomes a small, instant community of shared ideas, and it is also a way station for nurturing. This isn't a stage or arena for a cutting contest; it is a place where *work* occurs in relationship to ideas and process. Everything is talked about: workshop protocol, imagination, reading habits, language, principles of

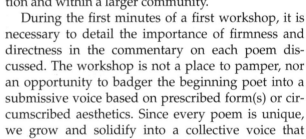

critique, tradition and innovation, form and technique, the individualism of each poem, the mechanics of revision, one-on-one conferences, poetry in translation and within a larger community.

During the first minutes of a first workshop, it is necessary to detail the importance of firmness and directness in the commentary on each poem discussed. The workshop is not a place to pamper, nor an opportunity to badger the beginning poet into a submissive voice based on prescribed form(s) or circumscribed aesthetics. Since every poem is unique, we grow and solidify into a collective voice that points out its positive and negative aspects. The poet is there to take notes, not to agree or disagree openly with the commentary, but to return to those recorded annotations at a later date and weigh his or her poems against them. The workshop isn't a platform for defending one's intent or motivations in composing a poem.

I wish it understood that when I rattle off my list of don'ts or pet peeves, they are mere suggestions: "Try not to use the word *that* in poetry . . . surprise yourself in order to surprise the reader . . . I agree with Richard Hugo, in his book entitled *Triggering Town,* when he says that the semicolon looks ugly in poetry ... do not resolve a poem nor allow a title to do so ... sentimentality is formless passion that controls or contains the poem's emotional thrust ... it is difficult to say *tears* in a poem ... write poetry in longhand, letting the hand transmit all its signals back to the brain ... see how many color adjectives can be extracted from the poem. Avoid using *I imagine* or *I remember.*

When Phillis Wheatley at seven or eight years old arrived from West Africa on the slave ship *Phillis,* she was purchased in July 1761 by a Boston merchant, John Wheatley, and given to his wife, Susanna, as a personal maid. She learned to read English and Latin literature, published her first poem in a Rhode Island newspaper in 1767; "On Imagination" appeared in her book, *Poems on Various Subjects* in 1773, making a bold claim:

Imagination! who can sing thy force?
Or who describe the swiftness of thy course?
Soaring through air to find the bright abode,
Th' empyreal palace of the thund'ring God,
We on thy pinions can surpass the wind,
And leave the rolling universe behind:
From star to star the mental optics rove,
Measure the skies, and range the realms above.
There is one view we grasp the mighty whole,
Or with new worlds amaze th' unbounded soul.

In this short excerpt, the fourth stanza, we see how Wheatley praises the power to imagine. It is on the wings of imagination that she's able to escape her earthly world.

One could say that each poem distills what imagination offers. So, it shouldn't surprise us when Muriel Rukeyser states the following in *The Life of Poetry* in 1949:

The relations of poetry are, for our period, very close to the relations of science. It is not a matter of using the results of science, but of seeing that there is a meeting-place between all the kinds of imagination. Poetry can provide that meeting-place.

In contemporary society, imagination is mainly praised when it is pragmatic or ties into some economic venture. Otherwise, imagination is often linked to daydreaming—"a waste of time," an impracticality—without realizing that every object produced rises out of abstract imagination that is first intangible and then made substantive. Young people are often ashamed to say that they write poetry, because it doesn't lead to screenplays and movies. At best, writing poetry is often viewed as a hobby. Another common attitude mistrusts "a good imagination" because that quality can enable a person to rebel or pose hard questions. There's no denial, imagination is often rather unruly.

At the beginning of the twenty-first century, in the heat of technological and social changes, perhaps one might be led to question the sacredness of imagination that Jacques Maritain poses (not that distant from Phillis Wheatley's notion) in *Creative Intuition in Art and Poetry* (New American Library, 1977):

> . . . we must say that imagination proceeds or flows from the essence of the soul through intellect, and that the external senses proceed from the essence of the soul through imagination. For they exist in name to serve imagination, and through imagination, intelligence.

It is as if humans are created to embrace poetry, that which Rukeyser refers to as "an outcast art," because poetry attempts to deal with mysteries so monumental we seem reduced before them. Our language becomes abstracted, and the workshop becomes a place where the participants are mindful of the concrete. Speaking about existential reality, William Van O'Connor in *Sense and Sensibility in Modern Poetry* (Gordian Press, 1973) writes, "But [people have] another side. [Their] imagination and determination elevate [and] spiritualize [them]." That is, imaginative powers set humans apart from other species, and simultaneously make us responsible for creating the tangible realities of our world.

In beginning workshops, each student prepares a glossary of terms: first written out in longhand, and then, typed: abstract, accentual meter, allegory, alliteration, allusion, anapest, ballad, blank verse, carpe diem, caesura, closed form, concrete, connotations, couplet, dactyl, denotation, dialect, dramatic monologue, elegy, end rime, end-stopped, envoy, epigram, exact rime, explication, feminine rime, figures of speech, fixed forms, foot, free verse, haiku, heroic couplet, hexameter, hyperbole, iambic pentameter, imagery, internal refrain, internal rime, irony, lyric, masculine rime, metaphor, meter, mixed metaphors, monosyllabic foot, narrative poem, octave, off rime, onomatopoeia, open form, persona, personification, Petrarchan sonnet, poetic diction, projective verse, prosody, quatrain, rap, refrains, rhythm, rime scheme, run-on line, satiric poetry, scansion, sentimentality, sestet, sestina, Shakespearean sonnet, simile, slant rime, spondee, stanza, stress, surrealism, syllabic verse, symbol, synecdoche, tactile imagery, terza rima, tetrameter, tone, tragic imagery, trimeter, triolet, trochee, verbal irony, verse, villanelle, visual imagery, and voice.

When discussing poems in the workshop, it is imperative that participants utilize a common vocabulary in critiques, discussions, or responses to reading assignments incorporated in each student's *Critical Response Journal*. The *Journal* grows into a logbook for all impressions, statements, and ideas about the various poems read during the semester-long workshop.

Often, I find myself telling workshop participants that you must know the form and rules of poetry before you can become an innovator or risk-taker. The poem's visual shape is determined by its arranged components, as well as by the patterned organization of rhythms and sounds. Two major categories of poetic forms are fixed (sonnet, sestina, villanelle) and organic (historically, shape or patterns evolve with the poem). In thinking about the long development of poetry, organic forms are probably more traditional than fixed forms. The first form assigned in the workshop is the haiku—at least seven, twenty-one lines. In lines one and three are five syllables, and seven in line two; the mention of a season establishes the poem's tone, though this isn't an iron-clad rule for the contemporary haiku—especially when written in English, which is merely an approximation of the form. This exercise focuses on the integrity of the stanza.

Usually, workshop students are not presented in-class exercises; rather, I assign out-of-class exercises and the writing of theme-based poems. For instance, they might write love poems during the fifth week or discuss how difficult it is to compose a mature love poem, especially after having read Neruda's love poems or lyrics by Robert Johnson or Bessie Smith. We talk about music and the meaning of poems, about how we come to trust what words are saying and how they make us feel. Each word becomes important. Workshop by workshop, we create space for what we have imagined, witnessed, and lived. We may also fruitfully discuss Rothenberg's *Technicians of the Sacred,* Rilke's *Letters to a Young Poet,* or Rich's *On Lies, Secrets, and Silence.*

Out-of-class exercises often resemble the ten listed below:

1. Write a praise or tribute poem. Consider what Pablo Neruda accomplishes in "Ode to a Lemon"—here are the third and final stanzas:

> Knives
> sliced a small
> cathedral
> in the lemon,
> the concealed apse, opened,
> revealed acid stained glass,
> drops
> oozed topaz,
> altars,
> cool architecture.
>
> So, when you hold
> the hemisphere
> of a cut lemon
> above your plate,
> you spill
> a universe of gold,
> a
> yellow goblet
> of miracles,
> a fragrant nipple
> of the earth's breast,
> a ray of light that was made fruit,
> the minute fire of a planet.

> [*Selected Odes of Pablo Neruda,* translated by Margaret Sayers Peden, Berkeley (University of California Press, 1990).]

Or, study Robert Hayden's "Frederick Douglass" as a model for the tribute:

> When it is finally ours, this freedom, this liberty, this beautiful
> and terrible thing, needful to man as air,

usable as earth; when it belongs at last to all,
when it is truly instinct, brain matter, diastole, systole,
reflex action; when it is finally won; when it is more
than the gaudy mumbo jumbo of politicians;
this man, this Douglass, this former slave, this Negro
beaten to his knees, exiled, visioning a world
where none is lonely, none hunted, alien,
this man, superb in love and logic, this man
shall be remembered. Oh, not with statues' rhetoric,
not with legends and poems and wreaths of bronze alone,
but with the lives grown out of his life, the lives
fleshing his dream of the beautiful, needful thing.

[*Collected Poems* (New York: Liveright, 1985)]

2. All artists imitate—painters, novelists, sculptors, musicians, actors—as a springboard to cultivating their own craft, perspectives, and voices. Write a poem that appropriates the operatic trajectory of Walt Whitman's "Song of Myself" in no fewer than fifty lines.

3. Sometimes the poet attempts to venture to another realm or reality to plumb everyday images of experience and imagination: "Close your eyes . . . take a few deep breaths . . . you are standing before a closed door, your hand on the doorknob . . . you turn the knob slowly . . . you enter . . . someone is sitting in a chair, but he or she doesn't see you . . . is there light coming into the room, through a window, beneath a door? . . . focus on the person's hands . . . the hands are busy doing something . . . remember the hands . . . look at his or her hair . . . let your eyes take in the entire room . . . return to the person . . . slowly back out of the room . . . close the door . . . now, write down everything you observed . . . first in lines of prose, and then in lines of verse."

4. It is the 1960s, and you are about to become a Freedom Rider. Look at twenty or thirty photographs that capture the actions of the period. View the faces carefully before constructing your monologue from the perspective of the person in a photograph. Try making the poem's narrator the opposite gender of yourself. Envision your poem as a small monument to those who marched to a different drummer.

5. Write a music-related poem. For models, read selections from numerous anthologies including *Sweet Nothings: An Anthology of*

Rock and Roll in American Poetry, ed. Jim Elledge (Bloomington: Indiana University Press, 1994) or *Jazz Anthologies,* co-edited with Sascha Feinstein. *The Second Set: The Jazz Poetry Anthology (1996); The Jazz Poetry Anthology* (Bloomington: Indiana University Press, 1991). For examples of jazz-related poems, read William Matthews, Jayne Cortez, Sascha Feinstein, and Amiri Baraka.

6. Write a non-sense poem. Employ play and wit—a music that expresses two or more moods moving from one to the other. Let a seriousness live within the playfulness of language, similar to that found in many folktales. Refuse to concentrate on the narrative; instead, let *sound* convey the poem's emotional thread. Use Lewis Carroll's "Jabberwocky" as its model.

7. Tension in poetry is important.
   a. Write a poem that attempts to incorporate several levels of diction, such as scientific phrases alongside street language, to generate playfulness. It may be necessary to choose a traditional form such as a ghazal, villanelle, or sestina.
   b. Write a poem that intertwines two emotions. Example: begin with something you hate, but end with something you love. In fact, this poem may become a "love poem" that doesn't mention love.

8. Write a poem that compares and contrasts Robert Lowell's "For the Union Dead" with Allen Tate's "Ode to the Confederate Dead."

9. From the menagerie of spirit animals—magical or real—write a poem without naming the animal; make it visible. If you wish, resurrect one from extinction so it will live through the imagination and power of poetry.

Dream Animal

He's here again. Is this hunger I smell, something like wildflowers and afterbirth tangled in sage? I press down on each eyelid to keep him here: otherwise, otherwise . . . But he always escapes the lair. Don't care how much I dance and chant rain across the mountains, it never falls on his back. Tiger or wolf, he muzzles up to me, easy as a Christbird walking across lily pads. As if he slipped out of a time machine, his phantom prints disappear at the timberline. I'm on all fours, with my nose almost pressed to the ground. A few galah feathers decorate clumps of tussock. Ants have unlocked the mystery of a bearded dragon, as they inch him

toward some secret door. I close my eyes again. Somewhere a kookaburra
laughs. In this garden half-eaten by doubt and gunpowder, honeyeaters
peck the living air. And here he stands beneath the Southern Cross, the
last of his kind, his stripes even brighter in this dark, nocturnal weather.

from *Thieves of Paradise*

10. Close your eyes, open the telephone directory, let your fingers find a name, open your eyes, and then meditate on the name. Get to know this person through your imagination: his or her personality, preferences, biases, attitudes, lifestyle, personal history, and so forth. Write a poem in forty lines that captures this person, using concrete details.

The ten above mentioned exercises are just a few of many that can help us tap into the magic of writing poetry. This assisted travel via the mind isn't a process of escape, but is one of confrontation and celebration, a naming ceremony. I agree with John Cowper Powys in his book *The Pleasures of Literature* (London: Cassell and Company, Ltd., 1938), in which he writes "magicians have never been able to control their angels and demons until they discovered their names. The origin of all literature lies here. A word is a magic incantation by which the self exorcises power—first over itself and then over other selves and then, for all we know, over the powers of nature." At least, such is the conjuring that often propels the poet's pen—maybe writing a line ten different ways before it seems almost right. Perhaps this is the reason group effort in writing poems is called a workshop. To borrow from a cliché, whenever there's power, there's responsibility: workshop participants learn to share the responsibility for arriving at truth and levity in language.

Each poem possesses a personality. Style. Of course, the topography of a poem says a lot about its personality. But what is great about world poetry is how so many voices and personalities can exist side by side, how E. E. Cummings's "since feelings first" is in the same anthology as James Wright's "A Note Left in Jimmy Leonard's Shack," along with Emily Brontë's "Prisoner." The Aristotelian sense of style evolves out of a person's whole body of work and is not applied to a particular poem. Compare and contrast Emily Brontë's poetry with Emily Dickinson's. The Platonic sense of style refers to the poet's sense of word choice to achieve intention and meaning, which readily concerns the beginning writer: Anglo-Saxon or Latinate, concrete and abstract, formal or colloquial, literal or figurative. Beginning poets, in their attempts to sound natural, are nevertheless accountable to the art's demands, that is, to enlarge the tone and meaning of contemporary language.

Jeanette Winterson states, "Poetry, poetic fiction, is not an artificial language (or at least when it is, it ceases to be poetry), but it is a heightened language." She further elaborates, "It is recognizably the language we use but at a pitch beyond the everyday capacities of speech" (*Art Objects: Essays on Ecstasy and Effrontery.* New York: Knopf, 1996). Winterson's comments are astute. However, William Carlos Williams's "The Red Wheel Barrow" keeps beckoning, saying, *Look at me etherized on this white space:* "so much depends upon a red wheel barrow glazed with rain water beside the white chickens." Is this "heightened language," the diction associated with poetry? Of course, "The Red Wheel barrow" itself is the answer to the question. There's something more: Everything seems to depend on how Williams broke his line to create tension through silence and subtle grace:

so much depends
upon

a red wheel
barrow

glazed with rain
water

beside the white
chickens.

The poem seems suspended in spacious silence. The language rings pure, uncorrupted by embellished gesture, insincerity, or disguise. In this sense, one also thinks of Ezra Pound's "In a Station of the Metro": "The apparition of these faces in the crowd; / Petals on a wet, black bough." Again, this isn't an example of heightened language. Each line, as is true in every well-worked poem, conveys patterned emotions and feelings: The poem becomes an entity within its design. In a nonself-censoring way, language is aware of its rhythm(s) as it moves naturally (trying not to call attention to itself as a construction) through the lines—the syntax—the nerves inside language.

When form and content grow into one, language becomes organic, and then the poem possesses the capacity to surprise. Surprise penetrates language without being grandiose or overly embellished.

After beginning poets have imitated some of poetry's endeared masters, I encourage them to develop their own voices. I don't like to see members of a workshop writing the same poem, even though they may share similar aesthetics—and not for the sake of being different but of being true to one's self. Of course, an individual's voice has much to do with culture, class, temperament, and any number of factors, but ultimately it distinguishes one individual from another within a rather complex world. And let us not forget time. The times in which one is writing bear upon the poem's sound and tone.

One way to examine voice is to look closely at poetry in translation. I encourage workshop participants to look beyond Robert Frost's infamous statement "Poetry is what is lost in translation" by suggesting that their minds and hearts have to embrace the larger world, that isolationism is unhealthy no matter the discipline or domain. I give them a few names of poets who have been translated into English: Osip Mandelstam, Anna Akhmatova, Paul Celan, Jean Follain, Pablo Neruda, Federico García Lorca, Miroslav Holub, Aimé Césaire, César Vallejo, Octavio Paz, Dante, Sappho, Nguyen Quan Thieu, Yehuda Amichai, Li Po, Wislawa Szymborska, Joyce Mansour, and others.

Often the differences in translations are slight. Yet, these variants suggest much about the fluidity of language—how many ways something can be said. This can be illustrated by three translations of the first stanza of Eugenio Montale's "Dora Markus":

It was where the wooden pier
at Porto Corsini juts into open sea
and one or two men, all but motionless, cast out
or haul in their nets. With a wave
of the hand you signaled toward the other shore,
invisible, your true country.
Then we followed the canal far as the docks
of a city glittering soot,
there in marshflats, where an inert springtime
sank out of memory.

—translated by Reg Saner

It was there, where the wooden pier
sticks out over the high tide at Porto Corsini
and a few men, almost without moving, drop
and pull up their nets. With a stab
of your finger, you pointed out the invisible landfall
across the water, your true country.
Then we followed the canal back to the city dock
shiny with soot,
in a lowland where a catatonic April
was sinking, flushed of all memory.

—translated by Charles Wright
[both excerpts from *Poetry Reading: The Field Symposia*. Ed. David Walker,
Oberlin College Press, 1999.]

It was where the wooden bridge
spans the high tide at Porto Corsini
and a few men, almost motionless,
sink or haul in their nets.
With the flourish of a hand you signaled
your true country on the other, invisible shore.
Then we followed the canal
to the city dock, slick with soot,
in the lowland where a listless spring,
devoid of memory, was sinking.

—translated by Jonathan Galassi
[Eugene Montale: Collected Poems 1920–1954, *Bilingual Edition, translated and
annotated by Jonathan Galassi*. New York: Farrar, Straus and Giroux, 1998.]

Revision. Re-see. Re-visit. Re-invent. I think it was Ernest Hem-
ingway who said "we have to learn to kill our little darlings." For the
beginning writer, often the most difficult task is to re-dream the
poem's new shape and form. Many young poets attempt to argue
that revision undermines the poem's inspired rhythm and content.
But I suggest that inspiration isn't an intellectual blood letting, that
instead, a poem develops by one successive act after another and,
because of this process, reaches fulfillment.

We begin with the title: Does it illuminate the body of the poem,
does it nudge its meaning in a slightly different direction, creating
additional tension? I suggest that the title should not resolve the

poem. If anything, the most provocative titles dissolve parameters that inhibit expansion of a poem's impact. Moving to the body of the poem, we ask: Does the poem really begin with that first line, or is it the tenth line? What if the poem begins with the last line and ends with this middle line? Or, is the fifteenth line the entry into the poem, and therefore the beginning of an entirely new poem? Certainly, these choices become available depending on the poem and how it begs shape and further work.

Sometimes it is necessary for the instructor to pursue the fine points of a discussion that originated in the workshop. The one-on-one conference, lasting anywhere from twenty minutes to one hour, provides the moment for in-depth, individualized instruction. This is when each poem and its evolution are addressed, and the negatives and positives of the overall workshop experience are faced. One student's temperament is so different from another's that each particular voice and sense of aesthetics must be considered. An artist's obsessions are shaped both by experiences and observations: Jill writes long narratives almost exclusively about mountain climbing, fly fishing, and soccer; Jack's poems are primarily terse lyrics woven of succulent imagery about food, and his poems about racing involve sensitive and delicate imagery. Both of these young poets become more skillful in their revisions; abstractions are replaced by engaging details. Surprising endings propel the reader or listener up to the poem's beginning lines, forcing them to re-contemplate the convergence of meanings and associations.

It is in this setting where each student's reading habits are discussed more thoroughly. Of course, the suggested reading list for Jill is different from Jack's. There are, however, the following poets whom I suggest for everyone: William Blake, John Donne, William Wordsworth, Samuel Taylor Coleridge, John Keats, Walt Whitman, Emily Dickinson, William Butler Yeats, Paul Laurence Dunbar, Robert Frost, Wallace Stevens, William Carlos Williams, Ezra Pound, H.D., T. S. Eliot, Jean Toomer, Hart Crane, Sterling A. Brown, Langston Hughes, W. H. Auden, Theodore Roethke, Elizabeth Bishop, Robert Hayden, Gwendolyn Brooks, and James Wright.

Sometimes conferencing inspires a poet to reveal the subtopic hidden within the secret design of a poem. Of course, at this point of revelation, the poet is coaxed to become bolder and more revealing, but without being overly confessional or sensational. Or, the young poet reveals his or her true passion, which hasn't been written about: "Can I write about skin diving?" "But how can I write about biology?" There's no topic that is taboo in the workshop because a poem's content is shaped by aesthetics. I suggest that the poem's real engine is *need;* if not, the writing slips into the format of exercises that are always in progress. True, one might grasp the technical aspects of making a poem in the same way one might spend a lifetime studying the properties of graphite or meteors, hoping to fashion diamonds, but a workshop student cannot be assured that a good poem can be produced this way: writing poetry requires passion.

My student, Jack asks, "How do I get published?" I suggest that one shouldn't be so eager to seek publication, but if he truly trusts his poems enough to send them out into the big, bad world, here are a few pointers: Submit between three and five neatly typed poems, with an address at the bottom of each poem. Consult *The International Directory of Little Magazines and Small Presses* (DustBooks); "Never send a cover letter" William Matthews said to me in 1975; enclose a self-addressed, stamped envelope (SASE); avoid sending poems to a magazine or periodical you've never seen or read. Your submissions, then, join great numbers of others arriving at a journal's office. Regardless of how many rejection notices you receive, hard work and persistence eventually win out.

Many have questioned the so-called workshop poem. Writing on this very topic, fiction writer Hilma Wolitzer, commenting on Wallace Stegner's two-part statement on the teaching of writing ("1. It can be done. 2. It can't be done to everybody."), says, ". . . But there's a place in the classroom for other interested parties who, in their ardent analysis of one another's writing, become much better readers. And God knows we can always use more of them." (*The New York Times*, 31 January 2000).

Of course, I agree with Wolitzer. I can't see how one can expect to write poetry and not read. Poets read literature naturally, but students must be encouraged to read outside the discipline to nourish their poems, that is, from science-related texts, mythology, philosophy, history, geography, etcetera. Then they must be made fully aware that the discussion about writing poetry has been going on for a long time. We have only to recall the last three lines of Andrew Marvell's "To His Worthy Friend Doctor Witty Upon His Translation of the Popular Errors": "For Something guides my

hand that I must write. / You have translations's statues best ful-
filled, / That handling neither sully nor would gild." Or, they may
venture further back, to the Taoist, Lu Ji (261–303 CE), in *The Art of
Writing: Teachings of the Chinese Masters* (edited by Tony Barnstone,
translated by the editor and Chou Ping), who writes this about
"process":

Search for the words and sphere of thought,
then seek the proper order;
release their shining forms
and tap images to hear how they sing.
Now leaves grow along a branching thought.
Now trace a current to its source.
Bring the hidden into light
or form the complex from simplicity.
Animals shake at the tiger's changing pattern
and birds ripple off when a dragon is seen;
some words belong together
and others don't join, like jagged teeth,
but when you're clear and calm
your spirit finds true words.
With heaven and earth contained in your head,
nothing escapes the pen in your hand.
It's how to get started at first,
painful like talking with cracked lips,
but words will flow with ink in the end.
Essence holds content as the trunk lifts the tree;
language is patterned into branches, leaves, and fruit.
Now words and content match
like your mood and face—
smile when you're happy
or sigh when your heart hurts.
Sometimes you can improvise easily.
Sometimes you only bite the brush and think.

[edited by Tony Barnstone and translated by Ping Chou, Chi Wen Fu Lu,
Kendra Crossen, Peter Turner, Shambhala, 1996]

The wisdom of process Lu Ji captures is instructive in its daring
simplicity and ornamental phrasing. Without saying so, he shows us

the origins of consciousness itself. Language is alive. For the poet, each word represents sound and meaning; the music of meaning is shaped by words that fall left or right of a single word. Each word is an increment of the whole. Perhaps we are drawn to poetry because language vibrates (is an action), and we seem to search still for a language that will keep us whole.

Beginning poets will discover that their first like-minded community is often the workshop: this is where the personal becomes political, where exposure develops trust. Relating to a host of influences, this small community intersects a larger literary one made up of bookstores, coffeehouses, special collections in libraries, slam and spoken-word readings at umpteen venues across the country in small towns and big cities. Poets just becoming familiar with this extended literary community also read and subscribe to a host of literary magazines. As was mentioned, most literary journals are catalogued in the *International Directory of Little Magazines*. Poets may consult listings in free or accessible local publications that announce poetry readings. In order to learn about poetry festivals, programs at arts centers, conferences, writer retreats and colonies, or reading series, besides by word-of-mouth, literary publications such as *Poets and Writers Magazine* as well as web sites—for example, that of the Poetry Society of America (www.poetrysociety.org) and the Academy of American Poets (www.poets.org) provide an enormous array of resources and services. On National Public Radio's "Poetry Showcase" (*All Things Considered*), Cathy Bowman introduces the works of contemporary poets. All in all, poets emerging from their first workshops learn that a larger community of writers is there to embrace them. They merely must commit themselves to poetry.

In recent years,we have seen scores of obituaries elegizing the so-called death of poetry. Sometimes, W.H. Auden's infamous lines are quoted from "In Memory of W.B. Yeats," usually the first five words out of context: "For poetry makes nothing happen: it survives / in the valley of its making where executives / Would never want to tamper, flows on south / From ranches of isolation and the busy griefs, / Raw towns that we believe and die in; it survives, / A way of happening, a mouth," eds. Margaret Ferguson, Mary Jo Salter, and Joan Stallworthy. *The Norton Anthology of Poetry: The Shorter 4ᵗʰ* Edition. (New York: W.W. Norton, 1997). By all signs, poetry in America seems to be alive and well, still speaking its own 'mouth(s).' This is the case because, in part, poets themselves have become mentors, teachers, workshop instructors, and curators, and are active in poetry organizations. Together, a poet and a group of initiates cherish the art that sustains them.

V

Audience

Maxine Kumin

The days when people stood on chairs to catch a glimpse of Alfred, Lord Tennyson are gone, we are told, along with the snows of yesteryear. The poems, in those good old days of Palgrave's 1861 edition of his "Golden Treasury of the Best Songs and Lyrical Poems in the English Language," provided a commonality of experience in every literate household. "Hail to thee, blithe spirit" and "Let  me not to the marriage of true minds" were easily accessible to a generation that had psalms andhymns by heart as well. In a not-yet heterogeneous, multicultural population, the Bible and Shakespeare, along with Southey and Herrick, Keats and Shelley served as foundation stones for the education of the young.

In a pre-literate society, the poet was shaman, myth maker, historian. The tribe survived because the life of the individual was subordinate to the needs of the majority, and the poet communicated the tribe's values through storytelling. Some sort of rhyme scheme and refrain was a way of remembering myth and metaphor. Long before the troubadours of the Middle Ages rode from village to village, the lives and loves of the gods were handed down from generation to generation.

In an essay on the ghazal, a Persian/Arabic form written in strongly end-stopped couplets, the Kashmirian poet Agha Shahid Ali describes this gala event: "At a *mushaira*—the traditional poetry gathering to which sometimes thousands of people come to hear the most cherished poets of the country—when the poet recites the first line of a couplet, the audience recites it back to him, and then the poet repeats it, and the audience again follows suit." At the dedication of a new hydroelectric station in Siberia, as many as 40,000 people are said to have assembled to hear the Russian poet Yevgeny Yevtushenko recite his "The Bratsk Station" in praise of its construction, an act that also helped restore him to political favor. In Latin America, a poet can also be a statesman or a governor or senator and command large public attention, as did Pablo Neruda. In our own country, Jimmy Carter, a lifetime reader of poems, aspired to be a poet himself and sought instruction in poetry from established contemporary poets. In 1980, he and his wife hosted an extraordinary gala for poets, inviting almost one hundred to attend and twenty of this number to give brief readings. As one of the poets invited to read, I have vivid but staccato-like impressions of the event. Philip Levine, Sterling Brown, and I read for ten minutes apiece, in what I have ever since referred to as the Rutherford B. Hayes room. There, in a capacious china cabinet, is enshrined a trapezoidal turkey platter of substantial proportions used by President Hayes for serving the Thanksgiving turkey.

In 1998, Robert Pinsky, the Poet Laureate, a new designation for the post that was formerly called Consultant in Poetry to the Library of Congress, hosted another gathering at the White House, where selected poets were invited to read from the works of earlier bards. Alas, I declined this invitation. It was scheduled for the same evening as a reading I had agreed to give at a small public library in Massachusetts, ironically, the same library where Pinsky had read the previous year. Since the publicity had already gone out, I did not feel I was entitled to cancel my appearance.

These are examples of large public audiences paying homage to poetry as an art form—sit-down audiences in auditoriums or stadiums drawn in as for a play or sporting event. Occasional poetry—poetry glimpsed in subways or buses, poetry over the telephone for a nominal charge, poems for a quarter by cigarette vending machine—may have an even larger though more casual audience. For poetry functions through multiple avenues; not only does the poem have primacy on the page, it is also an oral, aural, and visual experience. To be present when a great poet reads a great poem is surely an epiphany, but there are many stations to visit along the way.

When I was an undergraduate in Cambridge, Massachusetts in

the late forties, public readings were still something of a novelty. The close of World War II thrust some remarkable soldier-poets on the stage: Richard Eberhart, Randall Jarrell, Howard Nemerov, Philip Booth, James Dickey, William Meredith, Karl Shapiro—and by the fifties, readings at colleges and universities not only became an accepted and ever more prevalent art form but also were often subsumed into the contemporary literature curriculum. Honoraria for these readings, usually in the $250–$500 range, typically came out of English departments' discretionary funds plus contributions from small endowments, alumni/ae associations, literary magazines, even local businesses. The dinner-before-the-reading, usually pre-paid with appropriate beverages at the best local restaurant, in time became something of a tradition that persists to this day. Members of the English, the comparative literature, even the philosophy departments, the provost, the vice-president and a few hand-picked graduate assistants often took part. Frequently, the nervous poet picked away at a spinach salad while the rest of the table attacked the roast beef special.

Today, videotapes of historic and contemporary readings have become commonplace. While these usefully supplement class assignments, nothing takes the place of a live appearance. Just as a play on television can only partially capture its essence, so a legitimate theater production, like a live reading, projects the drama to its highest realm.

I had the good fortune to attend readings by some poets who are now firmly fixed in the canon of American letters. On more than one occasion, Robert Frost read to an overflow crowd in Sever Hall, one of Harvard's largest auditoriums. Students crowded into the window wells, stood along the sides and across the back of the room as Frost indulged everyone by reciting his crowd-pleasing old favorites: "Stopping By Woods," "Acquainted with the Night," "Provide, Provide," "Birches." He didn't run his poems together, either. Wise performer, he paused after each one and said something by way of introduction to the next piece. Years later, at the annual Bread Loaf Writers Conference, he counseled us young poets on the staff to follow his example. If you don't give them breathing room, he said (I am paraphrasing), the audience will just coast on the next poem you read and not catch a word of it.

I also heard Auden in that same room at Harvard, and again at Boston College, facing that same rapt audience of hundreds who would live to tell their children and their grandchildren how wrinkled the poet's face was, how casually he was attired—it was his habit to wear bedroom slippers in place of shoes—how brittle and British his tone. Another famous British poet said of him in his last years, "Poor old Auden. Pretty soon we'll have to take off his face and iron it out to see who he is." And while he still read his famous "September 1939" to attentive audiences, his text open on their knees ("I sit in one of the dives/On Fifty-second Street/Uncertain and afraid/As the clever hopes expire/Of a low dishonest decade. . . ."), he dropped the penultimate stanza of this major poem. No longer would he intone the famous lines that ended: ". . . no one exists alone;/Hunger allows no choice/To the citizen or the police;/We must love one another or die." Disillusion had overtaken him.

Some years later, I was privileged to hear John Crowe Ransom read at Tufts University; it was one of his last public appearances. To my surprise, this giant of the Fugitive poets, master of meter, rigorous rhyme, and brilliant metaphor, was physically small. Pink-faced and bald, he rocked back and forth on the balls of his feet as he recited poems from memory. Hearing him say those carefully metered and tightly rhymed poems in his own voice, Southern to the point of caricature to a Yankee's ear and exquisitely enunciated, enhanced my appreciation of the poem on the page. I never read "Captain Carpenter" now without hearing the Ransom lilt in the final quatrain: "The curse of hell upon the sleek upstart/Who got the Captain finally on his back/And took the red red vitals of his heart/And made the kites to whet their beaks clack clack." The satisfaction of those "k" sounds lingers with me, as does the regional term "kites" for buzzards.

Randall Jarrell came to Boston; so did Dylan Thomas. Jarrell sported a frail, see-through beard, but his delivery was robust and his intelligence delighted his listeners. Thomas was sonorous, mellifluous and, it was rumored, tipsy, though it was hard to sort out alcohol from stage performance. Hearing his villanelle, "Do Not Go Gentle into that Good Night," hearing "Fern Hill" with its dingle, owls, and ricks have fixed these two poems in my memory just as he performed them.

The West Coast poet Robert Duncan read, turning pages with his left hand as he conducted the orchestra of his words with his right. Batonless, he used his entire arm to indicate stresses and caesuras as he articulated them. Even the white spaces on the page called for his raised hand stilled in midflutter. I was fascinated by his style, much as, years later, I would be caught and beguiled by an Allen Ginsberg recitation of "Howl." Ginsberg, who modeled himself on Walt Whitman, stays in my memory as the most visionary, excoriating, and outrageous performer of our time. Anne Sexton was a close contender for the title of most charismatic confessional poet of the time, rivaling Ginsberg for provocative, even seductive delivery.

Robert Lowell read, turning his profile to the audience, saying his poems distinctly but in a modest, almost diffident voice. A soupçon of Southern accent, perhaps acquired from the time he spent studying with the Fugitive poets, overlaid his Boston Brahmin pronunciation.

Howard Nemerov suffered such severe prereading jitters that we made several circuits of the snowy campus before I was privileged to introduce him to a Tufts University audience in the early sixties. Once on stage, all traces of nervousness disappeared. He had a way of distancing himself from the content of the poems with witty, offhand commentary; these little verses, he seemed to say, were written by some other person. His listeners were enchanted.

Anne Sexton and I went together to hear Marianne Moore at Wellesley College, although she was all but inaudible, speaking, it seemed, below the microphone and no one daring to interrupt to correct the situation. The tricorn hat was enough.

In those days we used to arrive at a reading with the poets' several books in hand. When he—it was almost always a male—announced the title of the next poem we would rush to the table of contents to locate the poem, then follow faithfully word by sacred word.

I regret that I never heard Elizabeth Bishop or Louise Bogan give a public reading, although I had the good fortune to share a supper in Harvard's Leverett House with Miss Bishop, and John Holmes once took George Starbuck, Anne Sexton, and me to visit Louise Bogan in her cabin at the MacDowell Colony. From this latter event came a poem, describing us.

REVISITING THE MACDOWELL COLONY

The same cabin, the same stone fireplace,
red oak blazing in its sooty bin,
and just outside, October trees on fire
in the same slant of the five o'clock sun.
In the rocking chair, Louise Bogan,
girlish with company back then.

In the straight chair, theatrically puffing,
our mentor, John Holmes, with pipe.
We three novices lined up on the lumpy cot
while water was coaxed to boil over the hot
plate and jasmine tea was served in the club
they would never, o never invite us to join
who signed the plaque above the hearth
as evidence of tenancy and worth.

I strain to read above the confident fire
names of the early-great and almost-great:
Rumer Godden, Padraic Colum
Nikolai Lopatnikoff;
too many pale ones gone to smudges.
Use a penknife, I advise my friend,
then ink each letter for relief
—as if a name might matter
against the falling leaf.

Muriel Rukeyser was a poet I admired deeply; in the early days of the Vietnam War, she took a public stance that was courageous and brought down on her head praise and contumely in equal measure. She was the first woman poet I read who was overtly political; this seemed very daring in the tame fifties. However, I heard her read only once, a valiant reading she gave toward the end of her life when she was suffering the aftereffects of a stroke.

My own experience as a poet in the public eye commenced, in a small way, before my first book was published in 1961. Asked to read at a meeting of the New England Poetry Club where I was a new, provisional member, I was catapulted into a state of panic. Although as an adjunct instructor in English at Tufts University, I was teaching freshman composition and American literature to indifferent phys ed majors and dental technicians, the prospect of reading my own work before a live audience terrified me. It did not console me to be told that many actors suffer extreme stage fright before every performance; that seemed only to validate my own fear.

Now, after forty years of facing audiences as diverse as snowflakes, I look back with compassion on this person who was racked by such terrible anxiety. Perhaps it is normal, perhaps pathological to face an audience with a degree of terror that arouses physical symptoms—

hyperventilation, shaking, tunnel vision—so severe they almost overcome the speaker. I confess that I took to downing two bloody marys in advance of evening readings. There was a thin line between reducing inhibitions to a point at which I could function and slurring words so that they were unintelligible, and I fear I did not always find it. Partly, I think, I was afraid to succeed in a male-dominated field. Partly, I felt exposed by the emotion of my poems, even the early, heavily latinate, metrically exact ones—such as "Halfway," the title poem of my first book, which opens: "As true as I was born into my mother's bed in Germantown. . . ."

The shorter poems were easier to get through before my voice began to shake. Longer poems that could be counted on to elicit audience response, such as "Fraulein Reads Instructive Rhymes" or "You Are in Bear Country" eased the way, and I came to rely on such poems to launch the program. The bear poem draws on language found in an admonitory pamphlet distributed at the entry points to various parks in the Canadian Rockies. The tone is earnest, the advice full of contradictions. Listeners slowly come to realize that a confrontation with a grizzly may prove fatal no matter what they do.

YOU ARE IN BEAR COUNTRY

Advice from a pamphlet published by the
Canadian Minister of the Environment

They've
been here
for thousands of years.
You're
the visitor.
Avoid
encounters. Think ahead.
Keep clear
of berry patches
garbage dumps, carcasses.
On woods walks bring
noisemakers, bells.
Clap hands along the trail
or sing
but in dense bush
or by running water
bear may not hear your clatter.

Whatever else
don't whistle. Whistling
is thought by some to imitate
the sounds bears make when they mate.

You need to know
there are two kinds:
ursus arctus horribilis
or grizzly
and *ursus americanus*
the smaller black
said to be
somewhat less likely to attack.
Alas, a small *horribilis*
is difficult to distinguish
from a large *americanus*.

Although
there is no
guaranteed life-saving way
to deal with an aggressive bear
some ploys
have proved more
successful than others.
Running's a poor choice.
Bear can outrun a racehorse.

Once you're face to face
speak softly. Take
off your pack
and set it down
to distract the grizzly.
Meanwhile back
slowly toward a large
sparsely branched tree
but remember
black bears are agile climbers
in which case
a tree may not offer escape.

As a last resort you can
play dead. Drop
to the ground face down.

In this case
wearing your pack
may shield your body from attack.
Courage. Lie still. Sometimes
your bear may veer away.
If not
bears have been known
to inflict only minor injuries
upon the prone.

Is death
by bear to be preferred
to death by bomb? Under
these extenuating circumstances
your mind may make absurd
leaps. *The answer's yes.*
Come on in. Cherish
your wilderness.

[*Maxine Kumin*, Selected Poems 1960–1990 (Norton).]

I have never failed to receive laughter and/or gasps of horror
whenever I reach the third stanza of "Fraulein": "Now look at Con-
rad, the little thumb sucker/Ach, but his poor Mama cries when she
warns him/The tailor will come for his thumbs if he sucks
them./Quick he can cut them off, easy as paper." [Maxine Kumin,
Selected Poems 1960–1990 (Norton).]

When did the terror ebb and where did it go? It's hard to say.
Somehow, repetition wore down my fear to a manageable nub.

Some venues were more hospitable than others. Reading sitting
down, thought by some to be chummy, is something I dislike doing.
It feels unnatural to me to say my poems as if the hearers and I were
having a casual conversation. A platform with a podium, an
adjustable microphone and light, and a glass of water were usually
provided, but there were, inevitably, lapses. At Stevens College in
Missouri I remember having to rest my books on a flimsy music
stand. Every time I put any weight on this contraption, it slowly sank
to the level of my knees. In Boston's Hynes Auditorium, I read my
poems against the clatter and sizzle of a cooking school demonstra-
tion on the other side of a folding partition. In upstate New York, a
fraternity party with a live band was taking place next door; some-

where else, during an afternoon reading, huge mowing machines drew close, receded and returned while I hurried to fit my words into the spaces between rows. On a Friday night in San Antonio, the microphone had been locked away before the custodian departed; I read in a large room at the top of my voice and was hoarse the next day. At Boston College, an inebriated priest jumped to his feet and recited one of my poems along with me before he was gently led away. For years, a deranged fan in Boston followed me from reading to reading. On one occasion she leapt up and denounced me loudly as an impostor.

In libraries and bookstores, there was often vocal competition from other patrons and customers as they wandered through the building. In massive auditoriums, a small audience could be lost, scattered to the four points of the compass. It was an overwhelming task for the poet to draw them together into the circle of the poem. A small, stuffy room, filled to overflowing, was always preferable. Once, on a State Department Arts America tour, I was invited to read at the U.S. Embassy in Tel Aviv. An enthusiastic overflow audience reached halfway up the stairs, packed the hall, and disobeyed all the fire laws. It would be hard not to read well under such welcoming circumstances.

In Holland, Michigan, arriving on a delayed flight and whisked from the airport to the reading hosted by Hope College, I found myself on stage in a renovated movie theater. Every seat appeared to have been taken. A student jazz group was warming up the crowd. I was overcome with paranoia; everyone would steal away when the poet rose and approached the podium. I was wrong. It was a memorable evening.

One of my duties at the Library of Congress in 1981–2 when I was Consultant was to draw up the list of poets to appear at the monthly readings. Many notable men had taken the podium over the past several years, but very few women had been invited. I was able to ask several outstanding women to give readings, among them, Josephine Miles, Audre Lord, Eleanor Ross Taylor, and Adrienne Rich. The line for Rich's reading snaked halfway around the building; closed-circuit television screens were hastily assembled for the overflow in a separate room. The valiant Josephine Miles, whose arthritic condition made it impossible for her to stand or indeed even to sit upright, read at a slant. I wish her work were better known today; she was a remarkable poet.

Does the size of the audience correlate with the success of the reading? Not necessarily. Sometimes the turnout for a poetry reading is small, sometimes surprisingly hearty. It isn't the size of the group that determines the level of response. One wintry day I read to a baker's dozen at a charming small library in rural Vermont, and the rapport was palpable. A sense of empathy filled the room making it a halcyon experience. At Bucknell University in Pennsylvania, only a handful of listeners braved a blizzard to hear several of us poets take part in a symposium. Again, the response was ardent though unexpected; we hardy few had reached a state of oneness that had nothing to do with the weather.

Rapport between sayer and hearer occurs or fails to occur, and sometimes it is not possible to know how the "pure, gem-like flame" came to life, or simply died away. There's a fine line between pandering to an audience and involving it. It's important to me to serve as poetry-evangelist in neutral or even unfriendly environments. To disarm adolescents is often a challenge. It becomes the poet's mission to reach even the bored, lethargic ones who are marking time at the back of the room. Many of them have been turned off poetry by overzealous or fearful teachers; many more have accepted the tv sit-com stereotype of the poet as fop or fool.

In the last four decades, I've faced a hundred different high school and prep school classes ranging from compulsory chapel attendance at St. Andrews School in Sewanee, Tennessee to a heterogeneous halter- and shorts-clad student body in Coral Gables, Florida. In every group there are a few who thrill to the poems, raise their hands to ask pertinent, even personal questions. In many cases, students will come up afterward to confess they've never heard a poet read her poems aloud before this, that they were astonished to be able to hear and understand the poems, that until now they had "hated" poetry because they couldn't understand it.

What had I done? Nothing remarkable. I talked about the genesis of some of my own poems, discussed a metaphor, explained an allusion. I had asked that they give every difficult poem three chances, three careful readings. If, after that, the poem failed to work for them, they should feel free to move on. Not every poem evokes the same response. This is art, I said, not science; there is no one path into the poem, nor is there always a hidden message within it. Take the poem at face value; read it for pleasure, for the story. In my opinion, every poem should offer the framework of a narrative—not a short story, not a plot complete with denouement, but the outline, the ghost-tale that suggests movement. (Other poets may strongly disagree with my premise, theorizing that language, description, emotion conveyed are enough to carry the poem forward.) Then let the other level arrive, enter into the ambiguity of the language, tease out the symbol, the metaphor. The poem requires nothing more than your open mind.

While talking to teenagers can be difficult, I prefer it to signing books for collectors, who arrive at the podium before you can step down. They have first editions of all your books, meticulously encased in plastic. Possibly they've read you, possibly they are only interested in your future market value—they expect to outlive you. There's no polite way to escape their importuning as they unwrap one book at a time. (I almost expect them to request that I wash my hands before I sign.) Meanwhile, the people who have bought one or two books from the table at the back of the room and want you to personalize your signature by writing "For Joan and Mike," must wait. Sometimes, too, the poet is faced with a scrapbook, journal, or diary in which all the visiting poets preceding her have written encomia in praise of the hosts. I always find my predecessors' comments far more laudatory and charming than I am capable of. Then, too, knowing that the next poet on the roster will have to read what I have written, induces in me a powerful writer's block.

What poems to read to what audiences is a judgment call. Of course the poet wants to seduce the listener, wants to carry him or her along on the journey from poem to poem, but there are bound to be pitfalls. Some in the audience will be moved by a love poem, an elegy, a political poem; an equal number may turn a deaf ear to such subject matter. At Brigham Young University, the poet is requested in advance not to read any poems containing profanity. Where a humorous description of bodily functions may be welcome in one academic setting, it may be offensive in another. While it is wise to make subtle inquiries of your host ahead of time—"are there any particular poems you would like to hear?"—few among us want simply to entertain or to gratify an audience's preconceived notion of our work. We want to present poems that delight with their surprisingly apt images, that provide settings and emotions in an identifiable context. Most of us have no desire to be opaque. We would like to build an audience, not bore it. We want to be heard; we would even like to be loved, but not at the price of talking down to the lowest common denominator. Achieving balance may be desirable. But for some, reading feminist poems, anti-war poems, lamentations and rants, historical narratives in blank verse, intricate triolets, or free-verse gay love poems overshadows all other concerns the poet may have about audience. I feel that the poet is entitled. The poet needs to be him/herself, come what may.

When I teach poetry seminars I always require my students to attend two or three public poetry readings in the area and write a brief report on one. I am trying to make the point to them that poetry is aural and oral as well as written. They also must read their own poems aloud in workshop, after having asked a fellow member to read it first. This gives the poet an opportunity to hear how the poem is perceived and then to apply the proper corrective in his or her own voice. For doesn't every MFA candidate in poetry cherish a secret hope of becoming the public figure invited to stand at the lectern and read his/her own work to a worshipful audience?

In the early seventies, Anne Sexton joined forces with a trio of rock musicians to form a group called Anne Sexton and Her Kind. I hated what they did; I felt that the music cannibalized the words and that to rise above them Sexton read ever more melodramatically, doing a grave disservice to the poems themselves. I did not know how popular this blended art form was to become, or how much my cranky ear might over time be trained to appreciate new conjunctions.

Today, music marries poems in a dozen different venues, ranging from cafes and bistros to the concert stage and the college auditorium. Is this blurring of distinctions between genres good for poetry? Well, if it exposes more people to the language of the poem, I reason, it can't be bad. Consider what has been done at the highest level of musical literacy with the poetry of Walt Whitman: Vaughan Williams's "Sea Symphony," Delius's "Sea Drift," William Bolcom's "Whitman Triptych," and perhaps best known, Paul Hindemith's requiem for Franklin Delano Roosevelt, composed in 1946, titled "When Lilacs Last in the Dooryard Bloom'd." What attracts composers is the melodic quality of Whitman's lines, his dramatic imagery, his essential "American-ness." Once viewed with disdain for his celebration of soldier and prairie, of himself and his homosexuality, Whitman has undergone rehabilitation. Scorned by Ezra Pound and Henry James, once derided as ninth-rate and banal, Whitman is now firmly lodged in the literary canon. [Paul J. Horsley, *New York Times*, May 16, 1999.] For the 100th anniversary of his death, more than 2,000 people jammed the Cathedral of St. John the Divine in

New York City to hear several well-known contemporary poets read Whitman's work aloud.

In an essay originally printed in *Harper's Magazine* in 1989, Donald Hall, one of our canniest poets, who is also an essayist and commentator on the literary scene, debunks the frequently heard charge that poetry is dead. "More than a thousand poetry books appear in this country each year," Hall states, although he is quick to grant that "poetry is not as popular as professional wrestling. More people write poetry in this country—publish it, hear it, and presumably read it—than ever before."

I suspect that Hall's "more than a thousand" books of poems has escalated considerably in the last ten years, thanks to the proliferation of small presses and the new poetry lists undertaken by virtually every university publishing house in the country. Nor is it only the number of books published. Farrar, Straus & Giroux, one of New York's most prestigious publishing houses, sold over 100,000 copies of Ted Hughes's "Birthday Letters," poems about the British Poet Laureate's doomed marriage to the famous suicided poet, Sylvia Plath, an American. [Martin Arnold, *New York Times*, January 14, 1999.]

And Alfred Knopf, another premier publisher, sold 250,000 copies of poetry books, both cloth and paper, in the preceding year, a figure that includes their Everyman Pocket Poetry series of thirty titles, featuring such icons as Emily Dickinson. [Martin Arnold, *New York Times*, 1999.] The reason for this growth industry? More prizes for first books, more small presses, more MFA programs in poetry encouraging poet wannabes to realize their dreams; more readings in bookstores in the malls as well as on university campuses, in community centers, cafes, even nursing homes; more public poetry slams with cash prizes for the poet whose poem receives the loudest applause; poems visible to the casual eye on subway and bus placards; poetry in the schools nurtured by young visiting poets underwritten by state arts councils and the National Endowment for the Arts. The language of poetry was at one time male, middle class, and white; now, it is polyglot, nongender-specific, multicultural, and not necessarily polite. Rap, for example, breaks more than the rules of grammar.

Poetry slams began at the Nuyorican Poets Cafe in East Greenwich Village, in New York City, in the eighties. As their name suggests, the early "slammers" were New Yorkers of Puerto Rican ancestry. The subject matter was often politically radical. Slam poems today are declaimed at the top of the poet's voice. They depend heavily on almost primitive layers of assonance and alliteration, as did such early English epics as "Beowulf" and "Gawain and the Green Knight." At the annual National Poetry Slam, up to fifty teams of four poets apiece compete for cash prizes.

Rap poetry, or rap music—either term is applicable—has expanded enormously in the last two decades. The poet and critic Dana Gioia sees it as the major new trend of the era. [Jesse McKinley, *New York Times*, May 30, 1999] He reminds us that rap is written in the same base meter as "Beowulf;" moreover, it is rhymed. The rhymes are not subtle; often they are as banal as the "June/moon/spoon" or "fire/desire" variety. The language is often violent, racist, chauvinist, and sexist. The prevailing rhythm thumps on the ear like bongo drums, perhaps suggesting that modern poetry has traveled full circle from its preliterate origins in chants and songs through centuries of written work to its present oral resurgence.

Frankly, I disagree with Gioia. Rappers and rap, with its raw bigotry, trite imagery, and dependence on the shock effect of obscenities, can hardly be seen as the new-age poetry of the people, replacing William Carlos Williams or Walt Whitman as the spokespersons for the common man. What rap reflects is social unease, economic disparities, and deficient education. The purpose that it serves is to call attention to these inadequacies. Perhaps, too, it is a safety valve for publicly venting bitterness.

And then there's Robert Pinsky's Favorite Poem Project. Conceived in his office in the Library of Congress as Poet Laureate, the Project's goal is to assemble an audio-visual archive of one to two hundred Americans reciting aloud their favorite poem. People have been invited to submit their favorite poem and expatiate on how they came to love it. As of this writing, more than 10,000 letters and e-mails have flooded in from every region and age group. On Valentine's Day—a traditional day often marked with verse, sometimes mere doggerel—an international web site for the project was launched at www.favoritepoem.org. These entries will be winnowed down to a workable number, to be recorded, along with the individuals' statements. Pinsky has made a very telling and poignant point with his project. Not only has it proven that the affectionate audience for poetry in this country is broad and lively, ranging from pipe fitters to sheepherders, school children to bankers to trapeze artists, but, as he is quoted as saying, "Imagine if we had an archive of this kind from the year 1900, or the year 1800." [from Maggie Dietz's article in *American Poet*, spring 99, Academy of American Poets bulletin.] If we had, it would have been an enormous cultural resource, providing insight into what Americans thought and felt. Now, posterity will have this archive from the millennium. Moreover, the project reinforces my personal passion for having poems by heart, providing, as it were, the very best imaginable audience of one. This same affectionate audience is evident in Russia as well. In 1999, that nation celebrated the 200th anniversary of the birth of Alexander Pushkin. Although Pushkin, who died in a duel at the age of 37, is Russia's most celebrated bard, the degree of poetic frenzy this bicentenary evoked had not been anticipated. Pushkin's visage appeared on posters and billboards, T-shirts and candy wrappers. Thanks to the enterprise of Yevgeny Gorelets, a freelance television producer, his best-known verses were recited daily by ordinary Russians who were filmed as they faced the camera. "Eugene Onegin," a romantic narrative poem of 389 stanzas, most of them 14 lines in length, was declaimed by "bakery workers, homeless people, politicians, actors, outlaw bikers, pedestrians, farmers, coal miners, hikers, prison inmates, students at an institute for the blind—all sharing a common love for Pushkin," according to an Associated Press dispatch by Mitchell Landsberg.

Technology, then, has tapped into a broader audience than could have been imagined fifty years ago. Electronic magazines make poetry accessible to a wide range of potential readers. Many poets have individual web pages, often established by their fans. What happens next on the poetry scene is a matter for conjecture.

Whether conveyed in cyberspace, printed on an actual page, or shouted aloud on the street, poetry requires an ardent attentiveness on the part of the audience. There's a kind of contract entered into between poet, the giver, and audience, the receiver, that goes beyond the limited attention span needed to watch a movie or a sitcom. The receiver of a poem has to be an active participant. "A great poem," says Lawrence Raab in an article titled "Poetry's Weakness," "provides many simultaneous pleasures, which are also demands—that we hear, that we think, that we imagine, that we connect." [*The Writer's Chronicle*, vol 31, no. 6.] Unlike other art forms in which the listener, visitor, viewer can play an active role or simply sit back passively and let the music, dance, drama, or painting wash over him or her, poetry makes demands on its audience. The hearer has to connect with the language. He or she may have a visceral response to its music, to consonance and alliteration, to meter and rhyme, but beyond these not inconsiderable surface delights, the reader and/or listener needs also to experience the surprises of metaphor and symbol, the way familiar words can be wrenched out of their old hiding places into new contexts.

I am not referring here to the language of Shakespeare's time, nor to the metaphysical love poems of George Herbert or John Donne, or even to the lush greenery of Dylan Thomas or Gerard Manley Hopkins, but to poems written in the colloquial speech rhythms of contemporary America. Not, as Marianne Moore wrote, "in Spanish, not in Greek, not in Latin, not in shorthand, / but in plain American which cats and dogs can read!" Perhaps poets in general are defensive about their audiences. Yes, we want them to comprehend a language cats and dogs can read, a language, we pride ourselves, that we are writing in, but it would be gratifying if they also understood our allusions in Latin or shorthand, if their ear and eye were trained to pick up rhythmic patterns, even rhyme schemes. A student fan once came up to me after a reading, full of enthusiastic praise for my poem, "Woodchucks." "And the best thing about it," he concluded, "is that you didn't force it into rhyme." The poem, in five stanzas of six lines each, is tightly rhymed *abcacb—right / Exchange / bone / airtight / stone / range*—however, I was not offended. A more sophisticated listener might have heard the recurring sounds. Rhyme, I feel, ought to occur subtly and naturally, in cat and dog, so to speak.

What audience are we writing for, who do we hope is listening to/reading us? The poet in prison, the academic in his or her office overlooking the college quad, the CEO, the assembly-line worker, the lover, house husband, mother . . . there are as many answers as poets. Sentenced to death by Queen Elizabeth, eighteen-year-old Chidiock Tichborne wrote his own elegy from the Tower of London.

ELEGY

Written with his own hand in the Tower before his execution

My prime of youth is but a frost of cares;
   My feast of joy is but a dish of pain:
My crop of corn is but a field or tares;
   And all my good is but vain hope of gain;
The day is past, and yet I saw no sun;
And now I live, and now my life is done.

My tale was heard, and yet it was not told;
  My fruit is fallen, and yet my leaves are green;
My youth is spent, and yet I am not old;
  I saw the world, and yet I was not seen:
My thread is cut, and yet it is not spun;
And now I live, and now my life is done.

I sought my death, and found it in my womb;
  I looked for life, and saw it was a shade;
I trod the earth, and knew it was my tomb;
  And now I die, and now I was but made:
My glass is full, and now my glass is run;
And now I live, and now my life is done.

It is hard to imagine the poise and strength of character that enabled this young man to compose three six-line stanzas rhyming *ababcc* in perfect iambic pentameter before his execution. It is not only a cry from the heart; he is addressing posterity

Four centuries later, the Turkish poet Nazim Hikmet, in "Some Advice to Those Who Will Serve Time in Prison," counsels ". . . it's your solemn duty/ to live one more day/ to spite the enemy. . . ." Here, the audience is quite simply those who survived the same ordeal or managed to avoid arrest in a police sweep. We cannot help but be moved by the work of so many political dissidents in Eastern Europe and now, increasingly, by oppressed minorities around the world. Poems by Chinese dissidents, for instance, have even given rise to a school known as the poetry of ambiguity, in which metaphor conveys the politics of opposition to the regime.

At the other extreme lie the poems of those who say they write only for themselves. They don't have an audience, they don't desire one. They are not professionals. They do not, for the most part, read the poetry of others. They write out of an inner need to express the intensity of their feelings. Somehow, this position has a disingenuous cast to it. Many of these "amateurs" who ask nothing of an audience do not confine their poems to diaries or journals. Some go on to publish their work privately, paying for 500 copies from a vanity press to distribute to their friends and relatives and, not infrequently, to published poets and critics as well.

As Raab points out in "Poetry's Weakness," one rarely hears a musician say, "I compose string quartets, but only for myself." The diary poem, he points out, is "in the service only of its creator, desiring no other reader . . . since the feverish moment of its composition may have been all that was necessary." Revision, for this writer, may be a violation of the feelings that prompted the poem. "If this is, in fact, the way many people who write but do not seriously read poetry view poetry," poetry is reduced to "a private confessional activity . . . a curious kind of emotional self-indulgence." Such views distance poetry farther from its potential audience, giving it an aura of pretentiousness and exclusivity.

In fact, the poem, like the string quartet, presupposes an audience. The story is not a story until it is told. Some poets may conceptualize the perfect audience of one; others may fantasize for themselves that crowd of 40,000 glistening in the summer sun of Siberia. Still others may have in mind a parent, a teacher, colleagues, both friendly and un-, a lover, a faceless murmuring group assembled in the local library.

Many of us turn away from this question, generally one of the top ten asked in an interview. My own answer is as equivocal as any. I write, first of all, to please myself, although "please" is not an adequate descriptive. Although aware of an audience, desiring a sympathetic, intelligent audience, like the diary poet, I write for self-gratification. The poem needs to be shaped. It has to meet my own standard for it before it can meet anyone else's, but I want it to be read, listened to, chewed on. In a sense, the poem is not finished for me until it has found an audience. Once in print, it acquires a certain authenticity it lacked while it was still in draft form. Once I have read it to a live audience, it acquires even more modeling. The breath rhythms become more apparent. There are caesuras (natural breath rhythm breaks within the line, indicated here with \ \) that I may have been subliminally aware of while I was writing but which now assume a more deliberate stance, becoming platforms, inviting the reader to pause, look back before going on ("They are weighing the babies again \ \ on color television. They are hanging these small bags of bones \ \ up in canvas slings. . . .").

If the poem is in form, if the rhyme scheme was hard-won, as is usually the case, presenting the poem to a live audience gives me an opportunity to rejoice in the gift of rhyme achieved without any wrenching from the natural word order. Ideally, the power of rhyme lies in its seemingly effortless ability to surprise the reader with its aptness, with imagery that presents a new view. I want to slow down, to enunciate modestly but accurately so that no words are swallowed and lost. "Morning Swim," written in rhyming couplets with almost no recourse to slant or approximate rhyme, tries to present a very small moment in time. It seeks to disarm the listener by way of its simple diction. It's a flashback, a distinct memory of a sensual event.

MORNING SWIM

Into my empty head there come
a cotton beach, a dock wherefrom

I set out, oily and nude
through mist, in chilly solitude.

There was no line, no roof or floor
to tell the water from the air.

Night fog thick as terry cloth
closed me in its fuzzy growth.

I hung my bathrobe on two pegs.
I took the lake between my legs.

Invaded and invader, I
went overhand on that flat sky.

Fish twitched beneath me, quick and tame.
In their green zone they sang my name

and in the rhythm of the swim
I hummed a two-four-time slow hymn.

I hummed *Abide with Me.* The beat
rose in the fine thrash of my feet,

rose in the bubbles I put out
slantwise, trailing through my mouth.

My bones drank water; water fell
through all my doors. I was the well

that fed the lake that met my sea
in which I sang *Abide with Me.*

If the poem is built on slant rhymes, I want to say them carefully so that the half-rhymes carry their weight ("and the pond's stillness nippled as if / by rain instead is pocked with life. . . ."). English is a rhyme-poor language, built around such restrictive Anglo-Saxon monosyllabic nouns as "life," "word," "fist" "tribe." "Life," for example, yields very few direct rhymes other than "knife" and "wife." "Strife" hardly fits my criterion of having occurred in normal usage at least once in the last two weeks. The same applies to "rife." "Fife" and "fief" are intriguing possibilities but require specific contexts. The minute the poet eases into slant rhyme by eliding the vowel sound, a thousand permutations for "life" suggest themselves: grief, loaf, safe, aloof, riff, scoff, and so on.

These are technical matters. So, too, is the question of the poem's length. It is hard for an audience to follow a long poem, particularly a philosophical one, without narrative guidelines. Without the text in front of them, listeners' attention strays; a line, an allusion is lost; bewilderment sets in. Sensing this, the reader feels abandoned, grows anxious, wants desperately to put an end to the disaster. I try to avoid presenting in public poems that run over two pages. I have only read "Letters," the crown of mother-daughter sonnets that opens my collection "Connecting the Dots" to an audience on one occasion. I feel it is too dense and perhaps too personal for regular exposure. "Marianne, My Mother, and Me," while historical, is so packed with detail that I think it is difficult for an audience to retain the information, decade by decade. Another long narrative poem that depends on historical content, "The Bridge-Builder," presents a further problem in that it is written in the lofty diction of the eccentric builder-engineer himself. This one, too, I tried only once. And an elegy for my brother, who died of ALS, called "The Man of Many L's" depends visually on the misspellings of such words as lilacs and oleanders for its effect, so that I feel simply to read the poem aloud does it a disservice.

Instinct tells me that shorter lyrical poems are better suited for reading aloud to a general audience. Shorter poems give the reader more latitude, allowing the poet to display a broader range of topics: love poems, elegies, political, ideational poems that border on polemic, pastoral and anti-pastoral poems, cityscape poems, poems about family constellations, and so on.

Building an audience in today's market, so to speak, depends to a large extent on where the poet is, geographically and chronologically, as well as on the poet's status in the literary community. The time-honored route by way of publication, first in small literary magazines, then in larger ones with a larger audience, then a chap-book or first book traditionally leads to acquiring an audience, first on the page and gradually, on the reading circuit. Geographically, the poet who wants a live audience will fare better in an academic set-ting, where readings are established routes on campus or in the nearby city. Chronologically, it helps to be either young and newly discovered, or old enough to have outlasted many of your peers. (I visualize the university committee sitting around the table, saying, Let's get Maxine Kumin this year while she's still around.) In the interests of ethnic diversity, more minority poets are being invited to take the podium.

In my lifetime, I have had the distinct pleasure of seeing the audi-ence for poetry by women grow from a tiny, secret cell of listeners, to, in some cases, overflow crowds. In the fifties and sixties, women writers were harshly criticized by male reviewers for overtly confes-sional poems. James Dickey, for example, attacked Anne Sexton's focus on such then-taboo subjects as menstruation, abortion, and menopause; Adrienne Rich regularly drew fire from critics who were offended by her lesbian stance. Carolyn Forché, whose photograph appeared on the cover of her stirring book of poems about the revo-lution in El Salvador, was attacked, presumably for going where no woman poet before her had gone and for allowing her face to appear on the jacket (in my experience, the poet seldom is consulted about what picture is to appear where). This was the price she paid for being pretty.

Some poets work through lecture bureaus that solicit bookings for you, negotiate your fee, make plane reservations, and supposedly tend to your special needs (a nonsmoking hotel room, a vegetarian menu). These agencies charge up to 30 percent of the poet's honorar-ium. The fee is almost always called an honorarium, (defined as payment given a professional person in a situation in which payment is not legally required), as poetry is considered a noncommercial enterprise, and perhaps also because the fee is often too minimal to be called anything other than an honorarium. I avoid lecture bureaus. I found over the years that making my own travel arrange-ments is less subject to error than forms filled out in duplicate and that dealing directly with my host makes it clear from the outset that I prefer the anonymity of a motel to the forced conviviality of a bed and breakfast. Also, I can make it clear that I am willing to meet with a class the morning after a reading or give an interview to the student paper, providing that they have some familiarity with my work, and so on.

Recently, in an interview for a college paper, the reporter set the tone immediately by volunteering, "I have one of your books, "Nurture," but I haven't read it." His first question was: "Would you say you write academic poems or metaphysical ones?" Taken aback, I asked him to define these terms. "I don't know what they mean," he said. "One of my professors suggested that question." Next came the three McQuestions of student interviewers: Who is my favorite poet, which poets have influenced my writing, which of my poems is my favorite. As usual, I equivocate, naming five or six favorite poets and several more, including the psalmists, who have influenced my writing. My favorite poem, I tell him, is the one I'm working on at the moment.

He understands that I am a nature poet. And that women in general write nature poems. I mention Robert Frost, W. S. Merwin, Gary Snyder, Wendell Berry. Frost is the only one he has heard of. In closing, he says he will "probably" come to the reading. They take attendance, and he could use the extra credit.

Not all student interviewers are as crass as this young man. But if the poet sallies forth on the reading circuit, this awaits him or her somewhere on the agenda. Somewhere, too, lurks the night on tissue-paper sheets in the only motel in town, the only window overlooking a bleak barrack of storage sheds, the dawn traffic rife (there's that rarely used rhyme word) with bawling hogs being hauled to the abattoir. On the room's tv, a sitcom featuring an effete character who is of course a poet. Welcome! You are a poet in the millennium in America.

But in all fairness, this scene is counterbalanced by some profoundly rewarding ones. Flowers, fruit and nuts, wine and cheese, even champagne ordered by the women's studies program or an independent reading group await you in Days Inns or Marriotts or in modestly elegant surroundings, sometimes a suite of rooms in Seattle or Chicago. Or, in the unavoidable instance when you are accommodated in the university guest room or the vice-president's house, a junior member of the faculty takes you home for a breakfast of Irish oatmeal the next morning. Two students meet your puddle-jumper plane in Minnesota or Oklahoma and convey you to a lookout tower to watch the sunset. The forest ranger is a Ph.D. candidate in biology and has all of your books. A poetry workshop you agree to sit in on is alive with exciting work. And, if you have attained my advanced age, former students step forward frequently in Newark or Newport, Boise or Buffalo to tell you how much they enjoyed your class, how important you were to them in making some major career decision, how, heaven forfend! they have named their first child after you. Welcome! This too is poetry in the millennium.

· VI ·

Tell Me How It Was in the Old Days

IN SEARCH OF THE POET

David Citino

When we need advice, if we're smart we go to someone with more experience than we have—usually, someone older. Mother. Father. Aunt Angelina. My Calabrian grandmother taught me her recipe for Easter lasagna made with tiny egg-and-breadcrumb-bonded meat-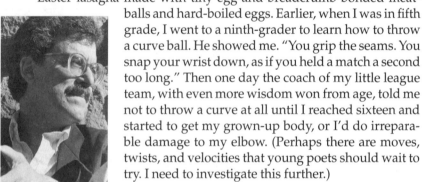balls and hard-boiled eggs. Earlier, when I was in fifth grade, I went to a ninth-grader to learn how to throw a curve ball. He showed me. "You grip the seams. You snap your wrist down, as if you held a match a second too long." Then one day the coach of my little league team, with even more wisdom won from age, told me not to throw a curve at all until I reached sixteen and started to get my grown-up body, or I'd do irreparable damage to my elbow. (Perhaps there are moves, twists, and velocities that young poets should wait to try. I need to investigate this further.)

Years later, an opposing coach, after his team had knocked me around quite smartly, my best pitches whizzing back past my ears, told me that he had alerted his team to the fact that, whenever I threw the curve, I tipped my hand by sticking out my tongue a little, as if I were concentrating.

"Son," he said to me, "you have to learn, when you throw the bender, to keep your damn tongue in your mouth."

Live and learn. I hadn't known that the art is to hide the art. A pitcher or a poet needs (I hope this doesn't mix the metaphor too violently) a poker face, so as not to announce to the batter or reader his or her intentions. I've never forgotten this kindness extended to an enemy—nor have I forgotten the importance to the poet of having a reader with a good eye and ear. Those paunchy, grizzled men sitting in dugouts are there for a reason. Those poets—women and men—sitting on benches back in the mists of time also are there for a reason. It's all about coaching and being able to take constructive criticism. The hardest lesson young pitchers and young poets have to learn is that their job is to listen, and to read, carefully.

The young have it over the older generations in everything but those degrees earned in schools of hard knocks. Many of the birds setting off on migrations and falling into the sea or getting lost under a maze of spinning stars—each year tens of thousands of birds never make it on their long and arduous journeys—are young ones who have never made the trip before. Birds, baseball players, and poets need to find out *what was* in order to understand better *what is*. I tell student poets that the best way to develop is to read poetry of all ages and all cultures, to ask of every poet, *Who in the world do you think you are?* The answer varies of course from poet to poet (as it does from pitcher to pitcher), but also from poem to poem.

The writer who tells us, tongue in cheek, "My mistress' eyes are nothing like the sun" in Sonnet 130, and the writer who has Lear say "Ay, every inch a king! When I do stare, see how the subject quakes," are both named William Shakespeare. Both (of him) are speaking of eyes, but are constructing themselves—writing themselves—in very different ways in the two examples.

Yes, one work is a sonnet and the other a grand tragedy. The (artful, public) lover and the dramatist are different people who view their art in different ways, though there are similarities between the two, of course. Each needs to take his audience into consideration, for one thing. Shakespeare was one of the many writers in London during the 1590's writing the sonnet, which was all the rage. Shakespeare knew that there were readers and listeners who would pay attention to pretty rooms (i.e., stanzas) full of beauty and wit. And Shakespeare knew well the wishes and needs of the audience that stood and sat in the theater for his plays.

I'm thinking here about more than the necessary fiction we use in speaking of the persona (the mask) or speaker of a poem as opposed to the poet himself or herself. With each poem the poet attempts to define "poet." Every poem is a partial definition of the poet. "This is what I think a poet can do," the poet says in a given poem. With each poem, the poet creates himself or herself. This poet's identity isn't the same from one poem to the next. Not at all. As Ralph Waldo Emerson reminds us, "A foolish consistency is the hobgoblin of small minds, adored by little statesmen and philosophers and divines. With consistency a great soul has simply nothing to do." The last thing a poet wants is to be consistent. Emerson's brief hymn to the changing of one's mind should be tacked up above every writer's desk. With each and every poem, a poet changes his or her mind about the meaning of poetry and perhaps about the meaning of the world—or has it changed by the act of creating.

All over college campuses in the first days of the academic term, and in opening chapters of so many books, teachers and writers take their audience back to the Egyptians, Greeks, Romans, and Arabs, to search out the earliest history of mathematics, chemistry, physics, or music. I've found this look backward especially helpful in a poetry class. When we use the word *poet* these days, we mean different things in the here and now: the sad, tousle-haired aesthete walking the shore of the sad ocean with his sad sheep dog; the bearded, well-endowed (I'm speaking of fellowships and awards here, not anatomy) academician reciting with world-weariness at the campus Sherry Hour; the slammer in her best black gripping the mike before the raucous, over-caffeinated coffee-shop crowd; and so many others.

But there's more to this classifying. We often use without realizing it the etymology, pedigree, and the history of the term. Let us go to those ancients to learn what *they've* learned about the art and craft.

Way back then, who was the poet?

THE MAKER

To the ancient Greeks, the poet was *poietes,* literally, maker. A poet is one who makes. The poem is a made thing. This fact seems elementary, but it provides today's poet with a necessary reminder of the nature of the *thing made* and of *the making itself.* To the Greeks, there were at least two ways of making—as there are to us. The poet is a creator, out of nothing, of art; and a maker, out of existing materials, of artifact, craft. Poetry is both art and craft. I was alerted early in life to the dual nature of the human attempt at making something beautiful and useful.

My grandfather was a carpenter. I spent much time when I was young watching him work. Because I was shorter in those elementary-school days, my face was very close—dangerously close—to the action of his saws and workbench. I witnessed with better than a bird's-eye view. As I watched, Grandfather showed me that he knew wood—knew it so well it seemed he loved it. His hands fit the boards, blocks, and flat planes so well, stroking up and down, and fit his tools, in ways that seemed to me masterful—and almost magical.

Those hands were old, and they bore the marks of a lifetime of labor, the danger of hammer and bandsaw. I was to learn later that, in Europe in medieval times, the craftsmen who built the cathedrals were known by the nickname of "Blue-nails." Anyone who wields a hammer—or a pen—understands where that name came from. Work, Adam's curse—and Eve's—is dangerous and sometimes hurts, but without it no real art is possible. Poets should be proud of the title "Blue-nails."

Grandfather was missing the tips of a finger and a thumb, and scars marked the backs of both hands. Those hands were lovely, even to the child I was. They were maps showing the way to a land where significant things were made. The hands were blessed with the fragrance of sawdust, the sheen of honest sweat. Through them, seemingly random things of this world were measured and were transformed to something useful, beautiful, planed and sanded, joined expertly, stained dark or blond. Chair. Table. Bookcase. Desk. Window-box. Someone *working* made these; I was witness to the beauty labor can bring.

So surprising, so unexpected were the artifacts that this carpenter fashioned, that I sometimes saw craft become art. The ancient Greeks recognized this twofold nature of creation. A god—or a poet or singer—can make things out of paper, papyrus, wood—even air passing over a string or through a reed. And through the imagination, a god or poet can create something out of nothing. There was a white piece of paper. A blank screen. Nothing else. Then a flash. A stroke. A mark out of darkness. Chaos begins to take shape. Sound. Form.

The poet needs to be a hard worker as well as an artist, blue-collar as well as white, wild and sweaty laborer and clean-nailed aesthete. He or she can't work on only one side of the ledger. The poets I most admire these days are those to whom writing seems to come not as something effortless or overly artful, but as a hard day's and night's effort, the result of a doggedness and determination to outlast the problems a poem represents.

How do words work, or fail to? What music can be made through the instrument of language? How do we measure a line? How are lines broken? Why ever do we need to break them? What is a metaphor? What does it do? Where does it take us? The answers to these questions, and so many others, poets need to find for themselves. The poet must serve an apprenticeship of reading, studying at the work-table of masters, before she or he is ready to make poetry.

There needs to be more than a bit of both artist (artiste, even?) and artisan to the poet. Of course it is much easier to speak of the craft, as anyone who has ever done time in a poetry workshop knows well. *Don't the iambics break down in line 13? Why is the fourth stanza so fat, the third so thin?* (Even, on a more mundane level: *Shouldn't "alot" be two words? Is it "its" or "it's" you mean here?*) Line breaks, rhythms, exigencies of form. A sonnet? That's easy. Fourteen rhyming lines of iambic pentameter. It's when we try to talk about the creation, the willing into existence of something palpable and living where before we could detect only blank space, the white page or blank screen, that we find ourselves with a severe case of aphasia, or at the least a prolonged spell of hemming and hawing.

We can consider various theories of creation. I've always been drawn to attempts to pin down the source of the artist's spark. Julian Jaynes, in *The Origin of Consciousness and the Breakdown of the Bicameral Mind*, argues that the primitive human did not know of the existence of consciousness—did not know knowing—so that a thought seemed to come from elsewhere, as the voice of a god out of a tree, a high place, a stream—out of thin air, even. Inspiration was, literally, a "breathing in" of something divine, something from the mind of god. Throughout history, women and men have seen inspiration as coming from either inside or outside. The poem is given to me from beyond or from so far inside me that the source is ultimately unknowable.

Make me, one child dares another, and something in the world or in our heart or on the blank screen or page challenges us to cross the line, to venture into unknown territory on a trek that will help us, in making the poem, construct the self. Perhaps it's the chaos, the inchoate poem itself, that eggs us on. *Make me.* We make and break our long or short lines of words all down the field of page.

THE SEER

For the Romans, a word for poet was *vates*, seer. This they meant in at least two senses, as we mean it today. The seer could read nature in the present, the special correspondences and signs of the natural world. Birds passing over the left shoulder or right, the entrails of those birds, the alignment of planets and stars, other marks by which gods spoke to woman and man. The seer was consulted before any significant undertaking: war, affairs of state and the heart. The seer could read the future in the textures, landscapes, and weather of the present.

That way of seeing is essential to a poet of today. We speak of a poet's *vision*, of the *focus* of a particular poem. So much depends on our being able to see. Now let me quickly say that I use seeing here not in the literal sense—we have of course the prime examples of the blind Homer and Milton, and my own eyes are too poor and lenses too thick for me to believe that one who tries to be a poet needs to be able to see in this way. Further, I use seeing to represent all the senses a writer needs in order to apprehend and then confront the world.

Rather than 20–20 vision, I mean that willingness to employ—to push—the senses in order to become nothing long enough to become something or someone else, of which facility I've always felt Keats was speaking in his expression "negative capability." It isn't easy to open the eyes fully to what exists around us. Thoreau writes, in *Walden*, "I have never yet met a man who was quite awake. How could I have looked him in the face?," and he asks, "Why level downward to our dullest perception always, and praise that as common sense?" The daily habitude of this life does seem to conspire to prevent our exercising our senses enough to *notice.* To say to another or to the world, "Yes, I see," is to grant that person or thing the right to exist; it is, in a very real sense, a declaration of the love a poet needs to have for the world as well as for her- or himself.

"I've nothing to write about," the young poet is fond of saying. "I don't travel or climb mountains or live an exciting or reckless life." "The real problem is not having too little to write," I tell them. There is far, far too much to write about. "I have traveled widely in Concord," Thoreau boasted. I have known worlds and worlds of Ohio, I can say.

Think of everything that has happened to you this day, from the moment you awoke. The remnants of a dream blew and swayed like morning curtains behind your eyes. You shaved and showered and ate your Cap'n Crunch or Count Chocula or bran muffin, thinking—musing—all the while. The hole in donut or bagel was a passageway to other worlds, memory and reverie. Songs played in your head, some with emotional moments attached—for we often keep time in our lives by the music accompanying our days, our ways and means—some now-nameless tunes, lullabies, commercial jingles from decades ago. *Use Wildroot Cream-Oil, Charley. See the USA in your Chevrolet.* . . .

Go look at something—really look, I like to say to students in my writing classes. Visit the Greyhound bus station Friday night and keep your eyes and ears open. Make four trips—one per season—to a cemetery, and sniff around. Close your eyes while you explore the face and hair and body of a lover. Listen—really listen—to Beethoven's Appassionata or Sinatra's voice and breath and phrasing, the plaintive wail of George Jones or the clear fragrance of Emmy Lou Harris. They're singing for you, with a special message. Listen, as if your life depended on it. Live your life as fully as possible, through the senses, the portals the mind uses to go out to and to admit the world. There is poetry in such sensory data.

THE POET AS VOYEUR

Speaking of seeing, think for a moment about how much we writers like to watch. It seems we live to snoop, eavesdrop, peer, ogle, stare, glance furtively. Those who write have a curiosity about those who live, just as, it seems to me, those who don't write are fascinated by writers—especially those who exhibit outrageous behavior: drinking, drugs, sexual gymnastics, whatever. How difficult it is to succeed at any two things done simultaneously. The writer's chief problem seems to be the clash of the writing with the living and, at the same time, the daily grinds of life with the activity of writing. To write is in one sense to pretend that we stop living for the duration of the writing or to feel throughout a life that the writing exempts us from the rules and responsibilities that other livers face. When we write we're most (and yet at the same time, it could be argued, least) human.

Thoreau, in *A Week on the Concord and Merrimac Rivers,* puts the problem—the split between life and art—this way:

My life has been the poem I would have writ,
But I could not both live and utter it.

Living and uttering, of course, are the twin (simultaneous) missions of the poet. Thoreau's poems, we know, were written, even as he accomplished a heap of living—his prose writing is pure, long-lined, unbroken poetry.

I'm reminded also, with regard to Thoreau's problem, that Noam Chomsky, the famed linguist, makes the distinction between *problems* and *mysteries*. With problems, we usually know what we don't know and need to find out, or at least we know what we can't do. With mysteries, we're in the deliciously thrilling state of having not a single clue. We struggle to solve problems in our poems; we are sustained in the effort by the great mysteries of existence. Thoreau, to attempt to see ways of solving problems in his life, went to the woods, where he found profound mysteries.

I had a teacher, a fiction writer, who, if such a thing existed, would have earned a black belt in voyeurism many times over. When he'd hear an interesting snatch of conversation, see a particularly lovely sunset, or look into a pair of striking eyes—whenever he saw or heard something particularly sordid or fine—he couldn't rest until he noted it on an index card. The cards were stored in filing cabinets in his office at the university and his study at home, arranged according to a system of his own devising. They seemed almost to take up all the light that tried to make it into his rooms; they were pieces of furniture filled with the raw stuff of art. This systematic record of his witnessing of the world eventually made it from the cards onto the pages of his stories and novels. But he spent so much time processing the world that he became, in my mind, a bureaucrat—a paper pusher—of his own epiphanies. I wondered how he had time for living, much less writing. I am reminded of the story about James Thurber, whose wife, at a party, reportedly walked up to him and growled, "Damn it, Thurber, stop writing!"

THE KNOWER

In Old Arabic, the poet was *sha'ir,* knower. (What *I* don't know could fill several libraries, I sometimes feel.) Well, what does the poet need to know in this day and age? Words, certainly. The nuts and bolts of the machine of language. I think of the story in the second creation account in Genesis in which God sits Adam down and parades before him each newly made creature. The author of this narrative describes a most interesting—and, I would submit, poetical—process: "And whatsoever Adam called every living creature, that was the name thereof." This story, which is supposed to symbolize our "dominion" over other living things (and what trouble this has caused all other life on Earth in our brief time), shows the importance of naming, so vital a power in the historical development of many cultures. (Toni Morrison is eloquent on the importance of naming in the African-American community, for example.) "Poetry is the way we help give names to the nameless so it can be thought," Audre Lorde said once to Adrienne Rich. Well, poets should know, it seems to me, the names of things: animals, insects, trees. Just as Adam announces, "Warthog, Weasel, Wildebeest," and the creature becomes itself in the mind of the namer as the very flesh becomes word, so too the poet creates the reality she or he wishes to bring into being, if only temporarily—through the act of naming. A poet is the parent and the words are the progeny.

How many of us could stroll through a woodlot and give the name (not the Latin classification, but just the familiar, popular designation) of each tree, wildflower, weed, bird, beetle? I remember how excited I was as a child to learn the lovely names of *chicory* and *Queen Anne's Lace* (the electric blue and latticed white adornments of so many summer highways), and further, to discover that I actually had an alternative in the designation of the latter—that I could, were I in a more roughly homespun, less lofty, perhaps even more American mood, transform Queen Anne's lace to *wild carrot*.

THE TRANSLATOR OF THE GODS

So much of the poet's responsibility to the world in former times involved the reception and communication to others of the tribe of messages from the gods. For whatever reason, God stopped speaking directly to all the Hebrews, so the prophet came into being, a man or woman who could hear the words of heaven and speak them to the people of the earth, often in poetical units called oracles. A good part of what Christians call the Old Testament—especially the prophetic books—is poetry, pure and simple. Either the prophets were poets, or God is. This the translators of the Authorized Version of the Bible, called the King James, did not fully realize, and thus in the most popular of all translations—one filled with what most readers think of as truly poetical renderings of religious thought in English—prophetic oracles and other passages of poetry appear as prose.

Moreover, in that same anthology of sacred writing that has had such a pervasive influence on nearly every aspect of our history and culture, the reader can find such shining examples of folk poetry as "The Song of Deborah and Barak" (a powerful and poignant narrative ballad) or "The Song of the Bow," David's deep lament composed right after he hears of the death of his enemy Saul and his dear friend (and Saul's son) Jonathan:

> I am distressed for thee, my brother
> Jonathan; very pleasant hast thou been
> unto me: thy love to me was wonderful,
> passing the love of women.
>
> [I Sam 1:26]

It is not only prophetical, historical, or religious poetry that we find in the Bible. The Song of Songs gives us the poetry of erotic love, as if to suggest that such communion can transform the human, at least for a time, into something divine:

> My beloved put in his hand by the hole
> of the door, and my bowels were moved
> for him. I rose up to open to my beloved;
> and my hands dropped with myrrh, and my
> fingers with sweet smelling myrrh, upon
> the handles of the lock.
>
> [Song of Solomon, 5:4]

THE ONE WHO BLESSES, CURSES

The Celts had their bards and minstrels. The bard, according to Robert Graves, was an official court poet whose function was to create efficacious prayers, blessings (to use on behalf of loved ones and friends), curses (to use on enemies, of course), and favorable "press releases" for the bard's lord or lady employer. The bard was something of a flack. Of course it needs to be pointed out that the lord or lady of the estate down the lane would have his or her own bards, so the best one could hope for was a kind of poetical balance of power.

Switching cultures rapidly, by way of an aside that I hope is illustrative of belief in the force and efficacy of words, I remember that during the Gulf War—that televised slaughter scored for CNN by John Williams for the voice of James Earl Jones—the Iraqi and Saudi poets hurled ancient, highly ritualized, blood-curdling verses at one another over the radio. Unfortunately for Saddam Hussein, the Iraqi poets weren't up to the task. Take *that*, Auden. Poetry makes nothing happen, you say?

But back to the Celts: the Celtic minstrel was a wandering musician (like the troubadour of Provence and northern Italy), a poet of the people who would set up at fairs or near the marketplace. A good performance of wit, word, and song might pry a few coins out of the audience; a bad one might result in the poet's being pelted with soup bones and rotten vegetables and sent packing. Still today some claim that they can see figures similar to the bard and minstrel in the government- or foundation- or university-supported publicly successful figure and the proletarian, scruffy, and rebellious poetry slammer or performance artist. It may be more difficult to tell the two apart at first glance, as either is as likely as the other to wear faded workshirt, boots, and jeans, or a more chic ensemble of all black, these being the two most popular outfits for poets these days. ("Step out in style this spring for your poetry reading and make a fashion statement.") It seems to me that for poets working today it would be of great benefit to strive to emulate both bard and minstrel; to take their profession as seriously as the ancient and honorable profession or vocation it is, yet never to forget where they came from: the city, precinct, tribe, neighborhood, the *people.*

THE MAGICIAN

In primitive societies the poet is the shaman, a man or woman in tune with the powers of nature. (Mircea Eliade's wonderful study *Shamanism* is a book, that every poet must read—more than once.) The shaman hears voices and sees visions early in life—this behavior, which in so-called civilized societies might be thought of as evidence of madness, is in fact the proof of the shaman's strength. He or she goes out into desert or woods to read, commune with, and receive the teachings of nature, and comes back, after a long fast (from food and civilization) charged with the primal and eternal powers of the natural world, with the eyesight of the falcon, perhaps, the cunning of coyote, the speed and near-miraculous agility of the nighthawk.

Perhaps there were shamans in my family tree somewhere back in history; this I've no way of knowing. I do know that my great-grandfather was the herb-doctor of his tiny and remote Calabrian village, a place called Serrastretta (Mountain Pass, in Italian), and he used poems, prayers, blessings, and curses in his vocation, curing villagers and livestock alike of their illnesses, warding off curses and the effects of *malocchio* (the evil eye), praying, performing the rites that make us human, working the white and black magic of tradition and words.

There is a family narrative I've always cherished—one of several stories told me by older kin once it became known throughout the family that I was beginning to think of myself as a writer—of a battle of magic between the herb doctor and a newly arrived young doctor from the medical college at Naples. Business was going well, even with the purveyor of the new medical science as competition. Great-grandfather was holding his own, the story goes, until the morning he woke to find his little flock dead on the hillside, the doctor having used his science to poison the old man's sheep and prove his the superior power in Serrastretta.

A true tale? How can I know? But it's one of those family narratives I need to believe. Great-grandfather's defeat has always represented for me something of a tragicomic rite of passage for the family, an explanation for the anger the older males of the family inherit, a propensity to cling to *vendetta* (a sustained, almost ritualized Mediterranean dislike and desire "to get even")—and my family's propensity to view life as grand opera—and all the old ways, even when the new thinking is everywhere on the ascendancy.

Always I find myself intrigued by stories that may be true. They become the truth, or my inclination is to assume them—make them—true. Ours is an age in which belief of any kind is unfashionable. We are a cynical tribe, to the point of expecting any hint of mystery or wonder to blow away like smoke after a little investigation. Poetry is, among other things, a place where belief is permissible, is possible, in fact, is required. In my writing, my reading, I ache to believe what the past is trying to tell me. It's not always possible to do so, but I feel a keen obligation to make the attempt.

CHARCOAL SKETCH OF AGED COUPLE
IN PEASANT DRESS, CIRCA 1880

Their child, Father's father,
took to sea in steerage
from wild Calabria, once a kingdom
ruled by nomad Normans, who

ages before their France
were Norsemen, fierce travelers
blown like cinders from bonfires
of home by prevailing gales.

In the eyes of ancestors
staring down the wall at me
as my hand makes its slow way
across this ruled page

I recognize a northern cold,
numb and alien unease
of wanderers huddled around
their frail, windy fire,

and at the same time
the sweet heat of storied South.
I find myself this night bound
to Ohio, where all that breathed

once huddled close in caves
as outside the glacier screeched.
I feel the earth tilt and lurch
in its incessant revolution

toward winter and beyond,
sky just behind my window
a map of the history of wishing.
What comings and goings lie ahead

for my own restive children?
I feel the family disease:
blood a few degrees too hot or cold,
home both before me and behind,

the need above all else to stay
and learn the lay and language

of this adopted land;
the ache to take leave.

[From *The Discipline; New and Selected Poems, 1980–1992* (Columbus: Ohio State Univ. Press, 1992)]

So we poets owe a debt to those who came before us. We carry right here in our genes (right here in our denim jeans, also) what we've inherited from the old ones.

THE ONE WHO REMEMBERS

Every poet knows Wordsworth's famous definition, from his Preface to *Lyrical Ballads:*

> . . . Poetry is the spontaneous overflow of powerful feelings:
> It takes its origin from emotion recollected in tranquillity.

Wordsworth grants to memory an important place in the making of poems. We experience something. At some later date, when we have the time (and the "tranquillity"), we recall the feelings generated by the experience and try to write them down. If we're successful, recollected emotion comes again, and our poem is suffused with it. If we get it right, the reader then feels the emotion we've remembered and relived.

The sixteenth-century Jesuit missionary Matteo Ricci, in order to gain access to the ruling families of China, offered them a method for improving memory that he had adapted from classical authors. The Memory Palace (see the excellent book of the same name by Jonathan Spence) is a method of memory, a mnemonic metaphor. The method instructed the one who wished to remember something to "place" it either in a well-known location (the top drawer in a chest in the bedroom, say) or in a specific imaginary place (a "bureau," perhaps, in which a number of important things can be stored).

I've been fascinated by this story for some time. I wrote a book of poems, *The House of Memory,* in which the *place* where remembered things are stored is of the utmost importance. Often, our memories reside in *sited* states. When I conjure up a face of the girl I was "going with" in eighth grade, I'm likely to remember her along with a hit song we danced to, the hang-out where we had pizza and Cokes together, the musty smell of the basement TV room where we spent time away from adults. Very few of my memories exist in *no* place.

Ezra Pound makes the distinction between "multitudinous detail" and "luminous detail" in a poem, the latter being that image that suggests so many others because it is connected somehow to the world, the universe, the collective experience of any number of people. We can make a list of all the images we remember from eighth grade, and try to fit as many as possible into a poem (the multitudinous method), or we can try for those few that glow with connections, that suggest others (the luminous method). So many lasting poems are made of recollected, luminous detail.

I read a tale in a recent (February 15, 1999) issue of the *New Yorker*, which put into perspective some thoughts I have about the poet. Alexander Stille writes, in "The Man Who Remembers," of Giancarlo Scoditti, an Italian anthropologist. Scoditti goes to the tiny coral atoll of Kitawa in the Trobriand Islands and, during several visits and prolonged stays over many years, comes to know the people, their language, and customs. So diligent is he as seer (and voyeur), so deeply does he study the lives of the residents, that as the old members of the tribe die and more of the young leave the island looking for work and lives of their own, he is christened "The Man Who Remembers." He records the dances, mating rituals, folkways. He does what an elder is supposed to do—remind and instruct and caution the young. Scoditti comes to know the islanders in some respects better than they know themselves. Stille takes us to Kitawa for a particularly significant moment:

> On Scoditti's most recent trip to the island, he found the last oral poet on the island lying emaciated and alone in his thatched hut, unwilling to transmit his art to his son or to other young islanders, because they didn't appear to respect Kitawa's traditions.

This poignant scene brings home for me the terribly important responsibility of the poet, especially in this increasingly unlettered and forgetful age. The poet is The One Who Remembers. Out of our respect for the lives and ways of others, we remember and record the events of yesterday and today, for ourselves, of course, to help us make sense of the lives we're living, but also for the readers of tomorrow. I wrote down the family tale about the herb doctor because I needed to feel that this history was telling me something about then and now.

So often, poetry comes from the attempt to record the important, the crucial.

When Giancarlo Scoditti joins with the other men on the island in decorating canoes, anointing his body with oils for the dance, singing songs and reciting poems, he crosses the line from voyeur to participant, from sympathy to empathy to full participant in the lives he is making history. He becomes the poet of the island.

THE POET AT HOME

"What are we coming to, John?," my mother asks my father as they drive through Kansas on their way from Ohio to their daughter's wedding in Colorado. They'd been listening to a radio bulletin about a particularly gruesome murder, and my mother is asking that anguished sort of rhetorical question we pose with increasing frequency in these days of spectacular and random acts of evil.

My father, numbed in that special way travelers through Kansas can be, locked in his own world behind the wheel as mile after mile of flat sameness blurs by, brought quickly to consciousness by my mother's inquiry, knowing he must answer, responds quickly with what he saw that moment as the undisputable truth. "Topeka," he says.

This family anecdote, told with glee by my mother countless times, always makes me think about the ramifications and complexities of that particular question and answer. What are we coming to? Where in the world are we?

I know the importance of that question to writer and reader. Writers play with time, of course, conveying us to any number of presents and pasts—whether it be yesterday or long, long ago—and even to the future. They look back, recapture past time, foreshadow, jump ahead. It's not only time management that makes art. The *where* of it all matters greatly as well. Every story, poem, play, and personal essay happens *somewhere*. Many novelists and storytellers are famous for the way they answer my mother's question, the way they make art out of where, place out of space. Writers have learned from realtors that what matters most is Location, Location, Location.

Virginia Woolf, in *Mrs. Dalloway,* creates the real (sometimes mean) streets of London, as did Dickens before her. James Joyce, of course, fills his pages with Dublin, down to individual shops and alleys and pubs. Faulkner invents a place that seems more authentic than real places, Yoknapatawpha County in Mississippi, and conjures up real characters, black, white, and red, to live there. Toni Morrison sends us to places miles and miles south of her native Lorain,

Ohio. Tony Hillerman's books bring us to the native Americans, the mountains and rites of Navajo country. Lucille Clifton is a poet of particular urban neighborhoods.

Poets too can answer my mother with their own truths, peddling their own wheres, as it were. Edwin Arlington Robinson gives us Tilbury Town, based on his native Gardiner, Maine, and introduces us to characters like Richard Cory, Miniver Cheevy, and Old Eban Flood. Mary Oliver, native of Ohio, now stages her poems against New England backdrops, individual woods and ponds. Robert Frost, Louise Erdrich, Sherman Alexie, Seamus Heaney—are, when it come right down to it, travel writers, and each knows his or her place like no one else. James Wright, even when he writes of Minneapolis or Italy, still tells us truths about Martins Ferry, Ohio. It's possible to write of home even when—some would argue *especially* when—we're somewhere else. The exile knows best what he or she is missing.

You can't go home again, Thomas Wolfe tells us. You can't avoid going back, I sometimes feel. Home is the place you never leave. I believe that each of us carries around inside one special place—a site imbued with primal feelings, a charged landscape we memorized by exploring it with our senses when they were new, when we were "trailing clouds of glory," as Wordsworth puts it. It may be the home town or that neighborhood, perhaps a single block, we remember from childhood. We recall who lived where, the kids we played with, which adults were especially nice and which sternly patrolled their lawns and flowerbeds against the wild neighborhood tribe of children. The homes of our friends had particular odors nothing like those of home. The water, the milk of home (not to mention the eggs, the chickens, the bread), tasted like nothing we've had since.

My place was—and therefore *is*—an ethnically checkerboarded, gritty industrial city divided West from East by a volatile, meandering river. It contained not just neighborhoods of black and white, but also Slovak, Slovene, Serbian, Italian, Puerto Rican, Jewish, Appalachian. Neighborhoods had their own bakeries, grocery stores, newspapers (in many cases in their own languages), places of worship, ways of praying, saying, and singing the name of God. Mine, in a very real sense, was Diversity City.

When I travel today to Chicago or New York, Dublin, or Rome, when I walk about in my adopted city, Columbus, I see and experience things in terms of the Cleveland of my youth. I can know them only because I know my home like the back of my hand, like my own name. When I write about any place, I'm really writing about the place I used to know. When I try to conjure up a face, a voice, a pair of hands, I see them in context. I try to put them in their place.

THE POET IN EXILE

"There's no place like home. There's no place like home." All this talk of home is fine. Yes, the poet tries all life long to get back. It's also true that home is a place you can't get to from here (to mishandle Wolfe). The poet is an exile, a stranger in a strange land. "There's no place like home." That's certainly true for Dorothy and Toto, but Andrei Codrescu stresses the importance for a poet of leaving home: "Twentieth-century poets . . . have viewed exile therapeutically. Freedom of the spirit was available only by leaving home. They answered the siren call of the Elsewhere for many reasons, but mainly because they were not able to breathe at home. The deep breath is the breath of travel, of speed, of horseback, of movement. . . . Freed of the tribe's conventions, the poet is free to express the critical dictates of his instant nomad passage" (*The Disappearance of the Outside: A Manifesto for Escape* Reading, MA: Addison-Wesley 1990, pp 54–5.)

James Joyce took his Dublin with him into exile, in his mind, and Auden fled England for the U.S.; Eliot went from the U.S. to England. Where these writers went seems less important than that they did go, the very act of going from what is familiar and habitual is a trip to the land of poetry. How strange. The more we travel, the better we see and know home.

The poet must travel. (The act of the poem is itself a going out and coming back.) The breath of traveling makes us children again, as opposed to the creeping age of stasis, of refusing to venture out. On the move, all our experiences are new and fresh, even the water tastes different, and the air, the language, and our days are imbued with magic.

In the writing workshop room, or back in our writing rooms, we are, or should be, in exile, thinking of home, staying put and going.

THE READER

The poet reads the world, the way Scoditti read and kept track of his islanders. For some years now I've tried to keep up with the news from my own tribe. *The New York Times,* a number of local papers,

Time and *Newsweek* and other magazines, and so many Web sites (especially Arts & Letters Daily and "Refdesk.com"—these are the ways I try to chronicle, to keep track of, what is happening to my world and to the me who inhabits it.

I bring the news to the writing workshop (just as I delivered the *Plain Dealer* to my Cleveland neighbors so many years ago).

> Amish Busted for Buying Cocaine from Biker Gang.
> Cezanne Still-life Nets $60 Million at Sotherby's.
> Truck Overturns, Releasing Millions of Bees.
> Man Charged After Corpse Is Left in Van at Strip Joint.

Week after week, the occasions of poems come in dark ink on newsprint. The news is bad, or ludicrous, or maddening, or wonderful—sometimes it's all of these at once. Almost always it inspires some commentary; often it brings poetry. My students—and I, writing along with them—have poems assigned from these stories of mischance, malfeasance, malevolence, and kindness. These are prompts. The results are exercises, but, as I'm fond of saying, I see poems move from the poet's Exercise Pile to his or her A-List after some serious revision. Wonderful poems are not written on demand, but the seeds of such poems can be found in the news, the messages, high or low, that bombard us daily.

Like the chronicler of the past, we attempt to keep track of the world, write events of the day into our work, so that at the end of a term we've amassed some kind of record.

> Fight breaks Out at Funeral.
> Dead Man Revives in Morgue.
> Eight Roman Ships Found Perfectly Preserved
> Parish Priest in Italy Struck Dead By Easter Bell.

Such headlines get under the skin, where they can travel from mind to heart to soul. Poets are supposed to be an otherwordly race who've fled to ivory (or ivy) towers or bowers because the world is a cold and hurtful place ("I fall upon the thorns of life! I bleed!," says Shelley in "Ode to the West Wind")—a place where they don't belong.

Writing poems from the news keeps a poet in the world, where he or she belongs. Of course, our reading—the way we let the world in—can include, in addition to newspapers and magazines, tabloid rags and *Scientific American,* catechisms and physics texts, billboards and gravestones. I lived for some years next to a cemetery in Marion, Ohio (in which were buried Warren G. Harding, his wife, and at least one of his mistresses). This was the perfect place for one trying to be a poet, trying to be One Who Remembers.

READING THE GRAVES

Running here day after day
in the stone town beyond my yard,
I'm so close to earth's pure scents,
there's nothing I can't imagine.

I move past the infant citizens:
tiny graves, briefest lives
engraved on tablets, pennies
minted and lost the same year.

For no reason at all, I think
of my afterbirth and cord—
those pieces of mother and me
that my ancestors revered

as the infant's lost brother
and fate. I can almost believe
with the old Calabrians
that our nights and days

are tied in fearful ways,
that two windy darknesses
frame each frail light,
and stepping over the sleep

of an unchristened child
can give a body grave-scab,
fatal and unalterable disease
of palsied limb and clotted lung

until earth offers its children
the one palliative
for the one and only terror—
which only earth instills.

I'm four, Holy Cross Cemetery.
Each feast day we call on those

we converse with nowhere else
but in the plush caskets of dream.

At my feet under granite
lie the skeletons of my brothers,
Robert John and David John,
twins even in their new womb.

Still cornsilk-fine, their hair,
skulls in pretty bonnets.
The unlucky lungs that failed them
must be light as air by now,

their bones, not much larger
than a bird's, dressed up
in diapers and knitted booties.
What can it mean, such adult weeping?

I look down, broken-lined chaos
becoming the name I inherited when
a brother could call himself nothing.
Suddenly I can read. I can read.

[From *The Discipline: New and Selected Poems, 1980–1992* Columbus: Ohio State
U. Press, 1992.]

This is my attempt at a personal history of reading—which has
always seemed to me to be another sense—the sixth. Like the other
five, reading is a way we reach out to the world and also the way it
meets us half way. Poets need to be readers, in the largest sense of the
world. I've been reading the themes and essays—and of course the
poems—of my students for nearly thirty years. I've learned much
from these pieces of paper and computer screens—more than I'll
ever be able to write.

THE INVENTION OF SECRECY

The ancients were not able, save
for a few remarkable ones—
Alexander, Julius Caesar, Ambrose—

to read, or write, silently. I would
have written to you sooner, Cicero wrote
to a friend, but I had a sore throat.

Read to yourself, we say to children
still today. This they cannot do.
Saying the Latin answers at the Mass,

dressed in my white Sears shirt under
Medieval cassock and surplice,
Chuck Taylor Converse All-Stars—

to protect the sacristy carpet—
I heard some new music. The words
tasted nothing like Cleveland.

Ages ago, library, school, temple
were loud places where tongues flexed,
heart and lungs giving, taking,

the song and dance of subduing self
enough to put in our mouths words
of another body, words of our own.

Learning to read without even moving
our lips, we invented private life.
We created secrets of the dark hollows

of bone and flesh, a new selfishness,
deceiving ourselves into believing
that, alone, we could be complete,

silent, we would not grow too full.

[Published in *Poetry* 172.6 (1998): 334.]

THE POET AS ARCHEOLOGIST

Is there a place we can step where there is no fossil or remnant or relic
beneath us? The dark earth of so called "primitive" fires, bits of wing
and exoskeleton, tooth and bone, arrowheads, musket balls, bullets,
tabs from beer and soda cans. Our Earth, after so many eons of life
and death, tier upon tier, is rich with veins and lodes of those lives
who've gone before. The world is an offal place, when it comes right
down to it.

A book I heartily recommend to poets is *The Bog People*, by P.V.
Glob. In 1950, men cutting peat in a Danish bog uncovered the body
of a man with a noose around his neck. They thought they'd found
evidence of a recent murder, and called in the police, who in turn

asked Glob, a leading archeologist, to examine the body. Professor Glob, after careful study, determined that the man had been strangled and thrown into the bog some 2,000 years ago. His body was preserved through the tanning properties of the bog. *The Bog People* is a picture book—though there is a terribly powerful text as well—of Iron-Age women and men, well preserved, taken out of bogs. They are ancient, but seem to be of our own time. Punished for unknown crimes or thrown into darkness to appease a god, they are eternally alive, eternally dead.

It was such discovery from below that inspired Seamus Heaney to write his lovely and chilling bog poems, one of which is "The Tollund Man."

I

Some day I will go to Aarhus
To see his peat-brown head,
The mild pods of his eye-lids,
His pointed skin cap.

In the flat country nearby
Where they dug him out,
His last gruel of winter seeds
Caked in his stomach,

Naked except for
The cap, noose and girdle,
I will stand a long time.
Bridegroom to the goddess,

She tightened her torc on him
And opened her fen,
Those dark juices working
Him to saint's kept body,

Trove of the turfcutters'
Honeycombed workings.
Now his stained face
Reposes at Aarhus.

II

I could risk blasphemy,
Consecrate the cauldron bog

Our holy ground and pray
Him to make germinate

The scattered, ambushed
Flesh of labourers,
Stockinged corpses
Laid out in the farmyards,
Tell-tale skin and teeth
Flecking the sleepers
Of four young brothers, trailed
For miles along the lines.

III

Something of his sad freedom
As he rode the tumbril
Should come to me, driving,
Saying the names

Tollund, Grauballe, Nebelgard,
Watching the pointing hands
Of country people,
Not knowing their tongue.

Out there in Jutland
In the old man-killing parishes
I will feel lost,
Unhappy and at home.

[From *Seamus Heaney Selected Poems, 1966–1987* New York: Farrar, Straus
Giroux, 1990.]

We all are searching for our Tollund Man or Windeby Girl, the news
buried but breaking out beneath us. At the Italian funerals I re-
member attending as a child, the widow or widower or child would
sometimes attempt to get into the casket with the deceased. This is
overdoing it, certainly, but the news we want to report sometimes
comes from worlds other than the one we inhabit now. We want to go
there.

A midden is a term from archeology for a dunghill or refuse heap.
Researchers of the past have occasion to sort through such places for
evidence of what was. Poets, too, find middens a source—a place—
for their art. There are mounds and piles of potential poems just
beneath our feet.

THE POET IN THE KITCHEN

Especially during the holidays I'm reminded that writing a poem is much like preparing a meal. The poet may not always wear the funny hat, but he or she is still very much the chef. I assemble, arrange on counter and table, and then prepare the various ingredients. I measure, weigh, decant, top off, fold in, pour over. I beat, peel, pare, knead, squeeze, wring, pound, slice, chop. I sauté, brown, braise, bake, roast, performing that old dance whereby something raw and cold is brought, over a period time, to a state of heat, or at least doneness and completion, so that just in time I can meet others at the table where we've all come together to celebrate.

Let's say I want to write a poem about my family. I'll conjure up and assemble the ingredients: Nonna and Pop, their duplex on West 105th in Cleveland, their tales of life on the South Side before that, and in Italy before that. The warmth of her kitchen. The fragrance of her apron as she bakes bread, puts up in Ball jars tomatoes festooned with shreds of deep green basil, makes blood soup, cranks sausage into long casings of intestines she purchased at the slaughterhouse.

At sixteen, when I got my permanent driver's license, I would take Nonna to the import store, Giovanni & Mario's, near downtown. She'd been shopping there for half a century. I recall the potent force of garlic, olive oil in kegs and gallon cans, great baskets of live snails, tripe, dates, and figs—sights and scents I'll never get out of my head.

To get to my high school, I took a bus and the Rapid Transit from my home on the far west side of town. I then walked through the West Side Market on West 25th Street, past stalls of swinging cheeses and sausages, salamis and hams gleaming like stalactites in a great cave, and joints of meat, hog jowls and snouts, squid and gleaming fish whose baleful eyes seemed to turn to regard me as I passed by.

Grandfather had a garden out back of his house, with grapes on trellises above, little fig trees, and a crowd of vegetables in progress. He'd throw pebbles from the path to show me individual plants of which he was most particularly proud.

He worked for the B & O Railroad for 52 years. I remember the twelve pairs of tracks my little legs had to climb over to visit his signal shack, my fingers firmly trapped in the fat hand of my father. I know the rich stink and glow of the pot-bellied stove, in which he burned old railroad ties to keep warm, and the gnarled Italian cigars that took my breath away. The blare and glare of diesels, the U.S. Steel and J & L blast furnaces, Sohio's refinery flares, bellowing ore boats and tugs twisting up and down improbable curves of the Cuyahoga—these are my ingredients. So pure and elemental are they, each time I arrange them together I can make something with a different texture and taste.

I fuss and fume with these memories, recall and recall some more, fiddle, cut and paste, chop, grate and dice, head over to the oven of my feelings for these two dear immigrants with the thick accents and the world they created, which made me and mine.

If I'm lucky, if I watch the clock carefully, if I trust my training and taste through each step of the process, then I may end up with a poem pleasing to me and to others who will come to partake of it.

If I wish to cook the Christmas dishes Grandmother taught me, I proceed in similar fashion. For poets as well as comedians, timing is everything. I can't wait too far into December to visit the Italian specialty store—in Columbus it's Carfagna's on 161—for the essential parts of the meals. The store is packed—wall-to-wall paisans, often three generations pushing the cart down the terribly narrow aisles, looking over the offerings of holiday fare. We eye each other and recognize the familiar features of the tribe, most of us less than tall, dark and curly haired, dark eyed. I take a number and enter the throngs at the long fish and meat counter.

Back in the day, Christmas Eve was meatless, by church decree, and dinner consisted of various kinds of fish. I purchase a hard, flat slab of salted cod, *baccala,* of which always there is a goodly supply. This was—is—the fare of the peasant and poor immigrant. It keeps forever. I'll soak the fish for three days, changing the water often to wash away the salt, so that the finished product will wrinkle the noses of the children only a little. I select little tubs of shrimp and silvery smelt and perhaps a piece of whitefish, and of course clams or anchovies for the pasta.

I select hot Italian sausage and a stewing hen for the tomato sauce for Christmas Day lasagna. This dish is made with tiny meatballs that take forever to roll. Grandmother Carolina would criticize those of us who helped her roll the meatballs. They must be small as the fingernail of her little finger, she would show us. (I'm ashamed to say that today I crumble browned Italian sausage rather than use her more demanding and time-consuming method—sometimes I'm a lazy chef.) I prepare and add the hard boiled eggs and various cheeses for this lasagna, which is the signature dish of my family. It tastes of us, and we of it. It dates back to the grandparents in Calabria, to the grandparents of their grandparents in that land in the toe of the Italian boot.

Before I leave, after filling my cart with leaves of oregano, basil, Italian parsley—and some *fino vino* (Chianti Classico for the lovers of red, Pinot Grigio for the others), I purchase boxes of torrone, rectangular Christmas candies made of nougat.

When it's time to put together this year's version of the old Christmas poem of a meal, I go through the steps of preparation and execution, timing, boiling and stewing that I undertook for the poem I wrote about my grandparents, Michele and Carolina. A poem must have distinctive flavor. A good meal is a poem.

When it's time to eat and my family is arrayed around the table, which is laden with steaming sights and scents—and words—of the past, I know that the present family will be joined by the family that extends back into the past all the way to a peasant land where a meal is something like a gift, a communion, a poem.

The following poem I hope you'll find palatable for a holiday meal or at any time of the year.

THE POEM OF CHICKEN BREAST WITH FETTUCINE

After work has hollowed you,
sit a moment, thinking hard
of the simplest things. When
enough time passes, rise,

go into the kitchen.
Take two chicken breasts.
Pound, dust with pepper, salt,
dredge lightly in flour,

brown in a heavy skillet
with olive oil *Extra vergine*—
fragrant as Tuscan autumn—
with chopped garlic

and Crimini mushrooms
redolent of dank woods.
Add a half cup of Pinot Grigio,
bright as late sun,

and lemon, squeezed
by hand so the liquid

blesses your fist. Cover,
simmering no more than

twenty minutes. Thoughts
of cream, butter, cheese,
intricate timbales?
Put them out of your mind.

This will be so simple
it will take you back to what
you were. Serve over
pasta. Kiss with basil

and parsley that swayed
in a garden moments before,
grated *pecorino Romano.*
Sit now with someone

you care for, or could,
given the right words,
heat, savor, light—blessings
meant to be shared.

THE POET AS NOTHING AT ALL

One of my favorite poems of Emily Dickinson is (R.W. Franklin's)
No. 260.

I'm Nobody! Who are you?
Are you—Nobody—Too?
Than there's a pair of us?
Don't tell! They'd advertise—you know!

How dreary—to be—Somebody!
How public—like a Frog—
To tell one's name—the livelong June—
To an admiring bog!

[*The Poems of Emily Dickinson. Reading Edition.* R.W. Franklin, ed. Cambridge:
Harvard UP, 1999.]

This playful (yet at the same time serious) bit of warning brings me
back to Keat's "negative capability," mentioned above. The poet can
be so filled with the world, with a particular subject, passion, or

obsession, that inside there isn't any *there* there (as Gertrude Stein is said to have said about Oakland, California). At times the poet needs to be the serious empath, to empty her or his self. Dickinson intended—I firmly believe—that no one else read her poetry, but through a twist of fate we have it. We've become the "admiring bog" she warns other poets about. And, like the bogs of Seamus Heaney, we can help preserve the words of this Nobody for ages to come.

So perhaps it isn't true that a poet is no one at all. So who, then, *is* he or she? My favorite poetical attempt to understand the poet—a real Poet Poem—is by Gary Snyder.

As for Poets

As for poets,
The Earth Poets
Who write small poems,
Need help from no man.

The Air Poets
Play out the swiftest gales
And sometimes loll in the eddies.
Poem after poem,
Curling back on the same thrust.

At fifty below
Fuel oil won't flow
And propane stays in the tank.
Fire poets
Burn at absolute zero
Fossil love pumped back up.
The first
Water Poet

Stayed down six years.
He was covered with seaweed.
The life in his poem
Left millions of tiny
Different tracks
Criss-crossing through the mud.

With the Sun and Moon
In his belly,

The Space Poet
Sleeps.
No end to the sky—
But his poems
Like wild geese
Fly off the edge.

A Mind Poet
Stays in the house.
The house is empty
And it has no walls.
The poem
Is seen from all sides,
Everywhere,
At once.

[from *No Nature: New and Selected Poems*. New York: Pantheon, 1992.]

It might prove a useful exercise for a poet to find his or her own meaning on the scale Snyder provides. Is the Mind Poet the summit that the poet, after long labor through the other stages, attains? Are we poets all of these, "Everywhere, /At once"?

CONCLUSION: THE POET AS HUMAN BEING

I've been looking outside, elsewhere, erstwhile, back in once-upon-a-times, in this search for the roles—perhaps even the souls—of the poet. Of course, the writer looks inside first. There are a number of aspects of the poet, but only one self. A writer can't sit down at desk or keyboard and consciously choose his or her hat. ("It's Thursday. My day to play the Seer. Tomorrow is Shaman Day.")

I offer these various views of the poet as models, as ways of figuring, even as frameworks out of which a poet can find the subjects and the words. I think again of Thoreau's lines about "living" and "uttering." He was able to do both. In fact, he forced himself to live so passionately that his life at times became a poem.

There is a way of life that a poet can pursue in which she or he looks at the world as opportunity. "What do I have to write about?" a poet asks. "My self. And therefore, everything," should be the only acceptable answer.

Contributors

David Baker is the author of eight books, most recently *Changeable Thunder* (poems, University of Arkansas Press, 2001) and *Heresy and the Ideal: On Contemporary Poetry* (essays, 2000). He holds the Thomas B. Fordham Chair of Creative Writing at Denison University and teaches also in the low-residency MFA program for writers at Warren Wilson College. Among his honors are fellowships and awards from the John Simon Guggenheim Memorial Foundation, the National Endowment for the Arts, Poetry Society of America, and Society of Midland Authors. He is Poetry Editor of *The Kenyon Review*, and lives in Granville, Ohio, with Ann Townsend and their daughter, Katherine.

David Citino is Professor of English and Creative Writing at The Ohio State University. He is the author of eleven books of poetry, among them *The Invention of Secrecy* (Ohio State University Press); *The Book of Appassionata: Collected Poems* (Ohio State); *Broken Symmetry* (Ohio State), named a Notable Book of 1997 by the National Book Critics Circle; *The Weight of the Heart (Quarterly Review of Literature* Poetry Series); *The Gift of Fire* (University of Arkansas Press); and *The Appassionata Doctrines* (Cleveland State University Poetry Center).

Citino graduated from Ohio University (B.A.) and Ohio State (M.A., Ph.D.). Among his honors and awards are a Poetry Fellowship from the National Endowment for the Arts, the first annual Poetry Award from the Ohioana Library Association, a Major Fellowship from the Ohio Arts Council, the Exemplary Faculty Award from the OSU College of Humanities, and both the Alumni Distinguished Teaching Award and the Alumni Professional Achievement Award from Ohio State University.

Citino is former director of the Creative Writing Program at Ohio State, and former editor of *The Journal*. He has given readings and talks and has directed workshops at colleges, libraries, and community centers around the country. He currently serves on the Board of Trustees of the Greater Columbus Arts Council, and as Poetry Editor and member of the Editorial Board of Ohio State University Press, as Facilitator of the Literature Panel of the Ohio Arts Council, and as member (and former president) of the Board of Trustees of Thurber

House, the writers' center located in the restored boyhood home of James Thurber in downtown Columbus. He writes on poetry for the *Columbus Dispatch.*

Billy Collins is the author of five books of poetry, including *Questions About Angels* (University of Pittsburgh, 1998), *The Art of Drowning* (University of Pittsburgh, 1995), and *Picnic, Lightning* (University of Pittsburgh, 1997). His most recent collection is *Sailing Alone Around the Room: New and Selected Poems* (Random House, 2001). He has won numerous awards, including a National Endowment for the Arts grant and a Guggenheim fellowship. He is a professor of English at Lehman College and a visiting writer at Sarah Lawrence College.

Yusef Komunyakaa was born in Bogalusa, Louisiana. Besides workshops in the writing of poetry at Princeton University, Komunyakaa has taught seminars and sessions on craft at Bread Loaf, the Corliss Lamont Series, the Dodge Festival, Fine Arts Work Center in Provincetown, Folger Shakespeare Library, Julliard, Marin Poetry Center, the National Arts, Club, PEN, Poets House, Poetry Society of America, Prague Summer Seminars, the Robert Frost Center, San Miguel Poetry Week, Squaw Valley Community of Writers, The Tennessee Williams Festival, The Vermont Studio Center, William Joiner Center, as well as in high schools and university creative writing programs. His most recent books include *Talking Dirty to the Gods* (poems, Farrar, Straus & Giroux) and *Blue Notes: Essays, Interviews and Commentaries* (University of Michigan Press). Among his other titles are *Thieves of Paradise,* a finalist for the 1999 National Book Critics Circle Award, and *Neon Vernacular: New and Selected Poems 1977–1989,* winner of the 1994 Pulitzer Prize in poetry. Forthcoming is *Pleasure Dome: New and Collected Poems, 1975–1999* (Wesleyan, 2001). He was elected to The Board of Chancellors of the Academy of American Poets in 1999.

Maxine Kumin was born in Philadelphia in 1925, acquired a BA and MA from Radcliffe College in '46 and '48. She has published 11 collections of poetry, including *Selected Poems 1960–1990* and *Connecting the Dots* (1997), five novels, most recently an animal rights murder mystery, *Quit Monks or Die!,* and four books of essays, most recently *Always Beginning* (2000). Her awards include the Pulitzer, the Aiken Taylor Poetry Award, The Poet's Prize, and the Ruth Lilly Poetry

Prize. Maxine and her husband live on a farm in New Hampshire, where they have raised horses and vegetables, and maintained a sugar bash (for maple syrup) since 1976.

Carol Muske (Carol Muske-Dukes in fiction) is author of six books of poetry, most recently *An Octave Above Thunder, New & Selected Poems,* Penguin, 1997. Her two novels are *Dear Digby,* (Viking, 1989) and *Saving St. Germ,* (Penguin, 1993).

In spring of 2001, Random House will publish her third novel, *Life after Death.* She is a regular critic for *The New York Times* Book Review and the *LA Times Book Review* and her collection of reviews and critical essays, *Women and Poetry: Truth, Autobiography and the Shape of the Self* was published in the "Poets on Poetry " series of the University of Michigan Press, 1997. Her work appears everywhere from the *New Yorker* to *L.A. Magazine,* and she is anthologized widely, including in *Best American Poems, 100 Great Poems by Women.* She is professor of English and Creative Writing and director of the new Ph.D. program in Literature and Creative Writing at the University of Southern California. She has received many awards and honors, including a Guggenheim fellowship, a National Endowment for the Arts fellowship, an Ingram-Merrill, the Witter Bynner award from the Library of Congress, the Castagnola award from the Poetry Society of America and several Pushcart Prizes. She lives in Los Angeles.

Ann Townsend won the Gerald Cable Prize for her first book of poetry, *Dime Store Erotics* (Silverfish Review Press, 1998). Her poems, short stories, and essays have appeared widely in such periodicals as *Five Points, The Nation, The Paris Review,* and *Poetry.* Among her awards are the Discovery/*The Nation* Prize, the Stanley Hanks Poetry Prize, and a grant in fiction from the Ohio Arts Council. She holds a Ph.D. from Ohio State University, and is Associate Professor of English at Denison University, where she also directs the Jonathan R. Reynolds Young Writers' Workshop. She lives in Granville, Ohio.